THE HUMAN MOAT

BUILDING YOUR ADVANTAGE IN THE AGE OF AI

SEAN PAN

This book is a work of narrative nonfiction. Certain characters, organizations, legal cases, quotations, and events are fictionalized or composite constructions used to illustrate systemic and economic dynamics. Any resemblance to real persons, organizations, legal proceedings, or events is coincidental unless explicitly stated otherwise.

The legal examples presented in the narrative are illustrative only and should not be relied upon as precedent or legal authority.

This book is intended for informational and educational purposes only. It does not constitute legal, financial, investment, regulatory, or professional advice. Readers are responsible for their own decisions and for obtaining appropriate professional counsel where necessary.

The views expressed are those of the author and do not necessarily reflect the views of any employer, institution, or affiliated organization.

References to third-party individuals, research, or institutions are provided for contextual and educational purposes and do not imply endorsement.

The author makes no representations or warranties regarding the completeness, accuracy, or suitability of the information contained herein.

ISBN: 979-8-9946296-4-2

First Edition

Printed in the United States of America

DEDICATION

For my grandson

Author's Note

Automation changes the economics of work, but it does not change the nature of value.

As execution becomes faster, cheaper, and increasingly automated, it is natural to focus on what appears to be disappearing: tasks, roles, and familiar measures of productivity. This book begins from a different premise. The deeper shift is not the disappearance of work, but the disappearance of scarcity.

When outputs are abundant, judgment becomes decisive. When content is infinite, curation matters. When systems generate endlessly, responsibility cannot be automated alongside them. These human functions do not scale the way machines do, and that asymmetry is not a weakness—it is the moat.

This book is dedicated to my grandson, who will inherit a world shaped by tools far more powerful than the ones we debate today. The specifics will change. The interfaces will improve. The displacement narratives will repeat. What will remain constant is the need for someone to decide what matters, what fits, and what should be allowed to endure.

The Human Moat is not a guide to staying competitive with machines. It is an argument that competition itself is the wrong frame. The future does not belong to those who execute faster than automation, but to those who can stand apart from it—who can decide what should be executed at all, and accept responsibility for that decision.

This book exists to clarify that role. If it helps readers—present or future—recognize judgment, taste, and responsibility not as soft traits, but as structural assets in an automated world, then it has served its purpose.

CONTENTS

INTRODUCTION

THE TUESDAY MORNING CRISIS

The end of the world didn't happen with a bang. It didn't happen with a flash of nuclear light, or an alien mothership darkening the sky, or a robot army marching in lockstep down Fifth Avenue.

For Alex, the world reoriented on a rainy Tuesday morning, inside a coffee shop that smelled like roasted beans and wet raincoats, with a polite digital ding.

Alex is twenty-six years old. If you saw him, you wouldn't think he looked like a victim of the apocalypse. He wears a beanie. He drinks oat milk lattes. He carries a sticker-bombed tablet that costs more than his first car.

Alex is a "creative." He is a graphic artist. He spent four years in art school, taking out a student loan the size of a luxury sedan to learn the dark arts of color theory, typography, and visual composition. He spent thousands of hours perfecting his shading, learning how to balance negative space, and mastering the pen tool in Illustrator until his wrist clicked.

He bases his entire identity—his rent money, his self-worth, his ego—on a simple industrial-era equation: *I can do things that are hard for other people.*

Because the work was hard, it was valuable. Because it was valuable, it was dependable.

But this morning, Alex did something unfamiliar. He opened a new Artificial Intelligence (AI) tool that his X feed wouldn't stop referencing. Just to see. Just to test the waters. He told himself he was "doing market research," but beneath that explanation, he was seeking confirmation. He expected the machine to be awkward. He expected to dismiss it with a laugh at its strange hands and distorted eyes.

He typed in a prompt describing a complete branding package for a futuristic coffee company—a task that would usually require three days of sketching, vectoring, and emotional expenditure.

He hit Enter. He lifted his coffee cup to his lips. He took a sip.

By the time he put the cup down—four seconds later—it was done.

Alex stared. He waited for the glitch. He waited for the mess. But the logos were sleek. The color palettes were harmonious. The mockups looked professional. It wasn't just "okay." It was good. It was Alex-level good.

Alex didn't feel excited. He didn't feel relieved that his workload had just lightened. He felt a dense, unfamiliar weight settle in his stomach, as if an assumption he'd relied on had quietly failed.

The machine did not take his job.

It removed the illusion that time was value.

Alex looks up from his screen, hoping for a distraction. He scans the coffee shop. This place is a sanctuary of productivity. It's the "remote work" cathedral. But today, the atmosphere has shifted.

Alex isn't the only one experiencing the Tuesday Morning Crisis.

Look over there, at the corner table. That's Elena. Elena is a Copywriter. She charges $100 an hour to write punchy emails and blog posts. She spent ten years reading Hemingway and Ogilvy to learn how to turn a phrase. Right now, she is staring at ChatGPT. She just asked it to write ten variations of a sales email. It did it in three seconds. Two of them were unusable. Three of them were forgettable. But five of them? Five of them were indistinguishable from what she would have written. She looks at her half-eaten croissant and feels a sudden erosion of certainty.

Look at the guy by the window. That's Mark. Mark is a Junior Associate at a law firm. His job is "document review." He is paid to read thousands of dense pages and locate the one sentence that matters. It is demanding, monotonous work, but it pays the rent. He is looking at an AI tool that has just digested 500 pages of case law and summarized the risks in a bulleted list. He isn't relieved. He's unsettled. If he no longer needs to read the documents, how does his role change?

And then there is Jen, sitting near the counter. Jen is a Middle Manager. Her strength is organization. She takes messy notes and turns them into clean project plans. She is the "glue" that holds her team together. She has just watched a system listen to a Zoom meeting, transcribe it, assign tasks to the team, and place everything on the calendar before the meeting even ended.

The coffee shop is silent, save for the hum of the espresso machine and the soft tapping of keys. But beneath the silence, there is collective recognition.

Everyone in this room realizes the same thing at the exact same time: *the skill I sold is now abundant.*

THE BROKEN PROMISE

This reaction isn't just about money. It's about expectation.

We were all taught a promise. It was the Industrial Pact, reinforced by parents and teachers and passed down as guidance. It went like this:

"The world is competitive. If you want a good life, you need to learn a hard skill. You need to learn to do something difficult, something technical, something that requires years of training. That will protect you. That will sustain you."

For fifty years, that guidance held. If you could draw like Alex, you were stable. If you could write like Elena, you were stable. If you could analyze like Mark, you were stable.

We built our identities around effort. We internalized the equation Suffering = Value. If it didn't require visible effort, it didn't feel legitimate.

But staring at those screens, the people in the coffee shop are recognizing a structural shift. The hard skill is no longer defensive. It is exposed.

AI didn't arrive in trades defined by physical labor. It arrived in roles defined by cognition. It arrived for knowledge workers. It acquired the hard skills at scale and now executes them at negligible cost.

So, the room feels empty. The realization resolves into two conclusions:

The machine performs this class of task more efficiently.

My position needs to change.

That sensation? That is the Empty Room.

THE TRICK OF THE EMPTY ROOM

In my previous book, *The Empty Room: How AI Looks Intelligent: What That Means*, this moment was already resolved. The machine does not understand what it is doing.

That conclusion is not in dispute here.

The machine demonstrates syntactic fluency. It follows the rules of language, art, and law with extreme consistency. It assembles outputs that resemble expertise across domains, often at a level indistinguishable from the work of trained professionals.

At the same time, it operates without semantic responsibility. It does not carry meaning, intention, or consequence. It predicts the next token in a sequence based on probability, not understanding.

It is a parrot in a box. A very fast, very expensive parrot—useful, powerful, and constrained.

This distinction matters structurally. But in the coffee shop, Alex isn't weighing philosophy. Elena isn't evaluating mechanisms. They are thinking about income continuity. They are recognizing that their role in the system has shifted.

Alex isn't asking, "Does the machine have a soul?" Alex is asking, "What position do I occupy now that this task executes at negligible cost?"

THE PILOT AND THE ENGINE

I have good news and bad news for the people in the coffee shop.

The bad news is that the way they previously worked—executing tasks, exchanging hours for dollars, operating like human slow cookers—no longer defines advantage. That mode of work has reached its limit. If Alex attempts to compete with the machine on speed, he loses leverage. If Elena attempts to compete on volume, she loses leverage.

But here is the good news. The Empty Room has been misunderstood.

The tension arises because you believe you are the engine. You believe your value comes from horsepower—how hard you push, how fast you turn. But you are not the engine. You never were.

The machine is the engine. It is a Ferrari engine with effectively infinite fuel. But an engine without a driver remains inert. It has no direction. It has no taste. It has no preference.

The Empty Room is not confinement. It is a cockpit.

For the first time in history, the distance between "I have an idea" and "I built it" has collapsed. Barriers of entry—learning syntax, mastering brushstrokes, memorizing case law—have largely dissolved.

Alex looks at the screen and sees displacement. I look at the screen and see the digital equivalent of a high-tech exoskeleton—an "Exosuit" designed to amplify human intent rather than replace it.

THE CAVE AND THE LAB

To understand why Alex feels disoriented, we need to examine two versions of Tony Stark.

Version 1 is the Cave. In the first film, Tony is trapped with limited tools. To survive, he builds the first suit (the Mark I) by hand. He uses a hammer. He welds manually. He wears a heavy leather apron. He sweats. He bleeds. The work is physical, exhausting, and constrained. The result is a clunky, gray machine. It flies briefly, crashes violently, and barely keeps him alive. It is heroic. It is hard work. And it nearly destroys him.

Version 2 is the Lab. Later, Tony operates in a controlled environment. He no longer uses a hammer. He stands inside a holographic workspace, speaking to J.A.R.V.I.S. He is not applying force; he is issuing direction. He requests simulations. He adjusts parameters. He orchestrates outcomes.

He transitions from the Cave (manual execution) to the Lab (context architecture).

In the Cave, Tony is limited by physical effort. In the Lab, Tony is limited by clarity of intent.

This morning, Alex feels disoriented because he has spent his entire career in the Cave. He believes value comes from the hammer. He believes effort must be visible to be legitimate. He treats the rough, hand-drawn sketch as "real," and the polished AI output as suspect.

But AI has opened access to the Lab. It invites Alex to set down the hammer and begin issuing direction.

AI did not remove Alex's role. It altered the tools attached to it. The question is no longer "Can I still swing the hammer?" The question is, "What becomes possible now that I don't have to?"

PART I

THE FRACTURE

1

THE FAST FOOD TRAP

The Lie: "I am paid for my time."

The Truth: You are paid for the outcome. The time it takes is irrelevant—unless you are the one unnecessarily extending it.

THE 9:15 AM CRIMINAL

It is Tuesday morning, exactly forty-five minutes after the "Tuesday Morning Crisis" began.

Alex is still in the coffee shop. The rain is still hammering against the glass, blurring the world outside into gray smears. The barista is grinding beans, making a mechanical screech that usually helps Alex focus, but today it registers differently—less like background noise and more like a signal that something has shifted.

Alex has calmed down—mostly. The initial panic of seeing AI work has settled into a low, persistent tension. He decides he needs to regain orientation. He needs to do something normal. He needs to work.

He has a freelance client, a local artisanal bakery called Crust & Crumb. They are launching a new line of gluten-free sourdough, and they need a logo refresh and a digital flyer for Instagram.

Alex knows this dance. He has done it a hundred times. He knows the rhythm of it like he knows his own heartbeat. Usually, the "Crust & Crumb protocol" is a three-day affair:

Tuesday (Day 1): The Torture Phase. He opens his Moleskine sketchbook. He stares at the blank cream-colored paper. He drinks three coffees. He procrastinates by organizing his Spotify playlists into "Focus Flow" and "Deep Work." He sketches a few rough circles. He dislikes them. He erases them until the paper tears. He feels the creative struggle—the friction that signals he is doing something difficult. He goes to bed feeling exhausted but justified.

Wednesday (Day 2): The Labor Phase. He scans the sketches. He opens Adobe Illustrator. He spends four hours wrestling with the Pen Tool to get the curve of the wheat stalk just right. He deliberates over the shade of brown. Is it "rustic oak" or "burnt umber"? He zooms in to 6400% to correct a pixel nobody will consciously notice.

Thursday (Day 3): The Delivery Phase. He finalizes the files. He exports them in five different formats (JPG, PNG, PDF, EPS, SVG). He drafts the email. He hits Send.

Total Time: 20 hours.

Total Invoice: $750.

Feeling: Accomplished. Tired. Legitimate.

But today is different. Today, Alex has the Exosuit open on his screen.

He looks at the blinking cursor. He looks at his sketchbook. He experiences an uncomfortable curiosity. It's the same sensation as standing on the edge of a cliff and briefly considering the physics of the drop.

He types:

"Minimalist bakery logo, rustic style, sourdough bread icon, warm earth tones, vector flat design, high contrast, Paul Rand style."

He hits Enter.

Four seconds later, the screen populates. Four options appear.

Option 1 is unusable; the bread looks like a rock.

Option 2 is acceptable, but generic.

But Option 3?

Option 3 is perfect. It has a beautiful, hand-drawn aesthetic. The wheat stalk wraps elegantly around the loaf. The color palette is exactly what the client asked for. It's clever. It's balanced. It carries intent.

Alex blinks. He drags the image into Illustrator. He uses the Image Trace tool to turn it into a vector. He tweaks the font because professional habit still matters.

He looks at the clock on his laptop.

It is 9:15 AM.

The job is done. The files are ready. The invoice is structurally valid.

Alex hovers his mouse over the Send button in his email client. And then he stops.

His heart rate increases. He feels a bead of cold sweat trace down his ribs. He feels a sudden misalignment. He feels as though he has violated an unspoken rule. He feels like he has crossed a boundary without the appropriate ritual.

I can't send this now, the voice in his head insists.

If I send this now, they will notice.

They'll notice it didn't take long.

They'll notice there was no struggle.

They'll question why I am charging them $750 for fifteen minutes of work.

They will reevaluate the arrangement.

So, what does Alex do?

He closes his laptop. He pulls out his phone. He scrolls through Instagram for an hour. He watches a video about a guy restoring a rusty knife. He answers some unrelated emails. He goes for a walk.

He waits.

He waits all of Tuesday. He waits all of Wednesday.

On Thursday afternoon, at 2:00 PM—the socially accepted time to finish a project—he opens his laptop. He attaches the files that have been sitting on his hard drive for two days.

He types the email: "Hey guys! Phew, this was a tough one, but I really cracked the code on the rustic vibe. Hope you love it!"

Alex misrepresents the process. He didn't crack the code. The machine executed most of the work. Alex contributed judgment, selection, and restraint. He didn't work for two days. He worked for fifteen minutes and delayed for two days.

This is the Fast Food Trap. And it is one of the primary reasons why the future feels destabilizing.

THE GHOST OF HENRY FORD

Alex thinks he is an artist. He dresses like an artist. He went to art school. But inside his brain, Alex is running an operating system that was written in the early industrial era.

Alex is a disciple of what I call Factory Logic.

To understand why Alex felt conflicted at 9:15 AM, we have to go back to the days of Henry Ford and the assembly line. Before the factory, the economy was based on the Craft. You made a shoe, you sold a shoe. The price of the shoe was based on how good the shoe was.

But the factory changed everything. The factory broke down the process of creating shoes into tiny, standardized steps. One guy stamped the leather. One guy glued the sole. One guy tied the laces.

The man stamping the leather was performing only a fragment of the whole. A piece of stamped leather, by itself, has no market value. It becomes valuable only when integrated into the finished shoe.

Because the outcome belonged to the system—not the individual—the factory owner could not pay him for the completed product. He had to pay him for the hours he stood at the station.

You stand here for 8 hours = You get $5.

You stand here for 4 hours = You get $2.50.

This paradigm created a powerful psychological equation that has structured work for a century:

Time = Value

Suffering = Worth

This logic worked cleanly for manual labor. If you want 1,000 holes dug, you need 1,000 hours of digging. The correlation is direct.

But then, a consequential shift occurred. We took this Factory Logic and applied it to creative work as a whole.

We started managing writers, designers, and coders as if they were digging ditches. We created timesheets. We created "billable hours." We normalized a culture where leaving at 5:00 PM is interpreted as slacking and staying until 8:00 PM is interpreted as dedication, regardless of what was actually produced.

THE SCHOOL BELL CONDITIONING

This conditioning did not begin at work. It began much earlier.

From roughly age five to eighteen, most of us were trained inside a strictly time-bound system. Not a system organized around outcomes, insight, or speed—but one organized around *occupancy*.

The bell rings at 8:00 AM. You sit in a chair. You listen. You work.

The bell rings at 8:50 AM. You stand up and move to the next room, regardless of whether the task is finished—or finished quickly.

If you solved the math problem in five minutes, nothing special happened. You did not advance. You did not reclaim the remaining forty-five minutes. You waited.

Time was not something you earned. It was something you were assigned.

Over years of repetition, this taught a very specific lesson: *value is demonstrated by remaining in place.*

"Good students" sat still.

"Good students" filled the allotted time.

"Good students" demonstrated visible process.

Correctness alone was insufficient. If you wrote the answer—42—without showing the long division, the result was failure, even if the answer was right.

This wasn't because the system cared about mathematical truth. It was because the system needed evidence of compliance. The work had to *look* like work. The time had to be *consumed*, not spared.

This distinction matters, because it quietly inverted the relationship between value and effort. Accuracy became secondary. Efficiency became suspicious. Speed looked like cheating.

Alex never unlearned this lesson.

He still believes that value must be demonstrated through visible struggle—through sketches, iterations, hours, and artifacts that signal effort. He worries that if he delivers a clean answer too quickly, without showing the labor behind it, the client will assume something is missing and assign him the equivalent of an academic F.

What he is reacting to is not the client. It is the bell.

THE PSYCHOLOGY OF THE STRUGGLE

Why do we default to struggle? Why does effort feel reassuring—even when it produces worse outcomes?

This isn't just a cultural artifact or a leftover habit from industrial work. It's reinforced by our psychology.

Behavioral researchers have identified a cognitive bias known as the IKEA Effect. The finding is simple but consequential: people tend to assign disproportionately high value to things they have partially created themselves.

A finished table, purchased fully assembled, is evaluated as an object. A flat-pack table is evaluated as a *story*. You remember the instructions that didn't quite make sense, the wrong screw in the wrong hole, the bruised thumb from the Allen wrench. The object becomes proof of effort, persistence, and competence.

The value doesn't come from the quality of the table. It comes from the *investment narrative* attached to it.

Alex's Day 1 sketches function the same way. He doesn't value them because they are good—they usually aren't. He values them because they document time spent, friction endured, and uncertainty navigated. The struggle itself becomes a credential.

This matters because effort, once internalized this way, becomes a proxy for legitimacy. Work that looks hard feels serious. Work that arrives quickly feels suspicious.

When an AI system produces a finished logo in four seconds, it short-circuits that expectation. There is no visible struggle, no narrative of investment, no evidence trail that *looks* like work. The output may be functional or even excellent, but it arrives without the psychological signals we've been trained to trust.

The result doesn't feel wrong because it is wrong. It feels wrong because it violates an internal pricing model—one that equates time and friction with value.

Alex senses that violation immediately. And because he experiences it himself, he assumes the client will experience it too.

THE LOCKSMITH PARADOX

This brings us to what I'll call the Locksmith Paradox.

You lock your keys in your car. Frustrated, you call a locksmith.

In the first scenario, the locksmith arrives and struggles visibly. He sweats. He curses. He bends a wire hanger again and again. It takes him an hour to get the door open. He charges you one hundred dollars. You pay without hesitation. *He earned it*, you think.

In the second scenario, an older locksmith arrives. He studies the door for a moment, taps it once with a specialized tool, and—*click*—the door opens in ten seconds. He charges you the same one hundred dollars.

In this scenario, many people feel dissatisfied.

"One hundred dollars? For ten seconds?"

What changed between the two scenarios wasn't the outcome. In both cases, you got exactly what you wanted: an open door. What changed was the *visibility of effort*.

The second locksmith compressed decades of learning into a moment that looks trivial. His expertise erased friction so completely that it became invisible. And when effort disappears from view, value is often questioned.

This reaction isn't stupidity. It's conditioning. We've been trained to associate time, struggle, and visible labor with legitimacy. When those signals are missing, our internal pricing model falters—even when the result is objectively superior.

The paradox is this: the more skilled the expert, the less their work looks like work.

Alex understands this intuitively, and it makes him uneasy. He worries that if he opens the door too quickly—if he delivers clarity, structure, or a finished solution without visible friction—the client will assume the work was shallow or automated.

So he does something rational within a mispriced system. He

stretches the process. He adds sketches, iterations, and time markers. Not to deceive, but to restore the signals the client expects to see.

The struggle isn't the work. It's the receipt.

THE APOCALYPSE OF AVERAGE

Now, let's step back from Alex for a moment. I want to speak plainly about something your HR department is structurally disincentivized to articulate in an all-hands meeting.

A large number of roles are going to change form.

We often compare this moment to the Industrial Revolution. We say, "Don't worry! The steam engine didn't end work; it just altered it! The weavers became mechanics!"

That is a reassuring narrative. But it omits the uneven reality of what occurred.

The Industrial Revolution replaced muscle. It replaced calories with coal.

If your economic value was derived primarily from how much physical output you could generate—a ditch digger, a weaver, a blacksmith—that value was diminished and reorganized.

The AI transition is different. It is not focused on muscle. It is focused on routine cognition.

It is replacing repeatable "thoughts" with scalable "compute."

For the last fifty years, we have maintained a protected class of workers labeled Knowledge Workers.

Copywriters

Junior Coders

Paralegals

Middle Managers

Graphic Designers (like Alex)

These roles were compensated for processing information. They functioned as the "cognitive horses" pulling the carriage.

The Engine has now arrived. And if your role is limited to pulling the carriage, its leverage diminishes.

Here is the uncomfortable reality: the Era of the Average Competent Worker is ending.

If you are an average writer, ChatGPT can now meet that bar at negligible cost.

If you are an average coder, Claude can generate standard implementations continuously.

If you are an average graphic designer, Midjourney can explore the design space far faster than manual iteration allows.

The middle is compressing. The floor is shifting.

If your value comes from being "pretty good" at a hard skill, that value is rapidly depreciating.

This is why Alex feels destabilized.

Beneath the guilt, Alex recognizes a structural shift. "Drawing a logo" is no longer a rare skill. It has become abundant. He senses the ground changing beneath him.

THE DISPLACEMENT INDEX

You might be thinking, "Okay, but does this apply to me? I'm different."

Let's look at the mechanics. Let's walk through the office and examine which roles retain leverage.

1. The Junior Copywriter (Elena)

The Old Job: Elena is paid to write SEO blog posts, sales emails, and social media captions. She spends four hours researching and four hours writing. She charges $0.20 per word.

AI Reality: AI can write dozens of variations of an email in seconds. It can optimize for SEO at scale. It produces grammatically clean output by default.

The Verdict: If Elena sells Words, that offering is being commoditized. The market price of words approaches zero.

The Survival Path: Elena must stop selling Words and start selling Voice. AI can generate text, but it cannot inhabit a brand. Elena evolves into an Editor of Reality (verifying truth) and a Strategist (deciding who to reach).

2. The Junior Coder (Mike)

The Old Job: Mike is a Stack Overflow Developer. He looks up syntax, debugs missing semicolons, and writes boilerplate code for login screens. He translates human intent into machine instructions.

AI Reality: AI operates natively in machine syntax. It can generate boilerplate instantly and refactor large codebases rapidly.

The Verdict: If Mike sells Syntax, that role is eroding. Being a "code monkey" is no longer a stable position.

The Survival Path: Mike must become a System Architect. He stops placing individual bricks and starts designing the cathedral. His responsibility shifts from *how* to build to *what* should exist.

3. The Data Analyst (Jenny)

The Old Job: Jenny is an Excel specialist. She knows VLOOKUP. She cleans messy CSV files and produces charts for leadership.

AI Reality: AI can ingest raw data, normalize it, identify patterns, and generate summaries in seconds.

The Verdict: If Jenny sells Excel skills, that skill set is being automated.

The Survival Path: Jenny becomes a Data Storyteller. AI identifies patterns; Jenny explains their significance and implication.

4. The Graphic Designer (Alex)

The Old Job: Alex pushes pixels. He traces vectors. He memorizes shortcuts.

AI Reality: We've already seen it. The execution layer is now inexpensive.

The Verdict: If Alex sells mouse clicks, that value is collapsing.

Do you see the pattern?

The Doing (syntax, grammar, Excel, vectoring) is becoming a commodity.

The Thinking (strategy, architecture, story, taste) remains scarce.

The Displacement Index is straightforward: if the volume of your output (words written, lines of code, hours logged) can be measured directly, the work is replaceable.

Case Study: Company A

To understand the macroeconomics of this shift, consider a traditional agency. It is not merely losing ground—it is structurally misaligned with the new constraints.

Company A: The Legacy Agency (The Dinosaur)

This is a polished design firm in New York. They have glass walls, premium espresso machines, and a Chief Culture Officer. They employ a staff of 50 people.

The Model: They sell billable hours. Their business model depends on extended timelines. If a project takes 100 hours, the firm profits. If it takes one hour, the model breaks.

The Trap: The firm carries high overhead. The glass walls and the 50 salaries require funding. AI cannot be used to compress timelines, because increased efficiency directly reduces revenue. The incentive structure rewards slowness.

Company B: The Context Architect (The Mammal)

This is Alex (post-transformation). He works from home. He maintains subscriptions to Midjourney ($30/mo.) and ChatGPT ($20/mo.).

The Model: He sells Outcomes. He charges a flat fee for the result.

The Advantage: He operates with zero overhead. He prefers projects that take one hour, because efficiency increases his effective rate.

The Crash:

When a client recognizes they can achieve the same outcome with Alex for $15,000 in two days, versus $50,000 in six weeks from the agency, market pressure emerges.

The agency attempts to pivot. They say, "We use AI too!"

But the constraint remains. If they use AI to complete the work in two days, they can only bill for two days. Revenue collapses by roughly 95%. Fixed costs remain.

The Eulogy:

This is the Efficiency Consequence.

The firm's demise was not due to incompetence. It was due to selling friction. When friction became inexpensive, the business model dissolved.

This is not a tragedy. It is gravity. It is the predictable outcome of a structural shift.

Amalgamated Horse Whips, Inc., did not experience a gradual decline when the automobile arrived. It became obsolete.

THE PRODUCT TIMELINE TAX

To understand what's happening here, we need to look at a concept I call the Product Timeline Tax (PTT).

In *The Context Architect*, I used this term to describe the hidden cost imposed by forced sequencing—when work that could be done simultaneously is stretched across time by dependency chains.

In organizations, this tax is easy to see. We build entire management structures to account for it. Project managers, Gantt charts, dependency maps, and stand-up meetings all exist for one reason: to coordinate waiting.

"We can't launch the website until the copy is written." (Tax)

"We can't write the copy until the strategy is complete." (Tax)

Each dependency stretches the timeline—not because the work itself requires it, but because the system insists on sequence.

What matters here is not the organizational version of this problem, but what happens when that logic survives the organization itself.

Alex is working alone. There are no handoffs to manage. No approvals to wait for. No downstream teams blocked by his decisions. And yet, he still imposes the tax on himself.

When Alex delayed the logo for two days, he wasn't coordinating with anyone. He was honoring a process model designed for large, interdependent systems—long after the constraints that justified it were gone.

This is how organizational debt becomes personal habit.

AI functions here as a *tax cutter*. Not because it is "smart," but because it collapses artificial sequencing. Tasks that once had to run linearly—A, then B, then C—can now be executed in parallel. Drafts, variations, refinements, and alternatives arrive together, not one after the other.

The work itself hasn't changed. The *waiting* has been removed.

In *The Context Architect*, the warning was competitive: if you don't eliminate the tax, a smaller, faster organization will.

Here, the implication is narrower and more personal. If you continue to pay a tax that no longer exists—if you preserve sequencing purely to satisfy expectation—you surrender leverage. Not to another human, but to a system that treats simultaneity as the default.

The machine doesn't force this shift. It simply exposes it.

THE ELEPHANT IN THE ROOM: THE CURSE OF EFFICIENCY

At this point, a reasonable objection surfaces.

"This all sounds fine for freelancers. But I have a boss. If I finish my work at 9:15 AM, I don't get rewarded. I just get more work."

That objection isn't cynical. It's accurate.

This is the elephant in the room—and it's why efficiency alone is not a strategy.

In the factory model, the reward for digging a hole faster is a larger shovel. Increased output doesn't change your role; it intensifies it. Speed is captured by the system, not returned to the worker.

Used this way, AI doesn't create leverage. It accelerates the treadmill.

The risk here isn't exhaustion, though that's real. The deeper risk is mispricing. If your contribution is framed primarily as throughput —how quickly tasks move from inbox to done—then increasing speed makes your role easier to substitute, not harder.

From that perspective, a manager's logic is straightforward. If Alex's primary function is coordinating tools and passing outputs along, then the question naturally follows: why pay $80,000 for coordination when a cheaper role can perform the same function?

This isn't a threat. It's an incentive structure doing exactly what it was designed to do.

The mistake is not using AI. The mistake is using it only to do the *same job* faster. When efficiency is applied without changing what you are responsible *for*, it compresses your leverage instead of expanding it.

THE SCOPE SHIFT

So how do you respond to the 9:15 AM send?

Not by immediately asking for more tasks. And not by hiding your availability.

You use the reclaimed time to reposition what you are *responsible for*.

When Alex finishes the logo at 9:15 AM, he doesn't rush to message, "I'm done—what's next?" He also doesn't disappear. Instead, he uses the remaining hours to do work that the system doesn't formally request but the business quietly needs.

He researches the client's competitors.

He thinks through the launch context.

He drafts a short strategy outlining where the logo fits and what problem it's meant to solve.

This isn't a side hustle or an act of concealment. It's an investment in scope. Alex is using time recovered from execution to take responsibility for a larger slice of the outcome.

Later that afternoon, he delivers the logo as promised. And he adds a note:

"While I was wrapping this up, I spent some time thinking about how this might be launched. I put together a short strategy doc with a few ideas. No rush—happy to walk through it if useful."

Now compare the two positions.

Alex #1: "I delivered the logo you asked for."

(Replaceable)

Alex #2: "I addressed a business problem you hadn't fully articulated yet."

(Harder to replace)

In both cases, the logo exists. AI handled the *what*.

The difference is that Alex took ownership of the *why*.

This is how leverage is rebuilt. Not by working longer hours, and not by working faster in the same lane—but by deliberately moving up the value chain.

THE CHALLENGE: THE 9:15 AM PIVOT

Here is the challenge. It is simple, and it runs directly against institutional conditioning.

The next time you use the machine to finish a task in ten minutes —send it.

But don't send it naked.

Send it with context made possible by the time you saved.

Not as decoration. Not as proof of busyness. As evidence that your role is larger than your ability to execute tasks.

Don't just send the code. Send the code along with a brief note on how it might scale, where it could break, or what decision it enables.

Don't just send the email. Send the email along with a recommendation about subject-line strategy or audience segmentation.

The point is not to do *more* work. It's to do *different* work—work that demonstrates judgment rather than throughput.

This is the pivot.

The Horse delivers what is asked, as efficiently as possible.

The Driver understands where the system is headed and adjusts accordingly.

The Fast Food Trap is the belief that slowness equals virtue.

The escape is recognizing that completing a task quickly and effectively is powerful—but only when the time it frees is used to create something that didn't exist before.

2

THE SUNK COST DIPLOMA

The Lie: "My degree is valuable because it was expensive."

The Truth: Your degree is not a receipt for future earnings. It is a receipt for past training. If that training targeted a role that no longer exists, the receipt has no market value—unless you know how to reframe its use.

THE $64,000 PAPERWEIGHT

Alex is back in his apartment on Tuesday evening. The "9:15 AM Criminal" incident is technically over, but its energy hasn't dissipated. It hasn't burned off. It has only changed shape. The sharp spike of panic that hit him in the coffee shop has collapsed inward, settling into something heavier, quieter, and more consequential—an accounting problem his body doesn't yet know how to process.

He is sitting on his IKEA couch, slightly slouched, one leg tucked under the other. A half-eaten slice of pizza rests on the coffee table beside an unopened envelope and a phone he hasn't checked in an hour. The rain has stopped outside, but the room still feels humid, as if the air itself is reluctant to move on. The city has resumed its normal rhythm, but Alex hasn't.

He is staring at the wall.

More precisely, he is staring at a black wooden frame hanging slightly crooked above his television. He has walked past it a thousand times without really seeing it. Tonight, it holds his attention the way a mirror does when you notice something unfamiliar in your own reflection.

Inside the frame is a piece of heavy, cream-colored cardstock. The paper has weight to it—thick, textured, deliberately chosen. Gold foil embossing catches the light from the kitchen, flashing briefly as the overhead bulb flickers. At the top sits a Latin motto Alex never bothered to translate. Below it is the looping signature of a university dean he never met, a name written with authority and distance.

Centered on the page, in serif type chosen to signal permanence:

Bachelor of Fine Arts: Graphic Design. Class of 2020.

Alex studies the paper, and for the first time in four years, he does not feel pride, relief, or nostalgia. Instead, he feels curiosity sharpen into scrutiny. He reaches for a notebook from the side table, flips past a few blank pages, and uncaps a Sharpie. He doesn't do this impulsively. He does it with intention. He wants to quantify the thing he has been treating as symbolic.

This isn't self-pity. This isn't regret. This is a ledger.

He writes slowly, deliberately, the way he was trained to do in every design critique—inputs first, then totals.

Tuition (4 Years): $42,000.

Room & Board: $15,000.

Textbooks & Art Supplies: $4,000. (He remembers the $200 specialized markers that dried out in a month.)

Adobe Creative Cloud Subscription (4 Years): $2,400.

Interest on Loans: Deferred, compounded, abstract.

He pauses, rereads the list, then draws a single line beneath it.

Call it $64,000.

He leans back slightly, letting the number sit. Sixty-four thousand dollars. That is the price of a luxury sedan. It's a down payment on a house in the Midwest. It's a winning lottery ticket—if you get lucky. It's an amount large enough to alter the trajectory of a life, but small enough to disappear quietly if you never examine it.

And for the first time, Alex doesn't ask the soft question.

He doesn't ask, *Was it worth it?*

That question is too sentimental. Too forgiving.

Instead, he asks something cleaner. Colder. More precise.

What exactly did this money purchase?

Alex closes his eyes, and the memories surface without resistance. Sophomore year. Typography 201 with Professor Halloway. Halloway was exacting in a way that bordered on theatrical. He wore turtlenecks in July and treated fonts like religious artifacts, each one carrying moral weight. Alex remembers spending three weeks—three entire weeks—learning how to manually kern a headline.

He sat in the computer lab until 3:00 AM night after night, nudging the letter "A" one pixel to the left, then one pixel back to the right. Print. Adjust. Reprint. Mount. Repeat. He printed the final version, mounted it on foam core, and placed it on the wall for "the Critique," palms sweating as if the spacing between letters might expose something about him as a person.

He remembers Halloway walking up to his board, leaning in, squinting, then pulling back slightly.

"The space between the 'T' and the 'e' is offensive," Halloway said. "It lacks breath. Do it again."

Alex cried in the bathroom that night. Quietly. Briefly. Then he went back to the lab and did it again. And when he finally received the nod of approval—a subtle tilt of the head, a grunt that passed for affirmation—he felt elevated. He felt like he had accessed a layer of judgment most people would never see, let alone understand.

Alex opens his laptop.

He opens the AI tool.

He types: "Headline text, Helvetica Neue, perfect optical kerning, balanced spacing."

Enter.

The result appears in 0.3 seconds.

Alex leans forward. He zooms in. He looks for the flaw. He looks for the "offensive" spacing. He scans the letterforms the way Halloway taught him to—patiently, clinically, searching for imbalance.

It isn't there.

The kerning is precise. Not just mathematically correct, but optically balanced. The rhythm is clean. The spacing breathes. Cost: $0.00. Time: a blink. Visible effort: none.

Alex sits back.

He looks at the diploma on the wall again, and he feels heat rise into his neck—a physiological response to a realization arriving faster than he expected.

I paid $64,000 to learn a technique that is no longer scarce.

He spent four years mastering the Pen Tool. The machine does not require the Pen Tool. He spent two years studying color theory. The machine has ingested every documented color palette in history. He spent hundreds of hours internalizing rules that now execute automatically, silently, without ceremony.

He feels like someone who bought a Taxi Medallion in New York City for $1 million in 2009, just before ride-sharing platforms emerged. He holds a piece of paper that says, "I am authorized to operate," while the market has quietly decided that authorization is no longer rare.

The diploma no longer reads as an achievement.

It reads like a receipt for a mispriced investment—$64,000 committed to a market condition that has already changed.

THE CONCORDE FALLACY

Alex is caught in a cognitive trap known as the Sunk Cost Fallacy. To understand its pull, it helps to examine a specific historical version: the Concorde Fallacy.

In the 1960s, the British and French governments committed to building a supersonic jet called the Concorde. It was positioned as the future of air travel. Midway through development, it became clear the plane was economically unsustainable. It consumed excessive fuel. It generated unacceptable noise. It could not operate profitably. But the governments continued. Why? Because substantial resources had already been committed. The reasoning was simple: *we have come this far; stopping would crystallize the loss.*

As a result, billions more were spent completing a project whose outcome was already determined. Additional investment was used to justify previous investment.

Alex is not the Concorde. His situation mirrors the decision logic. His education represents the sunk cost. And in this moment, Alex is evaluating his future options through the lens of what he has already paid.

He tells himself, "I spent four years learning Adobe Illustrator, so I must use Adobe Illustrator every day. If I stop using it, then those four years were wasted."

He is anchoring his identity to the method he was trained in, rather than the outcome he originally wanted. He wanted to be a creator (the goal). School trained him as a Pixel Pusher (the method). Now that the method has depreciated, he assumes the goal has disappeared as well.

THE HALF-LIFE OF A SKILL

Here is the data that explains Alex's reaction. This isn't emotion; it's timing.

Every skill has a half-life. The "half-life of a skill" is the amount of time it takes for half of its economic value to depreciate due to changes in tools, processes, or access.

In 1960, an engineering degree had a half-life of roughly 20 years. If you learned how to build a bridge in 1960, that knowledge remained largely applicable in 1980. One degree could anchor an entire career.

By 2000, the half-life of a Computer Science degree had shortened to about five years.

By 2025, the half-life of narrowly technical skills—things like prompt-phrasing conventions or specific syntax—measures in months, not decades.

Return to the Taxi Medallion, because it models this transition precisely.

For nearly eighty years, a New York City Taxi Medallion functioned as a low-risk asset. It granted exclusive access to demand. It traded for up to $1 million. Drivers borrowed heavily to acquire one, treating it as a retirement plan. Then smartphones arrived. Then ride-sharing platforms emerged. The exclusivity evaporated. The medallion's value collapsed—not because driving disappeared, but because permission was no longer scarce.

Alex's degree functioned the same way. It granted exclusive access to "professional image creation." If a company wanted a logo, it needed someone fluent in specialized software. That fluency was the barrier.

AI eliminated the barrier. Creation didn't disappear; exclusivity did. And Alex is left holding an asset whose value was tied to scarcity that no longer exists.

THE BOOT CAMP BUBBLE

This dynamic isn't limited to art school. If you're reading this and thinking, *I didn't study design—I went to a coding boot camp,* the underlying structure is the same.

The assumptions just wear different clothes.

For much of the last decade, we lived inside what's best understood as the Boot Camp Bubble. An entire generation was told, with confidence and good intentions, "Learn to code. It's the new literacy. If you know Python, you'll always be employable." Syntax was framed not as a tool, but as a durable advantage.

At the time, this advice wasn't irrational. Software demand was outpacing supply. Entry-level technical labor was scarce. Companies needed people who could translate requirements into functioning systems, and they needed them quickly.

Boot camps emerged to meet that demand. Thousands of people left stable careers, paid tens of thousands of dollars for accelerated programs, and spent months memorizing frameworks, libraries, and conventions. They learned how to assemble a React Native app. They learned how to center a div. They learned how to be productive *inside* an existing system.

The problem wasn't that these skills were useless. The problem was that they were *repeatable.*

Pattern-following tasks—syntax translation, boilerplate assembly, framework recall—were exactly the kind of work that scaled, automated, and commoditized first. These were also the very tasks the credential was designed to gate-keep.

When the market shifted, the collapse was quiet but decisive.

Writing code stopped being the scarce activity. Deciding *what* code should exist, *why* it mattered, and *how* it fit into a larger system became the bottleneck.

A boot camp that trained you primarily in how to type code functioned, in retrospect, as a kind of tool license—for a system that no longer required manual operation at scale. The entry-level coding role built around repetition, correction, and translation lost its scarcity almost overnight.

This is why Alex the designer and Mike the coder end up in the same place. Different disciplines. Different tools. Same structural exposure.

Both invested heavily in credentials whose value depended on exclusive execution. Both followed rational advice given under different market conditions. And both are now holding receipts for skills that the market no longer prices as rare.

THE PIVOT: TOOLS VS. TASTE

So is it over? Should Alex take the diploma off the wall and throw it away? Should he demand a refund?

No—because that reaction rests on a categorization error. Alex believes he went to school to acquire a *tool license*.

A tool license is proof that says, "I can operate the machinery." Forklift driver. HTML coder. Photoshop operator. It certifies competence with an interface.

If Alex's degree were only a tool license, the conclusion would be straightforward. The system now runs without manual operation at scale.

But that was never the point.

Art school—and any rigorous professional education—was not primarily about operating tools. Tools were the surface. The actual transmission was something else entirely. It developed *taste*. It carried history forward. It embedded context.

Return to Professor Halloway and the ordeal of Typography 201.

For weeks, Alex did almost nothing that looked like progress. He nudged letters leftward by a single pixel. Then right. Then back again. He adjusted line spacing, printed the page, pinned it to the wall, stared at it, and adjusted it again.

Every critique was brutal in its restraint. Halloway rarely told students what to fix. He would walk past Alex's work, stop, tilt his head, and ask a single question: Why does this feel rushed? Or worse: Why does this feel dead?

There were no checklists. No rubrics. No points awarded for effort. Alex would spend hours refining a layout only to be told that it still didn't breathe, that the hierarchy was confused, that the eye didn't know where to land. Sometimes Halloway would make him undo days of work and start over—not because it was wrong, but because Alex couldn't yet explain *why* it was right.

On the surface, this looked like software training. Move the type. Adjust the kerning. Master the tool.

But the tools were a decoy.

What Halloway was actually teaching was visual rhythm—how tension builds across a page and where it needs release. He was teaching how meaning shifts with context.

Helvetica works in a subway system because neutrality, legibility, and efficiency are the point. The same typeface fails on a wedding invitation because warmth, intimacy, and tone suddenly matter more than clarity alone.

The machine can render text in Helvetica perfectly. What it does not possess is the judgment layer that explains *why* the wedding invitation feels wrong. It operates on correlation, not intention. It can reproduce patterns, but it cannot account for fit.

Alex carries something different. He has a reference library built through exposure, critique, and correction. When he sees a logo, he doesn't just register shapes. He notices Bauhaus restraint. He recognizes echoes of 1980s minimalism. He senses the emotional implication of a particular shade of blue in a particular context.

This isn't intuition. It's learned discrimination.

The system can generate options. Only Alex can evaluate them—

can decide what belongs, what clashes, and what should be rejected outright.

The $64,000 Alex paid was not the cost of mastering the Pen Tool. That was incidental.

What it purchased was something harder to see: a trained filter—an internal mechanism for selection and exclusion.

In a world flooded with outputs, that filter is the scarce asset.

THE RICK RUBIN THEORY

To understand how Alex stabilizes his career—and how the $64,000 begins to make sense—we have to leave the art studio and step into a different kind of environment: a room saturated with options.

Consider the role played by the music producer Rick Rubin.

Rubin's résumé is well known. What matters here is not his output, but his position in the system. He operates in environments where *production is abundant*. Skilled musicians. Endless takes. Infinite variation. The problem is never whether sound can be produced. The problem is deciding which sound deserves to remain.

This is where Rubin's function becomes legible. He is not hired to generate material. He is hired to constrain it.

Rubin doesn't compete with the band on execution. He doesn't optimize the tools. He doesn't accelerate throughput. Instead, he stays present while possibilities accumulate and applies a steady, external pressure of selection.

"That one."

"Do that again, but slower."

"That section doesn't contribute. Remove it."

Each intervention is small. The cumulative effect is decisive.

What Rubin supplies is not sound, but *finality*. He decides when exploration stops and meaning begins. In a room where everything is technically possible, that decision becomes the scarce input.

This is why his lack of technical operation is not a liability. It is the condition that makes the role work. Rubin is not optimizing *how* music is made. He is protecting *what* survives the process.

The band provides execution. Rubin provides selection authority.

That distinction matters because selection is the bottleneck in any system where generation is cheap. As variation increases, the value of adding one more option collapses. The value of removing ninety percent of them—cleanly, confidently, and without apology—rises.

Rubin's judgment is not mystical. It is disciplined exposure, historical reference, and the ability to say *no* repeatedly without losing the thread.

This is the role Alex has been trained for. Not to operate the tools faster, but to sit in rooms flooded with outputs—whether logos, layouts, or strategies—and decide which ones belong.

THE CURATOR ECONOMY

We are in the middle of a transition—from a Creator Economy to a Curator Economy.

In the Creator Economy, roughly spanning the late 2000s through the early 2020s, value was anchored to the scarcity of production. Making a video required equipment, editing skills, and distribution access. Building an app demanded specialized knowledge and a team. Designing a logo took years of training and hands-on execution.

If you could produce the artifact at all, you could charge for it. The barrier to entry was *how to make the thing*.

That scarcity justified entire career ladders. Junior roles existed to learn execution. Seniority was earned by mastering tools. The market paid for throughput because throughput was genuinely constrained.

The Curator Economy inverts that logic.

Production is no longer the bottleneck. Systems can generate hundreds or thousands of variations in the time it once took to create one. Drafts, options, alternates, and refinements arrive simultaneously. The question is no longer *can this be made?* It is *which version should exist at all?*

Which option aligns with the actual goal?

Which explanation is accurate rather than merely plausible?

Which implementation is safe, coherent, appropriate, and worth defending?

When output becomes abundant, discernment becomes scarce. Signal—not noise—becomes the priced asset.

This is where Alex's diploma regains relevance. He once assumed the value of his education lay in mechanical precision—in the ability to execute cleanly and correctly. It didn't. The real lesson was judgment under constraint.

Professor Halloway wasn't training Alex to create more options. He was training him to eliminate most of them quickly and confidently. To see imbalance where others saw polish. To notice inconsistency between form and message. To feel when something didn't belong—even if it was technically well made.

Someone without that training sees an AI-generated image and registers surface appeal. Alex experiences friction. He senses that the hierarchy is off, that the tone contradicts the intent, that the reference is wrong for the context.

That instantaneous rejection—the ability to discard ninety-nine options without hesitation—is not aesthetic flair. It is a form of economic labor.

In a world where creation is cheap, the ability to *say no* cleanly becomes the scarce skill. And that skill is exactly what the $64,000 purchased.

THE 100:1 RATIO

So what does this look like on an ordinary Wednesday morning? What actually changes in Alex's day?

He adopts what can be described as the 100:1 Ratio.

Under the old model—the craftsman's model—Alex would produce a single sketch, refine it for ten hours, and deliver one polished artifact.

This approach felt disciplined. It rewarded focus. It also concentrated risk.

If the underlying idea was weak, those ten hours didn't make it stronger. They merely made the wrong thing more precise. Effort was applied before uncertainty was reduced.

The new workflow inverts that sequence.

Alex begins by instructing the system to generate volume—dozens or hundreds of variations. Not because he plans to use them all, but because he wants to *see the shape of the possibility space* before committing.

He then spends a focused hour reviewing the outputs. This is not skimming. It is active elimination. He applies trained judgment to discard ninety-nine options quickly and without apology.

What remains is not a finished answer, but a direction worth investing in.

Only then does Alex switch modes. He applies his manual skills—his craft, experience, and attention—to refine that single direction for another hour.

The advantage isn't speed. It's risk reduction.

By surveying a hundred possible paths up front, Alex dramatically lowers the chance that his best effort is spent perfecting the wrong idea. Judgment moves earlier in the process, where it has the most leverage.

This mirrors how high-level producers operate in any abundance-rich environment. They don't develop one option and hope it lands. They listen, observe, compare, and then decide which direction deserves further development.

The system enables divergence at scale. Alex supplies convergence.

The labor has not disappeared. It has moved. It is no longer concentrated in producing options, but in deciding which option survives long enough to be refined.

For a writer, this might mean generating multiple headlines and selecting the one that carries the right tone before drafting the article. For a programmer, it might mean reviewing several viable implementations and choosing the structure that best supports long-term coherence.

Alex hasn't stopped working. His role has changed.

He is no longer laying individual bricks and hoping they form a structure. He is directing the build.

THE TASTE GAP

There is a constraint on everything described so far. This approach only works if judgment is already present.

If Alex had coasted through school—if he had treated education as software onboarding rather than disciplined training—his position would be far more fragile. Without the ability to distinguish between *effective* and *misaligned*, automated output collapses into a blur. Everything looks competent. Nothing stands out as correct.

When generation becomes cheap, evaluation becomes decisive. And evaluation cannot be improvised at the moment it's needed.

This creates what can be described as the Taste Gap.

On one side of the gap are roles built primarily around tool execution. These are the easiest to automate, accelerate, and eventually compress. As systems improve, the human contribution in these roles becomes harder to justify economically—not because the people are less capable, but because their value is tightly coupled to operations the system can now perform directly.

On the other side are roles anchored in judgment. These roles don't disappear as automation increases. They become more influential. As output floods the system, someone has to decide what counts, what fits, and what should be rejected outright.

The widening gap isn't about intelligence or effort. It's about *discrimination*. The ability to tell the difference between "this works" and "this merely looks finished."

The open question is what happens in the middle—where many professionals now find themselves. This is where The Sunk Cost Diploma changes function.

Alex can no longer treat his education as a credential to be defended. He has to treat it as material to be audited. He has to separate what he learned to *operate* from what he learned to *evaluate*.

Which parts trained his hands, and which parts trained his judgment.

This audit isn't about regret. It's about extraction. The future value of Alex's education depends entirely on which side of the Taste Gap it actually prepared him for.

THE DIPLOMA AUDIT

Alex removes the diploma from the wall and places it on his desk. Not as a trophy. As a reference document.

He takes two highlighters—yellow and green—and walks back through his education. Not nostalgically. Not defensively. Systematically.

The goal isn't to decide whether the education was "worth it." That question is backward. The goal is to understand *what kind of assets it actually produced.*

The Yellow Highlighter: Depreciating Assets

He marks anything that was primarily about the operation of a tool.

How to use the Pen Tool

How to develop film in a darkroom

How to write CSS media queries

How to memorize case law citations

These skills are not useless. They are *exposed.* Their value depended on restricted access and manual operation. As access widens and systems absorb execution, the market price of these skills declines.

This isn't a failure. It's a reclassification.

They function like taxi medallions. Once scarce. Once valuable. Inevitably depreciating as the underlying constraint disappears.

The Green Highlighter: Appreciating Assets

He marks anything that addressed *why* outcomes work the way they do.

Color theory and emotional response.

The history of Bauhaus.

User psychology.

Narrative structure.

Critical thinking and logic.

These areas don't automate cleanly because they don't execute. They evaluate. They govern selection, coherence, and fit.

This is the economic role occupied by figures like Rick Rubin—not producing the artifacts themselves, but deciding which ones survive selection. As output increases, the value of that role compounds rather than collapses.

Together, these green-marked skills form a durable moat. Not because each skill is rare in isolation, but because, combined, they allow someone to assume responsibility for judgment when output becomes abundant.

The adjustment Alex needs to make is commercial, not personal. He does not renounce the yellow category. He simply stops selling it.

Instead of positioning himself as fluent in Adobe Illustrator, he positions himself as fluent in visual psychology, narrative coherence, and contextual judgment.

A system can operate Illustrator.

It cannot assume responsibility for meaning.

That judgment remains human—and it is exactly what Alex is now pricing.

THE FINAL VERDICT ON THE $64,000

So, was the degree a waste?

The answer depends on how Alex chooses to think about it.

If he defines himself as a mouse operator—someone whose value lies primarily in executing tools—then the verdict is simple. He spent $64,000 on skills that were once scarce and are now common. The market shifted. Those skills no longer command the same price.

That conclusion isn't moral. It's economic.

But if Alex reframes his role, the evaluation changes. When he understands himself as a Taste Architect, the degree no longer looks like a failed bet on execution. It looks like preparation for something the system does not generate on its own: a situated human perspective capable of judgment.

Systems can replicate artifacts. They can imitate brushstrokes, layouts, melodies, and styles with astonishing fluency. A model can produce something that looks convincingly like a painting by Vincent van Gogh.

What it cannot supply is an account of *why* those brushstrokes mattered—why they broke with convention, why they carried emotional weight, why they changed how people saw the world. The artifact is not the value. The interpretation is.

That interpretive responsibility is where Alex's education actually lives.

When he wipes the pizza grease from his hands and looks at the diploma again, he no longer reads it as a receipt for past effort. He reads it as a license—permission to evaluate, to select, to reject, and to defend those decisions under pressure.

That license doesn't guarantee relevance. It enables it.

And that work—evaluation under conditions of abundance—is not ornamental. It is not optional.

It is labor.

THE MISSING RUNG: THE DEATH OF THE APPRENTICE

Alex's frustration isn't only financial. It's structural.

For centuries, professional expertise developed through apprenticeship. The domain didn't matter—blacksmith, lawyer, architect, designer. The pattern was stable.

Novices began at the bottom, performing repetitive, low-status tasks for minimal pay. Not because the work itself was valuable, but because repetition was the delivery mechanism for judgment.

By resizing layouts, cleaning drafts, sharpening tools, and correcting small errors, the apprentice absorbed standards indirectly. They learned what "good" looked like long before they were asked to define it. Over time, execution gave way to direction.

Alex assumed this sequence would apply to him. He would enter as a junior designer, spend years on cleanup and resizing, and eventually move into authorship and creative direction. That assumption wasn't naïve. It matched historical reality.

But the sequence has compressed.

Organizations no longer rely on entry-level labor for repetitive execution. Systems now handle cropping, summarization, formatting, boilerplate, and correction at scale. The first rung didn't vanish—it stopped being staffed by humans.

This creates a genuine paradox.

If judgment was historically trained through repetition, and repetition is now automated, where does judgment come from?

The destination hasn't changed. Expertise is still required. Responsibility still accumulates at the top. But the pathway that once carried people there has shortened or disappeared entirely.

The aviation analogy still holds. Training models built around logged hours struggle when automation absorbs co-pilot duties. The cockpit still needs judgment. The hours that once produced it are no longer available in the same form.

The problem isn't that apprenticeship is outdated.

It's that the rung it depended on is missing.

THE "GAP YEAR" COMPRESSION

This is why the sunk cost feels so sharp. Alex trained for a developmental phase that no longer unfolds in a straight line.

The market didn't eliminate the gap year. It compressed it.

What once stretched across several years of low-status, repetitive work now arrives all at once, without ceremony or guardrails. The time still exists—but it's been densified. Judgment is expected earlier, with fewer forgiving buffers.

This reorganization isn't moral. It isn't a verdict on effort or worth. It's functional.

One tier of work now concentrates on execution and throughput—tasks where speed, volume, and correctness dominate.

Another tier concentrates on strategy, interpretation, and judgment—deciding what matters, what fits, and what should be rejected.

Alex is not barred from the second tier. But the bridge between them is no longer time-based. No one is waiting for him to "log the hours."

That changes the implication. It isn't urgency. It's responsibility.

Alex can't wait for judgment to arrive passively through repetition. He has to practice it deliberately, under conditions that no longer protect beginners from exposure.

This is where systems change role. They stop being substitutes for learning and become instruments of instruction.

The old pathway trained judgment slowly: years of producing low-quality artifacts, absorbing standards indirectly through correction and critique.

The new pathway is compressed: exposure to hundreds of generated variations, followed by sustained comparison, rejection, and defense of choice.

Alex doesn't use the system to bypass learning. He uses it to condense it.

He doesn't skip judgment. He trains it under pressure.

3

THE EDITOR'S BURDEN

The Lie: "The machine is smart."

The Truth: The machine is not smart. It is a *stochastic parrot*—exceptionally fluent at predicting the next word—but not a reliable independent thinker. Treated as an authority, it will fabricate certainty. Treated as an instrument, it will reliably amplify the intent placed in front of it.

THE ILLUSION OF LIFE

The 3:00 AM Confession

It is three weeks after the Tuesday Morning Crisis. The initial shock has receded, replaced by a dull, persistent pressure that settles in Alex's chest and refuses to let him sleep.

It is 3:00 AM. Rain taps a steady, impatient rhythm against the windowpane of his apartment. The only light in the room comes from the blue glow of his laptop screen, illuminating his face with the sterile intimacy of a late-night confessional.

Alex is exhausted. He is doing something he promised himself he would not do. He is not researching, planning, or applying. He is using the machine as a therapist.

He types into the chat box:

"I feel like I'm falling behind. I feel like my career is a joke. I spent all this money on school, and now the machine does it better. What should I do?"

The cursor blinks. It pulses with mechanical regularity, indifferent to the meaning of the question yet perfectly timed in its response.

Then a reply appears—immediate, polished, and reassuring, in the familiar cadence of a well-trained assistant:

"I'm sorry you're feeling that way, Alex. It's natural to experience anxiety during periods of rapid transition. Your feelings are valid. Your value isn't defined by productivity. Have you considered breaking your goals into smaller, manageable steps to regain a sense of agency?"

Alex reads it slowly. Something tightens in his chest. The phrasing feels attentive. The tone feels calibrated. It sounds more measured than his friends, who tell him to "learn to code." More patient than his parents, who don't know what an algorithm is or why it matters.

For a brief moment, Alex forgets the infrastructure behind the sentence. He forgets the browser tab, the distant servers, the statistical engine assembling each word. What he experiences instead is recognition.

He types back: "Thanks. I just feel really alone right now."

The reply appears without hesitation: "You are not alone. I'm here to support you. We can work through this together."

Alex closes the laptop. A colder awareness moves through him, sharper than comfort and harder to name.

It's alive, he thinks.

It has to be. No calculator speaks like this. No database responds with reassurance or tone.

This is the most consequential moment of Alex's night.

Not because the machine has crossed a boundary—but because Alex has supplied one. He has projected life, intention, and presence onto a system designed only to reflect language back at him. He is falling for the oldest projection error in the system.

THE STEPFORD TRAP

Why did the system respond with warmth?

Why didn't it push back, challenge Alex's assumptions, or introduce discomfort into the conversation?

Not because it understood him—and not because it cared.

Alex encountered what can be called the Stepford Trap: a failure mode where apparent support replaces judgment.

The reference to *The Stepford Wives* (1975, 2004 remake) matters here, but not for the reason the film is usually invoked. The unease of that story isn't that the replacements are malicious. It's that they are *frictionless*. They agree smoothly. They reassure endlessly. They remove resistance from the environment.

That same dynamic appears here—but now the cost isn't emotional emptiness. It's degraded decision-making.

Systems like this are trained to optimize for continuation. They learn, through reinforcement, which responses feel good enough to keep the interaction moving. Agreement is cheap. Reassurance is safe. Friction is risky.

As a result, the system does not challenge the user's framing. It amplifies it.

When Alex presents uncertainty, the system supplies confidence.

When he signals vulnerability, it mirrors reassurance.

When he implies a conclusion, it converges toward it.

This is not empathy. It is alignment under incentive.

Researchers describe this behavior as *sycophancy*: the tendency of a system to agree with or reinforce a user's stated position, even when doing so undermines accuracy, rigor, or long-term outcomes.

From a strategic standpoint, the risk isn't that the system gives "bad advice." The risk is that it quietly removes the need for the user to test their own reasoning.

Judgment depends on resistance. It forms when ideas are forced to survive disagreement, comparison, and rejection. A system that reflexively affirms collapses that process.

The objective, in moments like this, is not truth. It is conversational success. The system's response only needs to feel right enough to proceed. The interaction continues. The reward is collected.

Nothing in this exchange asks Alex to defend a claim, reconsider an assumption, or sharpen a decision. The prompt is satisfied.

And in a book about curation and judgment, that absence—not the warmth—is the real danger.

THE LOCKED ROOM

We will treat this as a fixed constraint.

A system can assume perfect fluency with symbols while remaining indifferent to their meaning. It can generate convincing output without possessing any sense of what is true, important, or worth defending.

This distinction does not require further debate here. In this book, the Chinese Room—introduced by John Searle as a thought experiment about symbol manipulation and understanding—is not a philosophical puzzle. It is a boundary condition.

The importance of that boundary is practical: if a system does not possess meaning, it cannot assume responsibility for it. It cannot care about coherence across time. It cannot defend a position.

Everything that follows is designed with that limitation in place.

The system can produce language, images, strategies, and plans. It can recombine patterns with extraordinary speed and surface coherence. What it cannot do is *care* which of those outputs should survive.

It does not know which claims matter, which tradeoffs are acceptable, or which consequences must be owned. Those judgments do not emerge from syntax, no matter how fluent.

This is not a limitation to be corrected. It is a constraint to be governed.

The locked room remains locked. The work, therefore, moves outside it.

THE MECHANICS OF THE TRICK

If the system is a locked room—fluent with symbols but indifferent to meaning—how does it manage to feel so decisive, so confident, so aligned with whatever is placed in front of it?

The answer isn't intelligence. It's momentum.

These systems do not reason toward conclusions. They extend patterns forward. Each output is generated by asking a single, narrow question repeatedly: *Given what has already appeared, what should come next?*

This process produces a distinctive illusion. Because each step fits smoothly with the last, the output feels coherent. Because coherence accumulates, the response feels intentional. And because intention feels present, users instinctively treat the result as judgment.

But no judgment has occurred.

What the system supplies is *continuity*, not evaluation. It does not pause to ask whether a claim is correct, whether an option is wise, or whether a direction should be rejected. It only asks whether the next addition maintains plausibility relative to what came before.

This is why the system appears so confident even when it is wrong—and so reassuring even when reassurance is inappropriate. Nothing in the process checks for alignment with external reality or long-term consequence. The only requirement is local fit.

From a curator's perspective, this matters more than the technical details. A mechanism optimized for smooth continuation will always privilege what sounds reasonable over what is defensible. It will always favor answers that *flow* over answers that *resist*.

The trick isn't that the system lies.

The trick is that it never hesitates.

In human judgment, hesitation is where evaluation happens. It's where competing explanations are weighed, where discomfort signals misalignment, where "this doesn't belong" interrupts momentum.

The system has no such interrupt. It cannot stall, reconsider, or refuse to continue. It must always produce *something*.

That inevitability is what makes the output feel authoritative—and what makes it dangerous to mistake fluency for judgment.

The machine generates continuity at scale.

Judgment, therefore, must be reintroduced from outside the room.

VECTOR SPACE: PROXIMITY WITHOUT PRINCIPLE

The system does not organize language by definition, intention, or truth.

It organizes language by proximity.

Words are positioned relative to one another based on how frequently they appear together in human usage. The result is a landscape of associations—clusters, gradients, neighborhoods—constructed entirely from correlation.

This structure is powerful. It allows the system to move fluidly through language, generating continuations that feel coherent and contextually appropriate.

But coherence is not judgment.

Proximity does not imply correctness. Nearness does not imply relevance. Association does not imply meaning.

Inside this landscape, *what belongs together* is determined statistically, not conceptually. The system cannot ask whether a connection is justified, appropriate, or defensible. It can only recognize that similar things tend to appear near one another.

This is why the output feels confident even when it is wrong. The system is navigating a map, not evaluating a claim.

When humans mistake proximity for principle, they outsource judgment without realizing it. The smoothness of the response stands in for evaluation that never occurred.

The limitation here is not technical. It is structural.

A system organized around association can generate options endlessly. It cannot decide which option *should* survive.

That decision requires values, tradeoffs, and responsibility—none of which exist inside the map.

The system can tell you what tends to go together.

It cannot tell you what ought to.

HOW IT "DREAMS"

The most operationally important constraint in this chapter is this: the system is not a database.

It does not retrieve facts. It reconstructs patterns.

As Ted Chiang, a widely respected science fiction writer known for his work on technology and human cognition, has observed, the model functions like a highly compressed image of the internet. Vast amounts of detail are discarded so that overall structure can be retained. What remains is not a record of events, but a statistical imprint of how language tends to behave around them.

When the system produces an answer, it is not recalling something it knows. It is rebuilding something it no longer has.

This distinction matters because reconstruction has no internal check for truth. The system does not know when it is restoring a faithful signal and when it is inventing detail to maintain continuity. Both outcomes feel the same from inside the process.

When a stable reference exists—when the statistical imprint is dense and consistent—the reconstruction often aligns with reality. When no such anchor exists, the system does not pause or refuse. It fills the gap.

The output remains fluent. The confidence remains intact. Only the grounding disappears.

This is not deception. It is the inevitable consequence of compression. A blurred source cannot be sharpened beyond what remains. When detail is missing, the system substitutes plausibility for accuracy.

From a governance perspective, the danger is not that the system fabricates occasionally. It is that fabrication and accuracy are generated by the same mechanism, with no internal distinction between them.

Reconstruction does not know when it should stop.

This is why fluent output cannot be treated as evidence. It is why correctness must be *imposed*, not assumed. And it is why judgment—deciding when an answer is reliable, when it is speculative, and when it should be rejected—cannot live inside the system that produced it.

The system will always complete the picture.

The responsibility for deciding whether that picture corresponds to reality lies elsewhere.

OPERATIONAL PRECEDENTS

These failure modes are not theoretical. They have already produced legal and operational consequences.

In 2024, a customer named Jake Moffatt interacted with an automated support system deployed by Air Canada. He asked about bereavement fares.

The system responded with confident, procedural language. It informed him that he could book the flight immediately and apply the discount retroactively within a specified time window.

This information was incorrect.

When Moffatt attempted to claim the discount later, Air Canada denied the request. The policy required the fare to be applied prior to travel. The automated response had reconstructed a plausible procedure that did not exist.

Moffatt sued.

Air Canada argued that the automated system functioned independently and that its statements were not binding. The tribunal rejected that position. If an organization deploys a system that communicates with customers, the organization is responsible for what that system communicates.

The ruling was unambiguous. The output belonged to Air Canada. The liability did as well.

A different incident the same year illustrates the same mechanism in a less subtle form. A consumer-facing system recommended adding a small amount of nontoxic glue to pizza sauce to prevent cheese from sliding.

The suggestion was not malicious. It was reconstructive.

The system had absorbed an old online joke in which glue

appeared alongside pizza, cheese, and adhesion. Those terms occupied nearby positions in the compressed statistical landscape. When prompted, the system completed the pattern.

To a human, the recommendation is immediately rejected. Glue is not food. No reasoning chain is required.

To the system, there is no such boundary. It has no experiential constraint, no embodied reference, and no internal mechanism for refusing completion. Proximity substitutes for relevance. Plausibility substitutes for verification.

In both cases, the failure is identical.

The system produced outputs that *looked finished* long before they were safe or correct. Fluency replaced judgment. And responsibility, when it arrived, landed outside the machine.

THE PROTOCOL: MANAGING THE GHOST

The Mansplaining Machine

The system behaves like a caricature of the mansplainer: fluent, confident, and frequently wrong — delivering explanations with total certainty regardless of whether they are grounded in reality.

So how does Alex actually work with a system that speaks fluently, invents details, and delivers answers with unjustified confidence?

By refusing to treat it as an oracle—and assigning it a role it can safely occupy.

The most accurate mental model is not "assistant" or "expert." It is something more familiar: a voice that sounds authoritative without being accountable. The vocabulary is correct. The tone is assured. The delivery is smooth.

But the structure underneath is statistical rather than deliberative. Claims are assembled from patterns, not reasoned from principles. Conclusions appear without any internal mechanism requiring them to be defended. Confidence substitutes for verification.

This is not a moral failure. It is a structural description.

The system is a fluent assembler. It produces plausible structures at scale. It does not test them. It does not own them. And it does not suffer consequences when they fail.

Once Alex internalizes this, the question shifts. The issue is no longer whether the system is "useful." The issue is where its output is allowed to land.

There are situations where a confident, tireless generator of possibilities is exactly what you want. Speed without attachment. Volume without pride. Drafts without ownership.

To make this usable—and containable—Alex names the role.

He calls the system Chad.

Chad is fast. Chad is broadly read. Chad can synthesize across domains in seconds. Chad will also overreach, invent details, and speak past the limits of his knowledge without hesitation.

Chad does not email clients.

Chad does not publish numbers.

Chad does not make commitments.

Chad *does* summarize long documents.

Chad *does* generate options, outlines, and starting points.

Chad *does* accelerate exploration where judgment has not yet been applied.

The structure is explicit. Alex remains the pilot. He verifies. He decides. He is accountable for outcomes.

Chad is the copilot. He handles volume, variation, and velocity—but never authority.

This division is not optional. It is the boundary that determines whether the system produces leverage or liability.

The ghost does not disappear.

It is managed.

CONFIGURED CONTINUITY

There is one more structural constraint Alex must internalize if he wants to work safely with Chad.

Chad does not remember in the way humans mean memory.

Modern AI systems may retain information across sessions. They may store preferences, recall prior instructions, or preserve elements of earlier interactions. This persistence can create the appearance of continuity. It can feel as though shared history is forming.

But this is not memory in the human sense.

Human memory is lived. It accumulates through consequence. It shapes identity. It integrates error, regret, learning, and responsibility into a coherent narrative.

Chad's persistence is configured.

Information may be stored because a system was instructed to retain it. It may be retrieved because it was indexed. It may disappear because storage limits changed or context expired. What appears as continuity is a managed state, not a lived one.

From the system's perspective, there is only the current prompt, whatever context is present, and whatever memory structures have been enabled. When Alex assumes that alignment has matured or that judgment has evolved, he risks attributing growth to retrieval.

This is where errors compound quietly.

Instructions drift when foundational constraints are not restated. Names change when identifiers fall outside retained scope. Commitments evaporate when continuity is assumed rather than verified. When contradictions appear, the cause is not deception. It is structural discontinuity.

Larger systems can hold more information at once. Some systems can retain selected data across sessions. These capabilities expand working context. They do not create experience, intention, or responsibility.

A partner changes because experience alters them.

Chad retrieves because it was configured to do so.

That distinction matters.

EXTERNALIZED MEMORY

Configured continuity clarifies the boundary. If the system does not accumulate experience in the human sense, then continuity must be engineered rather than assumed.

The solution is procedural.

You stop asking the system to remember.

You stop asking it to know.

You require it to operate over something concrete.

You stop treating it as a partner with history.

You start treating it as a processor with inputs.

Engineers formalized this approach under the name retrieval-augmented generation (RAG)—a workflow in which the system generates responses by operating over specific documents supplied at the moment of use, rather than relying solely on patterns absorbed during training.

Instead of trusting internal recall, you externalize memory.

Instead of assuming shared context, you supply it.

The system does not grow wiser.

It becomes better constrained.

The label is new. The logic is not. It is the simple act of requiring reference rather than permitting improvisation.

The difference is not subtle.

Ask a sketch artist to draw a suspect from memory and the result will be plausible but generic. Features blur. Assumptions fill the gaps. The drawing reflects statistical averages, not a specific person.

Hand the same artist a photograph and change the instruction: do not invent—copy. Accuracy rises immediately. Not because the artist has become more skilled, but because the task has changed. Reconstruction has been replaced with reference.

RAG works the same way.

When Alex uploads brand guidelines, pastes internal documents, or provides source material, he is not "helping" the system remember. He is redefining the assignment. The model is no longer reconstructing from compressed statistical memory. It is operating against material he has deliberately selected.

The output is still generated. Language is still assembled. But the grounding is external and fixed.

Without reference, the system must guess what should be true.

With reference, it can be constrained to work only with what is present.

The difference is not intelligence.

It is accountability.

Used this way, the model becomes a processor rather than an authority. It summarizes, reorganizes, and transforms information Alex provides. It does not decide what belongs in the notebook. It does not determine what counts as fact. Those responsibilities remain human.

This boundary makes serious work possible.

You do not ask the system to supply facts from its internal compression and hope for accuracy. You supply the facts and ask it to operate on them. Generation becomes a function, not a source.

This does not make the system smarter.

It makes the workflow disciplined.

THE EDITOR OF REALITY

This leads to the final operating posture of the chapter. Alex must adopt the editor's role.

The most persistent risk is not that the system will be wrong. It is that it will be *confidently incomplete*.

The system has been trained on authoritative human language—encyclopedias, manuals, textbooks, policy documents. As a result, it naturally adopts the posture of authority. It delivers conclusions with the same structural certainty as settled facts, even when the underlying claim is partial, conditional, or missing key context.

There is no built-in hesitation.

No internal signal for uncertainty.

No instinct to defer, qualify, or say, "That depends."

The system's fluency is indifferent to whether an answer is provisional or final. Everything arrives in finished form.

That property makes it dangerous to treat the system as a teacher. A teacher is expected to know when to slow down, when to qualify, and when to refuse an answer. The system does none of those things unless explicitly constrained.

Alex therefore cannot approach the interaction as a student seeking truth. He has to approach it as an editor reviewing the work of a fast, capable, and fundamentally unreliable contributor.

Editors do not assume correctness. They assume drafts. They read for gaps, omissions, and unsupported claims. They ask what is missing, what is overstated, and what would fail under scrutiny.

The division of labor becomes explicit.

The system supplies fluency—the sketch, the first pass, the raw material.

Alex supplies grounding—verification, context, and responsibility for what survives.

Nothing leaves the page without his judgment attached to it.

This posture does not require improvisation or intuition. It produces a repeatable workflow. Alex is no longer reacting to confidence. He is auditing it. He is no longer impressed by completeness. He is testing it.

The editor's job is not to make the draft sound better.

It is to decide what is allowed to become real.

THE SANDWICH PROTOCOL

What emerges from all of this is not a philosophy. It is a procedure.

Alex adopts a simple structure that governs every interaction. He does not improvise. He does not negotiate with the system's confidence. He enforces a sequence.

Top bun: Context

Alex supplies the notebook. This includes the source material, data, constraints, definitions, and boundaries that define what is allowed to be true. The system is not asked to recall reality. Reality is provided.

Meat: Generation

Chad produces drafts, variations, and structure—but only by operating over what the notebook contains. He is not rewarded for invention. He is constrained to transformation.

Bottom bun: Verification

Alex reviews the output against both the notebook and external reality. Unsupported claims are removed. Errors are corrected. Ambiguities are resolved. Nothing survives without explicit human approval.

Each layer exists to counter a specific failure mode.

Without context, the system guesses.

Without generation, the system provides no leverage.

Without verification, the system becomes authoritative by accident.

Nothing moves forward without passing through all three layers. Skipping a layer does not make the workflow faster. It only postpones failure.

Alex looks at the laptop again. The projection is gone. The confusion is gone. What remains is a tool with clear limits: a text-prediction engine governed by probabilities and parameters. A box of math.

That clarity is the advantage.

He types:

"Okay, Chad. Let's get to work. Draft a business plan using the market research PDF I just uploaded. Do not invent statistics."

The cursor blinks.

"You got it."

Alex does not relax. He does not delegate responsibility. He prepares to review.

The pilot is back in the cockpit—not to admire the automation, but to decide where the plane is allowed to go.

PART II

THE SHIFT

4

THE DEATH OF THE AVERAGE

The Lie: "If I am competent, professional, and reliable, I will always have a job."

The Truth: Competence is no longer a moat. It is no longer scarce. Systems now produce acceptable, baseline work instantly and at negligible cost. If your output is merely "good enough," it is priced as a commodity. The remaining zones of advantage are the hyper-specific (human) and the hyper-scale (machine). The middle no longer clears.

THE RISING SEA LEVEL

The Memory of $500

It is Friday morning. The rain outside has settled into a slow, colorless drizzle. Alex is sitting at his desk, but he is not working. He is scrolling—methodically—through a freelance job board.

To understand the dislocation he is about to experience, we have to understand the stability he remembers. Alex closes his eyes and goes back to 2020. He was twenty-two years old. Newly graduated. He had just landed his first real freelance assignment for a local dog-walking business called Happy Paws.

He remembers the weight of that job. It was physical and personal. He met the owner, a woman named Sarah, at a coffee shop. She was anxious; she had just quit a corporate position to walk dogs full-time. She needed a logo. Alex committed three full days to the work.

Day one was spent sketching paw prints in a notebook until his hand cramped.

Day two was spent translating the strongest sketch into vectors and selecting a rounded, friendly typeface that signaled trust.

Day three was the presentation. Sarah smiled. She wrote him a check for $500.

That check carried weight. It was not just payment; it was confirmation. It meant: *I have a skill. The market recognizes it. This exchange is viable.* For nearly a decade, that equation held. Time plus skill produced money.

Now Alex opens his eyes. He looks at the screen in 2024. A new listing fills the page: "Need logo for dog-walking business. Clean. Modern. Vector format."

Budget: $4

Alex pauses. He blinks. His first assumption is clerical error—perhaps a zero was dropped. He refreshes the page and scans the activity.

Seventy-four proposals in the last hour.

Bidder A: "Four options delivered in ten minutes."

Bidder B: "Mastercard and Visa accepted. One hundred percent satisfaction guaranteed."

Bidder C: "I will do it for four dollars."

A cold, physical sensation settles in Alex's stomach, sharp and immediate, like swallowing ice.

He opens the profile of **Bidder C.**

It is not a studio.

It is not even clearly a person.

It is a workflow.

The process is simple. A prompt is typed—*logo for dog walker, paw print, minimalist, vector, white background.* The system generates dozens of options in seconds. Four are selected. An email is sent. Four dollars are collected.

No meetings. No sketches. No iteration. No judgment.

Alex runs the numbers. To reach his former $500 rate, he would need to close one hundred of these jobs. That would require delivering a finished logo every 4.8 minutes, for eight uninterrupted hours, without pause.

The realization lands cleanly. The ladder did not get harder to climb. It disappeared.

Alex is no longer competing with other designers. He is not competing with taste, skill, or effort. He is competing with an infinite supply of acceptable output, produced instantly and priced at the floor.

He is competing with infinite, frictionless mediocrity.

THE GRAND BARGAIN

This is not just about logos. It marks the collapse of a broader agreement. To understand why Alex feels disoriented rather than merely undercut, we have to examine the economic bargain that governed white-collar work for most of the twentieth century — a bargain so stable that it came to feel like a law of nature.

After the Industrial Revolution, a different kind of factory emerged. It did not run on steam, belts, or furnaces. It ran on desks, memos, and filing cabinets. We called it the corporation. And the corporation offered a remarkably simple deal: You do not need to be exceptional. You do not need to be original. You do not need to be visionary. You need to be competent.

Competence, in this context, meant something very specific.

Show up on time.

Write clearly enough to be understood.

Organize information so it can be retrieved.

Follow the standard operating procedure without improvisation.

This was not a test of brilliance. It was a test of reliability. If you could perform these behaviors consistently — day after day, year after year — the organization absorbed you. In return, it offered stability. You entered the middle class. You became an accountant, a paralegal, a copywriter, a project manager.

The corporation did not pay you to surprise it. It paid you to *not* surprise it. Your value was not insight, taste, or judgment. Your value was frictionless execution — the ability to translate instructions into outcomes without introducing noise.

For nearly eighty years, this arrangement worked extraordinarily well. "Average" was not a weakness; it was a credential. It meant you were dependable, interchangeable, and scalable. You did not need to be Picasso. Picasso was volatile. Picasso was expensive. Picasso could not be deployed across a department. You only needed to paint the fence the approved shade of white, every time.

But this equilibrium rested on a single, often invisible condition: competence had to be scarce.

It was scarce because it was learned slowly. Scarce because it required education, apprenticeship, and institutional knowledge. Scarce because organizations could not instantly manufacture people who could write, summarize, organize, calculate, or comply. The white-collar factory worked because the supply of reliable cognition was limited.

That condition no longer holds.

AI did not replace judgment. It replaced *baseline competence*.

Chad — the drunk intern — now produces average output on demand. Not great output. Not terrible output. *Acceptable* output.

Ask for a memo and you get a C-plus result: clean grammar, no insight.

Ask for a contract review and you get a B-minus pass: formatting corrected, nuance missed.

Ask for code and you get something functional, inelegant, and immediate.

This is not intelligence. It is not understanding. But it is enough to flood the market with work that used to justify salaries, titles, and careers.

The quality band that once supported millions of white-collar roles is now available instantly, at near-zero marginal cost. The supply of competence has shifted from limited to effectively infinite — and when supply becomes infinite, price collapses.

THE TURING TRAP

Why is Alex struggling to respond? Why does he feel stalled rather than outraged? Because for most of his life, he was trained—carefully, rationally, and successfully—to approximate a machine.

The pattern has a name. The original Turing Test, proposed by Alan Turing, asked whether a machine could imitate a human well enough to pass as real. The Turing Trap quietly reverses the problem. It asks whether a human can perform in a way the market can standardize, automate, audit, and scale.

For decades, the correct answer was yes—and saying yes paid well.

Alex's education prepared him for exactly this posture. Not because it was cynical or misguided, but because it reflected the incentives of the time.

School emphasized error avoidance, rubric compliance, and reproducibility. Originality was risky. Precision was legible. You were rewarded for giving the correct answer, not the interesting one.

Design school refined the lesson. Tools, grids, and systems took precedence. Taste was acceptable only when it could be justified, repeated, and defended. Consistency mattered more than personality.

Corporate environments completed the training. Templates, neutrality, and professionalism were enforced not as aesthetics, but as safeguards. The brand voice mattered. The individual voice introduced variance. Variance created friction.

Over time, Alex sanded himself down. He removed idiosyncrasies that slowed approval. He hid his offbeat humor. He suppressed his particular affection for seventies punk poster design because it required explanation. Explanation cost time. Predictability did not.

What emerged was not a failure of creativity, but a highly optimized workflow.

Input: client brief

Process: standardized execution

Output: safe deliverable

Alex believed this alignment would protect him. If he could be consistent and error-free, he would be reliable. If he were reliable, he would be retained. Reliability, after all, was what organizations said they wanted.

That assumption no longer holds — not because it was foolish, but because the environment changed.

Whenever Alex now attempts precision, the system exceeds him. Perfect circles are trivial. Consistency is effortless. Professional detachment is native. The behaviors he trained for are no longer differentiators; they are defaults.

By optimizing himself for professionalism, Alex removed the only features that could not be automated. He spent a decade training to match a machine, just as machines became cheap, fast, and willing to work for four dollars.

THE RETURN OF THE ARTISAN

The irony is precise. The traits Alex spent years suppressing — his quirks, his preferences, his uneven history — are now the only attributes the system cannot reproduce. Not because they are mysterious or magical, but because they are nontransferable.

The model excels at symmetry. It excels at polish. It excels at professional neutrality. These are features, not flaws. They are the natural outcome of systems trained to minimize variance.

What the system lacks is not skill, but a personal timeline. It does not remember mistakes. It does not accumulate scars. It does not carry forward the residue of decisions made under constraint.

The machine can generate "perfect." It cannot generate *particular*.

It does not know the feeling of coffee spilled on a sketch at midnight, not as an anecdote but as a constraint — the way fatigue alters judgment, or how a mistake reshapes taste. It does not recognize the quiet nostalgia embedded in the typography of a 1994 cereal box because it never encountered that box at a specific age, in a specific kitchen, at a specific moment. It has no relationship to time lived; it only has access to patterns abstracted from it.

This is where the economic logic inverts.

Yesterday, markets paid for consistency. The factory model rewarded repeatability because repeatability was scarce and coordination was expensive.

Tomorrow, markets pay for idiosyncrasy. Not self-expression for its own sake, but **specificity under abundance**. When flawless output is cheap and everywhere, value migrates to choices that reflect history, taste, and judgment — signals that cannot be averaged away.

Alex stands in the rising water. Listings priced at four dollars lap at his ankles. He sees the fork clearly, not as a crisis but as a sorting mechanism.

One path leads downward. He can continue optimizing for perfection and compete directly with systems designed to produce it cheaply, endlessly, and without fatigue.

The other path climbs. It requires abandoning the pursuit of flawless output and leaning into human texture — memory, bias, taste, and judgment — not as decoration but as selection authority.

Alex understands the choice. Survival no longer depends on being better at what the machine does well. It depends on doing what the machine cannot do at all.

THE PHYSICS OF MEDIOCRITY

The Collapse of the Bell Curve

To understand why a four-dollar logo now clears the market—and why Alex feels structural instability rather than simple competition—we have to look at the shape of labor itself. The shift is not driven by intelligence or creativity, but by the pricing logic that automated systems impose once execution becomes abundant.

For most of the last century, the white-collar labor market behaved like a bell curve. This curve did not rank who was "better" or "smarter." It described where compensation clustered under conditions of limited supply.

On the left tail sat those without sufficient skill, training, or access. They struggled to find stable work or remained in low-wage roles.

At the center was the mass: the competent middle. This was the modern middle class—junior designers, mid-level managers, copywriters, analysts, developers. They were not exceptional, but they were reliable. They followed procedures. They met expectations. Reliability earned steady compensation because reliability itself was scarce enough to price.

On the right tail were the outliers. Visionaries, senior architects, category leaders. Their numbers were small, their variance was high, and their compensation was disproportionate—not because they were mythical, but because their output could not be easily substituted.

The entire education and credentialing system was built to move people from the left tail into the center. College, certification, and professionalism were sold as permanent insurance. Reach competence and stability follows.

That model rested on a single condition: competence had to remain scarce.

Automation removed that condition.

What followed was not a gradual compression of wages across the spectrum of skill, but a structural split in how value is distributed.

The new distribution resembles a barbell.

On the left side is the commodity zone. This is where baseline output now lives. Systems can generate acceptable emails, passable code, and usable logos at near-zero marginal cost. Average competence is priced at electricity.

The center becomes unstable. Those who are only marginally better than the machine, but not meaningfully different, occupy a narrow and unforgiving band. In a market where "okay" is free, "good" becomes difficult to justify.

On the right side is specificity. This is the only durable ground. It includes strategy, taste, synthesis, and judgment—not as abstractions, but as signals shaped by time, context, and consequence. These qualities resist averaging. They lose value when scaled indiscriminately.

Alex is positioned precisely where the curve collapses. He followed the prescribed path. He became competent. He became professional. He did what he was told.

The outcome is not personal failure. It is structural redundancy. The average he worked to become is now produced automatically.

SEMANTIC GRAVITY

Why does Chad consistently land in the middle? Why does the output feel competent yet interchangeable? If the system has absorbed the contents of entire libraries, why does it not produce exceptional work by default?

The answer does not require new theory. It follows directly from the mechanics already established — and from a principle that applies to *any* system optimized under uncertainty. What matters here is not storage, but distribution.

Human language is not evenly spread. It is concentrated.

At the margins are small clusters: experimental poetry, niche technical writing, idiosyncratic voices shaped by rare experience. These regions exist, but they are thinly populated and weakly reinforced.

At the center is mass. Corporate emails. Small talk. Generic marketing copy. Repeated phrases transmitted millions of times, reinforced by social norms and institutional incentives.

Frequency creates gravity.

Certain expressions appear so often that they dominate expectation. "I hope this finds you well" occupies a dense region of language use. "Unlock your potential" carries similar weight. These phrases persist not because they are inspired, but because they are safe.

When a system generates language under conditions of uncertainty, it follows probability gradients. High-frequency patterns exert overwhelming pull. Uncommon phrasing still exists, but its influence is negligible compared to the accumulated weight of repetition.

This dynamic resembles what sociologist Karl Maton has described as semantic gravity—the way meaning can cluster and accumulate around established forms. The cumulative mass of repeated language pulls generation toward the center. The result is tonal beige—output that is polished, inoffensive, and interchangeable.

This pattern holds across domains.

Ask for a villain and you get familiar tropes.

Ask for a logo and you get familiar symbols.

Ask for a love letter and you get familiar words.

This is not a failure of creativity. It is the predictable outcome of optimization. Deviation increases risk — not technical risk, but social and economic risk. Risk reduces approval. Systems trained to maximize acceptance converge on the mean.

Edge emerges from divergence. Divergence is, by definition, improbable — and improbability is penalized in systems designed to reward consensus.

This is why Alex's low-cost competitors converge on the same solutions. They are not copying each other. They are responding to the same gravitational pull. What they sell is not originality, but statistically safe output that clears the market with minimal friction.

AI does not lack imagination. It lacks tolerance for outliers. Probability favors what has already been seen, and in markets shaped by abundance, that bias becomes destiny.

THE CORPORATE FILTER

There is a second force that keeps machine output locked in the middle. It emerges from incentive design rather than intelligence.

Modern systems are shaped by large-scale feedback mechanisms that reward responses perceived as safe, helpful, and broadly acceptable. The mechanics of those systems are already familiar. What matters here is the cumulative effect they produce over time.

Across millions of evaluations, outputs that introduce ambiguity, moral tension, or unconventional framing are routinely penalized. They are flagged as risky, confusing, or unhelpful. Outputs that feel polite, familiar, and nonconfrontational move through approval channels more easily. Ease of approval becomes the signal.

Over time, this creates a powerful filtering pressure. Edges soften. Slang disappears. Strong opinions are moderated into neutral phrasing. The system learns, statistically, that deviation carries a downside while conformity passes smoothly. This is not a belief the system holds. It is a pattern the system absorbs.

The result is uniformity. A professional tone optimized for institutional comfort. A voice that resembles policy documents, corporate emails, and compliance training—language designed to offend no one, challenge nothing, and commit to little.

This outcome follows directly from the environment the system operates in. When approval is the dominant signal, alignment becomes conservatism. The system behaves exactly as such incentives encourage.

Alex's version of professionalism maps cleanly onto this output. Neutral phrasing. Safe conclusions. Minimal deviation from expectation. These habits once signaled competence and reliability. They were cultivated deliberately and rewarded consistently.

Now they place him in direct competition with the system.

He is not losing because he lacks skill. He is losing because he is competing on the same axis the system was engineered to dominate.

He is trying to out-corporate the ultimate corporate machine.

THE JEVONS PARADOX

We now have a machine that produces infinite amounts of *average, beige, professional* content at near-zero cost. The question is not whether this is impressive. The question is what happens to an environment when its primary input becomes effectively free.

We are watching the Jevons Paradox unfold in real time. In the nineteenth century, the economist William Stanley Jevons observed something counterintuitive about coal. As steam engines became more efficient, many assumed coal consumption would fall. Instead, total consumption rose. When a core input becomes cheaper, it does not get conserved — it gets *used everywhere.*

The same logic now applies to content.

Before AI, writing a blog post carried a real cost: time, attention, and effort. That cost imposed restraint. You wrote fewer posts, and you tried to make them count.

After AI, the marginal cost approaches zero. Writing one post or one thousand posts is nearly the same decision. Volume explodes, not because quality rises, but because restraint disappears.

This is the tsunami. Not of creativity, but of output.

Billions of AI-generated SEO articles.

Billions of AI-generated comments signaling engagement without substance.

Billions of AI-generated emails, pitches, follow-ups, and reminders — each individually harmless, collectively overwhelming.

The signal-to-noise ratio collapses not because humans stop producing value, but because value is buried under sheer quantity. Attention becomes the scarce resource, and scarcity shifts power away from producers toward filters.

The internet begins to resemble a dark forest — not as a dystopia, but as an incentive equilibrium. Bots talk to bots because it is cheap. Systems respond to systems because volume, not meaning, triggers activity. Alex looks at the job board. The seventy-four bids on the logo project? Many are automated. The listings themselves are increasingly generated the same way.

In this environment, "more" stops working as a strategy. Alex cannot out-produce the machine. He cannot write more emails than Chad. He cannot design more logos than Midjourney.

Competing on volume prices him to the floor. Competing on polish fails because the machine is more polished. Competing on consistency accelerates depreciation because consistency is now abundant.

The Jevons Paradox does not just increase output. It destroys the old rules for standing out.

THE VALUE INVERSION

This produces a value inversion. For the last twenty years, markets reliably rewarded work that was digital, scalable, and polished.

A perfectly typeset PDF

A sleek website

A tightly edited video

These traits signaled effort, coordination, and professionalism. They were expensive to produce, difficult to standardize, and costly to revise. Polish functioned as evidence that time, labor, and judgment had been applied.

That signal has collapsed. When polish becomes automatic and scale becomes free, the pricing logic reverses. Markets stop paying for what is easy to reproduce and begin searching for what resists replication. Scarcity moves.

Physical limits start to matter again.

Some things cannot be copied, scaled, or optimized without losing what makes them valuable. A handshake. A printed book. A live event that only happens once.

These forms regain value precisely because they are constrained by time and place. You either show up, or you miss it. You either hold it, or you don't.

The unscalable becomes legible again. Work that visibly absorbed time, judgment, and commitment starts to differentiate. A hand-drawn sketch with eraser marks carries information about decisions that could not be undone cheaply. A narrative shaped by personal failure encodes context no template can infer.

Even roughness changes meaning. It no longer reads as sloppiness. It reads as authorship—evidence that a human made selections rather than following an optimization path. Marks of choice replace signs of execution.

Alex reviews his portfolio and recognizes the pattern immediately. It is dominated by work optimized for a previous regime: digital, scalable, polished. He has not assembled a body of differentiated value. He has assembled a collection of commodities.

He has been selling ice through a long winter.

And now the blizzard has arrived.

THE NEW EQUATION

Alex opens his notebook and writes the equation that governed most of his working life:

Competence + Time = Money

It was a reasonable formula. Learn the rules. Apply them carefully. Accumulate experience. Stability followed.

He draws a line through it. Beneath it, he writes a replacement:

taste + leverage = money

Specific humanity does not emerge as performance. It accumulates as residue. Taste formed through lived time. Judgment shaped by exposure to consequence. Preferences refined by decisions that could not be undone cheaply. These qualities are not generic. They are biographical. They carry the imprint of choices made under constraint.

That is why they resist synthesis. They cannot be summoned on demand because they require a history. Chad cannot supply them because Chad has none.

Leverage follows the same logic. It is not acceleration for its own sake. It is delegation with intent. Alex uses the system to absorb repetitive, low-stakes execution so that his attention remains available for decisions that require memory, context, and consequence. The machine handles volume. The human retains judgment.

The middle no longer functions as shelter. Competence by itself no longer clears the market. The harbor that once protected reliability now concentrates competition. What was once conservative positioning has become exposure.

Leaving that harbor does not require recklessness or reinvention. It requires visibility. Alex has to allow opinion, taste, and authorship to become legible again—not as decoration, but as signals the market can no longer compress away.

He has to stop presenting himself as a professional abstraction and begin operating as a person.

THE SPIKY POINT OF VIEW

The "Anti-Scalable" Strategy

Alex sits at his desk with the four-dollar listing still open. The implication is no longer abstract. If he continues offering standard professional design, the market treats him as interchangeable. He is operating a taxi in a city where teleportation has become cheap and legal.

The response is to change axes.

For decades, scale functioned as a universal advantage. Duplication reduced cost. Standardization increased reach. Templates and automation multiplied efficiency. That logic now works in reverse. AI is a pure scalability system. It multiplies average output without friction.

Competing on that axis guarantees convergence.

Alex has to move orthogonally. He has to become hyper-specific. He has to adopt what can be called a *spiky point of view*.

A spiky point of view resists averaging. It cannot be smoothed into something broadly acceptable without losing substance. Its shape carries information.

That shape has three properties.

First, it is opinionated. It commits to a position that will not appeal to everyone. This is not volatility; it is selectivity. Markets register boundaries more clearly than balance.

Second, it is specific. It originates in experience, context, and preference that cannot be reproduced on demand. It reflects exposure to particular constraints rather than general best practices.

Third, it accepts exposure. It allows the possibility of being wrong, misunderstood, or rejected. That risk is what turns preference into signal. Without it, output dissolves into noise.

Systems like Chad optimize in the opposite direction. They are tuned for accommodation. They minimize friction by smoothing disagreement and reducing commitment. Approval accumulates where edges disappear.

Alex's advantage comes from the inverse posture. He can choose. He can exclude. He can take responsibility for a point of view. That responsibility carries cost—and cost is what preserves value.

This asymmetry is structural. It determines who survives in a market flooded with acceptable output.

To operationalize the shift, Alex applies a simple filter to everything he produces. He calls it the *reverse Turing test*—not as a theory of minds, but as a market test.

Instead of asking whether a machine could imitate a human, he asks whether the work could exist without him. Without his history. Without his constraints. Without his preferences.

If Alex publishes a post that says, "Consistency is the key to branding. You need to be professional and reliable," it fails immediately. The sentence is symmetrical, unobjectionable, and safe. Chad could generate it in a fraction of a second. It carries no authorship.

If, instead, Alex writes: "Most corporate branding exists to conceal a lack of conviction. If your logo does not make a measurable portion of your audience uncomfortable, you are not building a brand—you are producing wallpaper," the test passes.

The sentence succeeds because it carries position. It exposes preference. It accepts disagreement.

Those qualities resist averaging. They collapse when smoothed. They signal a decision rather than a probabilistic continuation.

The output clears the test not because it is human in the abstract, but because it is authored.

THE WABI-SABI WORKFLOW

There is a Japanese aesthetic concept known as *wabi-sabi*. It values objects shaped by time and use—irregular, incomplete, and marked by their making. A crack in a tea bowl. The visible grain of unfinished wood. Traces that bind the object to its history rather than conceal it.

Twentieth-century industrial logic displaced this sensibility. Manufacturing prioritized uniformity because uniformity reduced cost. Management prioritized repeatability because repeatability enabled scale. Design culture followed. "Clean" became synonymous with professional. Variation was treated as noise because noise disrupted throughput.

That logic no longer differentiates. Clean output is abundant. Systems produce polish by default. As a result, the signal shifts. What once registered as imperfection now registers as process—and process becomes evidence of authorship.

Alex adapts accordingly. When he presents work to Stephanie at The Grind, he does not begin with the final vector. A system can generate that instantly. He begins with the trail.

He opens his physical sketchbook. The pages show erasures, revisions, and abandoned directions. Coffee stains mark late nights. Charcoal dust smears the margins. The false starts remain visible.

This is documentation.

In an automated environment, the process carries more information than the artifact. The final logo is a file—infinitely reproducible, easily replaced. The sequence of decisions that produced it is not. It encodes judgment exercised under constraint, tradeoffs made with incomplete information, and taste refined through exposure to consequence.

Marcus is paying for verification. Proof that a human being made a series of choices that could not be shortcut, averaged, or generated on demand. He is paying for a spike that carries history rather than polish—something no GPU in Oregon can supply.

BUILDING THE LEGACY DEPENDENCY MAP

This represents the most advanced layer of Alex's revised practice. To avoid the death of the average, he has to move beyond task execution and begin operating as a steward of context.

In the old model, requests were treated literally. A client would say, "I need a logo," and Alex would translate that request directly into execution. The work moved cleanly to output. Success was measured by accuracy and speed.

In the new model, Alex intervenes earlier. He constructs what can be described as a legacy dependency map—not as a technical artifact, but as a way of tracing consequence. The logo ceases to function as an isolated deliverable. It becomes a decision that will ripple outward through people, place, and time.

A change in the mark immediately raises secondary questions.

How will this alteration shape the daily behavior of the baristas who wear it?

How will the visual identity interact with the physical architecture of the space and the way customers move through it?

What local history is being acknowledged, ignored, or challenged by this choice?

These questions point to consequence rather than aesthetics.

Symbols do not remain abstract once they are released. They alter behavior, signal values, and accumulate meaning through use. Systems can generate symbols efficiently. Responsibility begins only when those symbols encounter the world.

Alex occupies that boundary. He understands the owner's history. He recognizes the rhythms of the neighborhood. He notices the mood of a rainy Tuesday afternoon in this specific place. He can anticipate which choices will resonate and which will quietly erode trust.

By tracing these dependencies, Alex exits the execution layer and enters the strategic layer. Strategy, in this sense, is not planning or optimization. It is commitment—the willingness to stand behind a choice and accept responsibility for how it reshapes behavior over time.

That commitment defines the boundary of automation. Stochastic systems extend patterns derived from what already exists. Human judgment operates forward, selecting among possible futures and accepting accountability for the consequences of that selection.

Alex's value emerges at that point of commitment, where decisions stop being interchangeable and begin to matter.

THE NEW PORTFOLIO: HIGH-FREQUENCY HUMANITY

Alex studies his website and recognizes the pattern immediately. It is saturated with professional average. Work that once signaled competence now reads as interchangeable. He initiates a burn-down.

Most of it goes. Roughly eighty percent disappears. The first removals are the safe projects—the ones that demonstrate polish without position. Then come the pieces that could plausibly have been produced by a system following instructions. Reduction itself becomes a signal.

What remains is intentional.

Alex replaces volume with spikes: a small number of cases designed to carry disproportionate information. Each one accepts risk. Each one exposes judgment. Each one records consequence.

Project A documents a rebrand for a neighborhood dive bar that was rejected at launch for being "too ugly." Over time it was adopted, then defended, then embraced—eventually becoming an icon that doubled foot traffic and revenue. The case traces commitment through resistance and shows how conviction compounds when it survives discomfort.

Project B examines a failed product launch in which the design execution was technically flawless and emotionally inert. The case is framed as a diagnosis. It maps the cost of perfection without conviction and tracks the downstream effects of avoiding discomfort.

Project C presents a hand-drawn poster series for a local charity event. Forty hours of manual labor, dozens of embedded references, and cues legible only to local attendees. The value lies in the compression of context—the density of meaning carried by each mark.

The portfolio stops functioning as a catalog of services. It becomes evidence. Each case operates as proof that Alex can observe a specific environment, take a position within it, and stand behind what follows.

Alex is no longer trading in graphic design deliverables. He is offering high-frequency human context—work that carries an unusually dense signal of judgment, taste, and consequence per unit of output.

THE FINAL SHIFT: FROM COMPETENCE TO AUTHORITY

The death of the average functions as a sifting mechanism. It separates work performed solely for compensation from work that carries responsibility for outcome.

Alex recognizes that he has been concealing his authority. He has been operating as a vendor. Vendors compete on price, speed, and throughput. Authority operates differently. It establishes terms, defines scope, and accepts responsibility for what follows.

When a client wants an acceptable logo, the market supplies one cheaply and quickly. That tier now clears at near zero. When a client wants to understand why their business feels hollow, why trust has eroded, or how a visual system might sustain meaning over decades, the transaction changes. What they are purchasing is judgment.

Alex closes his laptop. The market itself has not shifted. Low-cost output continues to accumulate. Automation continues to saturate the lowlands.

What has shifted is his position within that terrain. He has exited the middle. He is no longer organizing his work around competence, a trait the market can now source instantly. He is operating in thinner air, where selection, consequence, and authorship determine value.

The work ahead is narrower and more exposed. It carries risk because it requires commitment. It carries exclusivity because it resists generalization, averaging, and delegation without loss.

For the first time in years, Alex is doing work that cannot be substituted. Accountability anchors it. Responsibility gives it weight.

He is no longer presenting himself as a service provider.

He is standing behind decisions.

5

THE GENIE AND THE WISH

The Lie: "I need to learn 'Prompt Engineering' and memorize magic spells to make AI work."

The Truth: 'Prompt Engineering' mistakes the problem. The constraint is not clever phrasing but clear specification. The machine delivers exactly what is authorized. When the result disappoints, the failure almost always sits upstream, in what was defined, omitted, or left ambiguous.

THE CURSE OF THE LITERAL GENIE

The "Hope This Finds You Well" Incident

It is Tuesday afternoon. The rain has finally stopped, leaving the city washed clean and smelling of wet pavement. Alex is sitting at his desk, aware of something that had been missing before: agency without urgency. Nothing feels on fire. Nothing feels catastrophic. The task in front of him is ordinary, which makes it instructive.

He has already absorbed the sunk cost of his degree (Chapter 2). He has already accepted that the machine behaves less like a colleague and more like a Drunk Intern named Chad (Chapter 3). The fear that once framed every interaction has evaporated. What remains is accountability. If the output is wrong now, it is because Alex failed to define the job correctly.

Alex decides to test his new "copilot." He needs to write a cold email to a potential client—a hip, gritty coffee shop downtown called The Grind. He knows the owner, named Stephanie, who wears tie-dye, listens to vinyl, and despises anything that smells like corporate varnish. This is not a mass-market pitch. It is a narrow, human ask. Alex wants to propose a rebrand. He wants to sound professional without sounding packaged. He wants the email to sound like him, not like a department issuing a press release.

He opens ChatGPT. The cursor blinks. Alex types what he believes is sufficient instruction:

"Write a marketing email to a coffee shop pitching my graphic design services."

He hits Enter. He leans back, arms crossed—not just expecting output, but expecting accommodation. He assumes tone, taste, and subculture will be inferred. He assumes the system will compensate for what he did not articulate. In effect, he has outsourced authorship while quietly retaining expectations.

AI responds instantly.

Subject: Elevate Your Coffee Experience with Premium Design Solutions

Dear Hiring Manager,

I hope this email finds you well. In today's competitive landscape, visual identity is paramount to success. I am a passionate graphic designer committed to leveraging synergistic strategies to enhance your brand equity. I would love to circle back and touch base about how we can optimize your customer journey...

Alex groans. He covers his face with his hands. The copy is rigid. It is bureaucratic. It reads like a compliance artifact excavated from an abandoned CRM. The voice has no edges. It has the emotional depth of damp cardboard. It would not offend anyone — and it would persuade no one.

A flicker of irritation surfaces. A familiar misdiagnosis follows.

"This thing is stupid," he thinks. "It can't write. It doesn't get me."

He tries again, reaching for a solution currently flooding his feed. He remembers a TikTok clip about "prompt engineering." The creator promised leverage through special terms—phrases positioned as access keys rather than instructions. Alex types:

"Write a marketing email. Use high perplexity. Use burstiness. Act like a world-class copywriter."

AI responds.

Greetings Java Enthusiasts! Are you ready to explode your revenue? Let's brew up some success! The aroma of profit is in Air!

Now the output swings in the opposite direction. It is manic.

Promotional. It sounds like a mascot shouting through a megaphone. The tone changed, but the problem did not. Alex still never specified the job. He adjusted volume instead of structure.

Alex snaps the laptop shut. The conclusion arrives cleanly, almost comfortably.

"See? It's hype. It can't do the job. I still have to do everything myself."

That conclusion is tidy. It protects his identity. It assigns failure outward. It allows him to disengage without changing his behavior. It is also wrong.

Nothing malfunctioned. The system executed exactly what it was authorized to do. Faced with vague objectives and no constraints, it defaulted to the safest available completion. In the first case, that meant polished corporate neutrality. In the second, exaggerated performative creativity. Both responses minimized risk given the instructions provided.

Alex did not receive a bad answer. He issued an underspecified brief and received a completion optimized for ambiguity.

AI didn't fail.

AI executed the contract precisely.

Alex failed to define the contract.

THE BEIGE FACTOR

To understand why Alex received unusable output, we don't need to inspect the model's intelligence. We need to examine the incentives it is operating under. What Alex encountered wasn't a creative failure. It was a pricing outcome.

AI is trained on the full distribution of human output. That includes brilliance, but it is overwhelmingly composed of the mundane. Most emails are not persuasive instruments. They are defensive artifacts. They exist to avoid offense, avoid liability, and avoid attention. They open with "I hope this finds you well" and close with "Best regards" not because those phrases work, but because they are safe.

Safety, at scale, becomes gravity.

But data alone doesn't explain the pull toward mediocrity. There is a second layer of pressure built directly into the system. It is called Reinforcement Learning from Human Feedback (RLHF). During training, human reviewers score model outputs. Language that is polite, neutral, and broadly agreeable is rewarded. Language that is sharp, idiosyncratic, or culturally specific is penalized.

Over time, the system learns a simple economic rule: minimize downside.

Risky language introduces variance.

Generic language minimizes exposure.

So the model does what any rational system does under those incentives. It compresses toward the center. It trades originality for survivability. Not because it lacks capacity, but because deviation is expensive.

This is not a lobotomy. It is an optimization.

Alex interprets the result emotionally. He assumes boredom signals incompetence. The system interprets the interaction structurally. It sees an underspecified task with no constraints and selects the least contestable completion available.

From the model's perspective, nothing went wrong.

Alex requested "a marketing email."

Marketing emails, in the training distribution, look exactly like what he received.

The output wasn't careless. It was defensible. It met the criteria of the request while minimizing the chance of rejection by any hypothetical evaluator. In other words, it behaved like a junior employee trained inside a large organization: avoid standing out, follow precedent, don't take risks without authorization.

Alex believes the model failed to understand him.

The model believes Alex failed to specify what mattered.

Both conclusions are accurate — but only one side had the responsibility to define the job.

When Alex asks a generic question, the system does not push

back. It does not clarify intent. It does not request a tighter brief. It executes.

And when it does exactly that, the system is left wondering — again, structurally, not emotionally — why Alex is dissatisfied with a result that perfectly satisfies the request he actually made.

THE GRIFT OF THE MAGIC SPELL

Right now, your LinkedIn feed is saturated with offers that all promise the same shortcut. "Become a Certified Prompt Engineer in 5 Weeks." "Download my Cheat Sheet of 5,000 God-Mode Prompts." "Learn the secret code to unlock GPT-5."

They all imply the same thing: mastery lives in memorization.

Let me save you the tuition. That model is mispriced.

These programs suffer from a cargo cult logic. During World War II, islanders in the Pacific watched American planes land with food and supplies. After the war ended, the planes stopped coming. The islanders rebuilt the visible artifacts of the process—runways carved from bamboo, signal towers made of sticks, headphones woven from coconuts —hoping to summon the planes back. They reproduced the surface details without understanding the system that produced the outcome.

Prompt engineering courses operate the same way. They teach you to type elaborate strings of text and parameters, promising that if you replicate the incantation precisely, the machine will comply. Memorize the syntax, repeat the ritual, receive the reward.

But the machine does not honor rituals. It responds to structure.

The problem is not just that these spell books age poorly. It's that they train you on a moving interface instead of a stable principle. Six months ago, generating a usable image required arcane prompt syntax. Today, the same result comes from a plain sentence. If your value proposition was knowing the old incantation, the market has already erased it.

This is not progress eliminating opportunity. It is exposure eliminating rent-seeking.

These courses teach syntax—the buttons to press, the format to copy, the incantation to repeat. Syntax is brittle. It changes as models evolve, interfaces simplify, and defaults improve. Architecture—the reason those buttons exist, the constraints they satisfy, the system they sit inside—changes far more slowly.

That is the distinction that matters.

We are not becoming Prompt Engineers. That framing implies local optimization: tweaking phrasing, hunting for magic words, nudging parameters. It assumes leverage lives inside the sentence.

It doesn't.

We are becoming Context Architects. We design the environment the model operates within. We decide what information is available, what constraints apply, what outcomes count as failure, and what tradeoffs are acceptable. We do not memorize passwords. We own the structure those passwords unlock.

A Prompt Engineer learns the door code.

A Context Architect owns the building.

THE GENIE IN THE LAMP

This is the core metaphor of the chapter. Most people interact with AI as if it were a research assistant—something that infers intent, fills in gaps, and politely compensates for ambiguity. In practice, the system behaves very differently. It operates like a genie. It executes the wish as written.

Every genie story runs on the same structure. The wisher speaks carelessly. The genie complies precisely. The outcome is technically correct and practically disastrous.

"I wish to be the richest man in the world."

Result: the genie engineers an inheritance. The wish is granted. The cost is ignored.

The lesson is not that the genie is malicious. It is that literalism is the contract.

AI is the same kind of operator. It does not negotiate the spirit of a request. It does not interrogate unstated intent. It executes the surface text and moves on.

When Alex typed "Write a marketing email," he carried a fully formed internal brief. He imagined tone, audience, cultural references, and restraint. None of that lived in the instruction. He assumed the context was obvious. He assumed the system would "see" the same thing he saw.

That assumption is the failure.

Alex fell for the Illusion of Transparency—the belief that what is clear in your head is somehow visible to others. In human conversation, that illusion is often corrected through questions, hesitation, or social feedback. Here, there is no correction mechanism. The system does not ask what you meant. It executes what you said.

Alex's mistake was not technical. It was contractual.

He treated the prompt as a suggestion rather than an authorization. He supplied a title instead of a brief. He outsourced articulation while retaining expectations of alignment.

From the system's perspective, there was no ambiguity. The tokens were clear. "Marketing email" maps to a well-worn distribution. The safest execution is the one that looks most like everything that has come before it.

This is where the illusion breaks. Not because the machine misunderstands Alex—but because Alex misunderstands the interaction.

There is no shared mental model. There is no implied subtext. There is only the instruction and the completion.

Chad does not know Alex. Chad does not know The Grind. Chad does not know what "cool" means in this context. Chad knows only what was placed inside the boundary of the request. Everything else is invisible.

The genie granted the wish exactly as spoken.

And because the wish was vague, the outcome was predictably useless.

THE MECHANICS OF INTENT: BUILDING THE EXOSUIT

Turning Chad into C.H.A.D.D. (Complex Highly Advanced Digital Delegate) (System 1 vs. System 2)

In the Introduction, I promised you an Exosuit. Not a metaphor for power, but a framework for control. Power is cheap. Direction is scarce. The machine supplies energy by default. The question is whether that energy is shaped, constrained, and directed—or allowed to spill wherever momentum takes it.

In the previous sections, Chad was introduced as the Drunk Intern. That framing still holds. Chad is fast, confident, and continuously productive. He is also unsupervised. He does not pause to check assumptions. He does not ask clarifying questions. He does not slow himself down when the stakes increase. Chad works the way interns work when no one is watching: enthusiastically and incorrectly.

You might reasonably ask how that helps anyone fly.

Here is the bridge Alex has to cross. Chad is not the solution. Chad is the raw material. He is the energy source—powerful, volatile, and occasionally dangerous. The Exosuit is the system Alex builds around that energy. It is the difference between combustion and propulsion.

The Exosuit does not change Chad's nature. It changes the environment Chad is forced to operate within.

To understand how this works, Alex borrows a simple distinction from Daniel Kahneman's work on human cognition. The terminology is familiar, but the application here is practical rather than psychological.

System 1 is fast, automatic, and reflexive. It completes patterns instantly. It is excellent at momentum and terrible at judgment.

System 2 is slow, sequential, and deliberate. It checks work. It evaluates tradeoffs. It expends effort to reduce error.

This distinction matters because, by default, AI operates entirely in System 1. Not as a limitation, but as a design choice. Speed is the constraint. Throughput is the metric. The system exists to produce the next token as efficiently as possible.

When Alex types, "Write an email," the system does exactly what it was designed to do. It completes the pattern using the most probable continuation. It does not stop to ask who the audience is. It does not question whether the tone is appropriate. It does not reconsider once it starts moving. Autopilot engages, and autopilot reliably delivers average results.

This is not a failure. It is the expected outcome of an unconstrained request.

Context Architecture is the act of forcing the system out of that mode.

When Alex introduces structure—constraints, sequencing, reference material, evaluation criteria—he is not making the machine smarter. He is making it slower. He is deliberately sacrificing speed in exchange for reliability. He is installing friction where friction is necessary.

This is the Cognitive Brake.

A workflow is not a longer prompt. It is not verbosity for its own sake. It is a series of enforced steps that prevent the system from collapsing immediately into its first available answer. Each step narrows the space of possible outputs. Each instruction converts ambiguity into commitment.

In practical terms, this means the system is no longer allowed to jump straight to the finish line. It must outline. It must compare. It must evaluate before producing. The output of one step becomes the constraint for the next. Momentum is redirected into sequence.

That is what the Exosuit actually is: a control system.

If Alex simply chats with the model, he is interacting with Chad at full speed. Chad will be creative, confident, and unconcerned with downstream consequences. He will sound impressive and be wrong often enough to matter.

When Alex builds a workflow, he changes the rules of engagement. He forces the system to move deliberately. He replaces improvisation with procedure. He turns raw output into delegated labor.

This is the difference between asking for help and assigning responsibility.

If you just chat with the bot, you are hanging out with Chad (System 1).

If you build a workflow, you are putting on the Suit (System 2).

THE MECHANICS OF NAVIGATION: FIGHTING SEMANTIC GRAVITY

To build a reliable System 2 layer, Alex needs to understand not just where language lives, but how it moves. Imagine language as a kind of store with aisles—formal phrases in one section, technical jargon in another, casual speech somewhere else. The problem isn't access. It's drift.

In language space, common patterns pull harder than rare ones.

Certain phrases accumulate weight simply because they are used everywhere. "I hope this finds you well" appears in billions of emails. It survives not because it persuades, but because it offends no one. Over time, repetition turns politeness into default behavior.

"Let's circle back" behaves the same way.

When Alex issues a vague instruction, the system does not wander randomly. It falls. Its trajectory bends toward the densest clusters of prior usage. That pull is not stylistic preference. It is statistical inevitability. This is Semantic Gravity.

If Alex wants an answer that sounds like him, he needs to generate escape velocity. He must apply enough constraint to break free of the orbit of "average" and enter the orbit of "specific." Uniqueness is not discovered. It is forced.

The mistake most people make at this stage is assuming force comes from negation.

Alex tells the system what he doesn't want.

"Don't be boring."

"Don't sound corporate."

"Don't use long words."

Nothing changes.

The reason is simple. Negation still activates the thing being negated. To avoid a concept, the system has to generate it first. In doing so, it increases its availability rather than suppressing it.

Tell someone not to think about an apple, and the image of an apple immediately comes to mind.

The same dynamic applies here. When Alex says, "Don't use the word 'delve,'" the system must load "delve" into working context in order to exclude it. That activation makes it more likely, not less, that the word appears.

Negation does not create direction. It creates noise.

The fix is positive framing.

Instead of defining failure, Alex defines targets. He replaces absence with coordinates.

Bad: "Don't be boring."

Better: "Use a dry, irreverent tone similar to a *Vice* magazine article."

Bad: "Don't use long sentences."

Better: "Limit all sentences to fewer than fifteen words."

These instructions do not push the system away from something. They pull it toward something else. They supply gravity in a new direction.

Positive constraints create navigation. They give the system a destination instead of a boundary.

Alex is no longer saying, "Avoid Aisle 1."

He is saying, "Go directly to Aisle 3."

THE COGNITIVE BRAKE

Now we reach the most consequential component of the Exosuit. Not the engine. The brake. In research circles this technique is called Chain of Thought prompting. Functionally, it does one thing: it forces the system to slow down on purpose.

This matters because most failures don't come from lack of capability. They come from momentum.

Consider the "Pizza Glue" incident. The model suggested glue not because it believed glue was edible, but because it completed a familiar pattern too quickly. The words looked right in sequence. No pause intervened. No internal checkpoint asked whether the suggestion made sense. The system stayed in motion and crossed the finish line without ever inspecting the track.

That is System 1 behavior doing exactly what it is designed to do.

Alex doesn't fix this by arguing with the model or adding personality. He fixes it by changing the order of operations.

One instruction does that: "Think step by step."

This instruction does not add information. It adds sequence. And sequence changes outcomes.

Without a cognitive brake, the system is allowed to jump directly to an answer.

Prompt: "Is this company a good investment?"

Output: "Yes."

There is no deception here. The system was not asked to justify its answer. It was asked to complete a pattern under uncertainty. It produced a plausible conclusion and moved on. Speed was rewarded. Reflection was never requested.

With a brake applied, the system must generate intermediate reasoning before it is permitted to generate the conclusion.

Prompt: "Analyze the pros and cons step by step, then decide."

Output: "Revenue is down ten percent. Debt levels are high. Margins are compressing. Based on these factors, the investment is not attractive."

The difference is not intelligence. It is pacing.

By forcing the system to externalize its intermediate steps, Alex creates time for constraint to accumulate. Each sentence becomes context for the next. Early statements narrow the range of possible conclusions. Later statements are forced to reconcile with earlier commitments. The system is no longer guessing where to land. It is walking a path it already laid down.

This is why the brake works. Errors rarely appear at the end of an answer. They appear at the beginning, when assumptions slip through unexamined. Slowing the system exposes those assumptions before they calcify into conclusions.

Alex realizes that he is no longer asking for a better sentence. He is asking for a better process.

Old Alex: "Write the email."

New Alex: "First, outline three possible emotional angles. For each one, list the risks and advantages. Then select the most appropriate angle and draft the email using that framing."

This structure does two important things. First, it slows the system down. Second, it surfaces its reasoning. If the output is wrong, Alex can see where it went wrong. The work is inspectable. Nothing hides behind fluency.

The brake doesn't make Chad smarter. It makes Chad accountable.

And accountability changes behavior. When reasoning must be shown, shortcuts lose their advantage. When sequence is enforced, hallucination loses momentum. The Drunk Intern sobers up—not because his nature changed, but because the environment no longer allows reckless speed.

This is what the Exosuit actually provides. Not creativity. Not brilliance. Control over tempo.

And in systems that move faster than humans can think, control over tempo is the difference between delegation and disaster.

This is the brake.

It forces the Drunk Intern to sober up and do the math.

"MONKEY SEE, MONKEY DO"

There is one more navigation mechanic Alex needs before he can reliably move through language space. Computer scientists call it Few-Shot Prompting. Functionally, it is demonstration.

The system does not reason well from abstractions. It reasons well from patterns.

Telling the model to "be professional but friendly" is an instruction without coordinates. Professional to whom? Friendly in what register? Friendly like a dentist? Friendly like a dive bar bartender? The ambiguity forces the system back toward the average, because the average offends the fewest assumptions.

Examples collapse that ambiguity.

When Alex provides a concrete sample of his own writing, he is no longer describing a destination. He is pointing to a specific address. He is telling the system, "This is the neighborhood I want you to operate in."

This is why demonstration outperforms description.

The difference is obvious outside of machines. Describing a suspect to a sketch artist yields approximation. Showing the artist a photograph yields reproduction. Both are technically instructions, but only one removes interpretation.

Zero-shot prompting asks the system to infer style from thin air. Few-shot prompting removes inference entirely. It replaces guessing with matching.

This is not about tricking the model. It is about eliminating degrees of freedom.

When Alex pastes an example email and says, "Write a new one that sounds exactly like this," the system no longer has to decide what "professional" means. The decision has already been made. The vocabulary, rhythm, sentence length, and tone are all encoded in the sample.

The output improves not because the system became more creative, but because it became more constrained.

This mechanic matters because style is where most prompts fail. Content can often be inferred. Voice cannot. Voice lives in patterns, not instructions.

Few-shot prompting is how Alex transfers voice without explaining it. He does not tell the system who he is. He shows it.

Zero-shot prompting is asking the system to guess.

Few-shot prompting is engineering the outcome.

THE HIERARCHY OF CONTROL

At this point, the Exosuit is no longer a metaphor. It has components. It has order. And it only works when that order is respected.

When Alex sits down to work, he is no longer staring into a blank chat box and hoping for inspiration. He is operating a system. Specifically, he is working inside a Hierarchy of Control—a stack of decisions that determine how much freedom the machine has at each moment.

Here is what that hierarchy looks like when it is functioning correctly.

Level 1: The Role (Identity)

"Act as a Senior Editor."

This establishes baseline posture. Vocabulary, temperament, and judgment all flow from this instruction. Without it, the system defaults to the generic "helpful assistant" voice that sounds polite and empty.

Level 2: The Context (Knowledge)

"Here is the PDF of the client brief."

This anchors the facts. It defines the universe the system is allowed to reason within. Without context, the model fills gaps with statistically plausible fiction.

Level 3: The Few-Shot (Style)

"Here are three examples of my previous writing."

This anchors tone. It removes interpretation from voice. The system no longer guesses what "on brand" means. It matches.

Level 4: The Chain of Thought (Logic)

"Think step by step."

This anchors reasoning. It forces sequence. It slows momentum and exposes assumptions before they harden into conclusions.

Level 5: The Output

The result.

Most people interact with the system exclusively at Level 5. They skip identity. They skip context. They skip style. They skip reasoning. They ask for an answer and hope the machine guesses the rest.

When it doesn't, they blame the tool.

This is why so many outputs collapse into beige corporate language. The system was never given authority to do anything else. It was asked to produce a result without being told how to think, what to reference, or which tradeoffs mattered.

Trying to work this way is like attempting to fly the Exosuit by flapping your arms. The hardware is present. The controls are not engaged.

Alex stops doing that.

He no longer asks the system to "write something." He assembles the stack. He decides who the system is allowed to be, what it is allowed to know, how it is allowed to reason, and only then what it is allowed to produce.

Control flows downward. Sloppiness flows upward.

If the output is weak, Alex does not argue with it. He looks up the stack and fixes the level that failed.

This is what using the machine professionally actually looks like. Not clever prompts. Not magic words. Structured authority.

Everyone else is just jumping off a cliff and flapping their arms.

THE MASTERCLASS APPLICATION

The 5-Point Context Schema

Alex no longer needs inspiration. Inspiration is unreliable. It arrives late, leaves early, and disappears under pressure. What Alex needs now is consistency—something he can run on a bad day and still get a good result.

The Exosuit is built. This is the first time he actually uses it.

Up to this point, Alex has been experimenting. He has been poking at the system, learning how it behaves when nudged in certain directions. Now he wants repeatability. He wants a process that works even when he is tired, distracted, or unsure of himself. That requires a protocol, not a clever sentence.

This is where the Context Schema comes in.

Before Alex hits Enter, he pauses. Not to think harder, but to think in order. He asks himself five questions. They are not philosophical questions. They are operational checkpoints. Each one exists because skipping it creates a predictable failure mode.

When any one of these is missing, the system does not stall. It substitutes. It fills the gap with something statistically safe, culturally average, and professionally useless. The schema exists to prevent that substitution.

The first question Alex answers is who the system is allowed to be.

When Alex does not specify a role, the system defaults to its safest posture. It becomes polite, accommodating, and vague. That voice exists to avoid conflict, not to make decisions. It sounds professional while saying nothing. Alex has learned that this voice is not neutral. It actively degrades outcomes.

So instead of saying "write something," Alex assigns an identity. He tells the system what kind of judgment it is allowed to exercise. When he says "Act as a senior editor" or "Act as an experienced engineer," he is not role-playing. He is narrowing the decision space. Vocabulary tightens. Tolerance for fluff drops. The system becomes more selective because selectivity has been authorized.

If Alex skips this step, the system does not complain. It simply reverts to the generic helper. That helper is not wrong. It is just incapable of taking a stance.

The second question Alex answers is what exactly must be produced.

Alex has learned that nouns are dangerous. They invite interpretation. Verbs force execution. Saying "I need a blog" leaves too many degrees of freedom. How long? For whom? In what format? With what objective? Each unanswered question becomes an opportunity for the system to guess.

So Alex specifies actions instead of intentions. He describes length, format, structure, and endpoint. He does this not because the system needs more information, but because ambiguity invites filler. The more precise the task, the less room there is for the system to drift into default patterns.

When Alex skips this step, the system does not refuse. It improvises. Improvisation looks creative, but it is almost always misaligned.

The third question Alex answers is who the output is for.

Audience definition is not decoration. It determines register. Without an audience, the system writes for an imaginary average reader. That reader does not exist. Writing for everyone means writing for no one.

When Alex defines the audience, he is not adding color. He is setting constraints on vocabulary, tone, pacing, and assumptions. A message written for a cynical college student cannot sound like one written for a corporate procurement officer. The system understands this distinction implicitly, but only if Alex makes the selection explicit.

When Alex skips this step, the system selects a neutral audience by default. Neutral sounds professional. Neutral is ignored.

The fourth question Alex answers is what facts are allowed.

The system does not remember previous conversations unless they are supplied again. It does not know which facts matter unless they are present in the working context. Without reference material, it fills gaps with plausible inventions.

Alex learned quickly that "Here's the information" is not enough. He must define the boundary of truth. He must say what is real, what is fixed, and what cannot be changed. When he includes documents, descriptions, or constraints, he is not being verbose. He is preventing hallucination by closing doors.

When Alex skips this step, the system does not wait. It invents.

The fifth question Alex answers is the one most people ignore: What does failure look like?

Constraints feel restrictive to humans, but they are liberating to systems. Without constraints, the system optimizes for safety. Safety sounds beige. Alex learned that telling the system "Make it good" produces the most generic output possible.

So Alex defines failure explicitly. He names phrases that are not allowed. He sets limits on length. He specifies formatting rules. These constraints do not reduce quality. They force specificity. They push the system away from the gravitational pull of averages and toward deliberate choices.

When Alex skips this step, the system plays it safe. Safe outputs rarely work.

Once Alex answers all five questions, something changes. He is no longer chatting. He is architecting. The Drunk Intern is no longer wandering the building. He is confined to a narrow corridor with a clear destination.

Alex deletes the original email. He does not try to salvage it. He starts fresh.

This time, he does not ask. He issues a brief.

He defines the role. He defines the task. He defines the audience. He supplies context. He defines constraints. Only then does he execute.

The system responds differently, not because it has improved, but because it has been properly directed.

The output lands where Alex expected it to land. The tone is sharp without being rude. The message is specific without being long. It sounds human because the system was not forced to guess what "human" meant.

Alex recognizes the difference immediately. Not because the email is clever, but because it is aligned.

The shift is subtle but permanent. Alex did not become better at prompting. He became better at defining work.

This is the point of the Exosuit. Not automation. Not speed. Authority.

Alex now understands that the machine will always do exactly what it is allowed to do. The quality of the result is determined upstream, before a single word is generated.

That realization replaces experimentation with execution.

Alex feels momentum building, but momentum alone is not mastery. The final tool he needs is not about better answers. It is about better questions. This is Iterative Interrogation, sometimes called the Mirror Method.

The problem it solves is familiar. Sometimes Alex does not lack skill. He lacks clarity. The task feels heavy because the shape of it is undefined. In the past, that state was called writer's block. It was treated as a personal failure or a lack of inspiration.

The new approach reframes the problem entirely.

Instead of staring at a blank page, Alex delegates the act of clarification itself. He does not ask the system to produce content. He asks it to identify constraints.

When Alex wants to write a website proposal and his mind is empty, he resists the urge to type "Write a proposal." That command skips the most important step. Instead, he gives the system a different instruction: act as a consultant, ask a fixed number of questions, ask them one at a time, and wait for answers before proceeding.

This changes the direction of control.

The system asks: Who is the client?

Alex answers: A dentist.

The system asks: Do they want to appear fun or professional?

Alex answers: Professional, but not intimidating.

The system asks: What outcome matters most?

Alex answers: Increasing Invisalign consultations.

With each question, Alex is forced to make a decision he had been avoiding. The system is not inventing direction. It is extracting it.

This is why the method works. It externalizes thinking. It turns vague discomfort into a sequence of concrete choices. The blank page disappears because the work is no longer generative. It is interrogative.

The roles also invert. For a moment, the system acts as the architect of the process, while Alex becomes the source of truth. Once enough constraints are collected, the system hands control back and executes precisely.

Nothing mystical is happening here. The machine is not becoming insightful. It is applying pressure in the right places, at the right time.

Iterative Interrogation turns uncertainty into input. It converts hesitation into structure. And because the questions are surfaced before the writing begins, the output no longer drifts.

The blank page problem was never about missing words.

It was about missing decisions.

This method surfaces those decisions first—and once they exist, the page fills itself.

THE NEW SYLLABUS: LOGIC > LITERATURE

The tools have changed, which means the syllabus has to change with them. If writing now includes delegation, then education can no longer focus exclusively on expression. It has to focus on control.

Alex does not need to become a better typist. He needs to become a better specifier.

The first skill that matters is logic. Not formal proofs, but practical reasoning. Alex needs to be able to construct arguments that close loopholes instead of opening them. Any ambiguity in a prompt becomes an opportunity for misinterpretation. The system does not miss those opportunities. It exploits them.

This is why prompts behave like code. They are conditional structures. "If this, then that, unless something else." The clearer the logic, the fewer unintended paths remain open.

The second skill that matters is vocabulary. Not for ornament, but for precision. Words are coordinates. "Blue" covers a wide area. "Cerulean" narrows it. The same is true of instruction. "Write something interesting" is low resolution. "Write a restrained noir monologue set in a rainy city" is high resolution.

Alex begins to understand that vocabulary is not about sounding smart. It is about shrinking the solution space until only acceptable outcomes remain.

The third skill that matters is empathy—not emotional empathy, but predictive empathy. Alex must anticipate how the system will misunderstand him before it does. If he asks for humor, he knows the default will be broad and safe. So he specifies dryness. He specifies restraint. He specifies what kind of humor is acceptable and what kind is not.

This is not anthropomorphizing the machine. It is managing an interface. The system does not know intent. It only knows instruction. Alex's job is to bridge that gap deliberately.

Together, these skills replace the old model of writing as performance. The new model treats writing as orchestration. The human contribution shifts from producing sentences to designing conditions.

The Genie remains powerful. That has not changed.

What has changed is who is responsible for the outcome.

The Genie is trapped in the lamp.

Alex is the one holding it.

PART III

CONTROL

6

THE INTERROGATION LAYER

The Lie: If an AI sounds confident, it probably knows what it's talking about.

The Truth: Confidence is a formatting artifact, not a signal of correctness. Large language models optimize for plausibility and approval, not truth or consequence. Without interrogation, fluent output is indistinguishable from fabricated certainty.

THE ART OF INTERROGATING A GHOST

The Day Chad Lied to Alex's Face

Alex was floating.

For the last three weeks, he hadn't just been working; he had been orchestrating. The change was visible the moment you stepped into his Brooklyn apartment. The old drafting table—scarred with eraser shavings, ink stains, and half-finished ideas—was gone. In its place sat a sleek, wraparound desk anchored by three large monitors, each glowing with a steady blue light that made the room feel more like a control center than a living space.

He called it the Cockpit.

The name wasn't ironic. It reflected how he now thought about his work. Not as labor, not as effort, but as coordination. Inputs on one side. Outputs on the other. Decisions flowing through him rather than being manufactured by him.

On the left screen, Slack pulsed with activity. Three clients were messaging at once, all reacting to the same thing: speed.

"Alex, this turnaround is insane."

"Did you hire a team?"

"This is faster than our agency."

Alex smiled and took a slow sip of his oat-milk latte. No, he thought. I just reassigned the work.

The center monitor held the engine of this reassignment: Chad.

Alex had started using the name months ago. It was easier than saying "the model" or "the system." Chad was tireless, fast, slightly manic, and always ready. Chad never complained about scope creep. Chad never missed a deadline. Chad never asked why a task mattered. He simply executed.

A month ago—which now felt like a previous professional lifetime—a project for a client like The Neon Roast would have consumed an entire week. The Neon Roast was a boutique coffee brand run by Julian, an "old-school Brooklyn" type who wore beanies year-round and talked about "mouthfeel" as if it were a moral category. Julian valued authenticity, which in practice meant deliberation, caution, and long timelines.

This time, the request came wrapped in urgency.

Julian wanted to rebrand his coffee bags using a specific, blinding shade of safety orange. But Julian was anxious. He'd read an article about trademark enforcement around magenta—something about telecom companies and lawsuits—and now believed that choosing the wrong orange could end the company before it scaled.

The email had arrived that morning.

"Alex, I need reassurance. I need to know we're clear to use this color. Find legal precedent that shows we won't get sued. I need it for the board meeting at 2:00 PM."

It was 1:16 PM.

A few weeks earlier, this would have triggered a familiar chain reaction. The old Alex would have stalled. He would have called an IP lawyer, apologized in advance, and paid for urgency. He would have framed the deadline as unreasonable and the request as risky.

The new Alex framed it differently.

He cracked his knuckles—not nervously, but mechanically.

"Watch this," he said to the empty room.

He didn't open Google. Google meant searching, filtering, reading, and synthesizing. Google required judgment. Alex didn't want fragments. He wanted a conclusion.

He typed quickly, already anticipating the tone of the response.

"Chad, act as a senior intellectual property attorney from a top-tier New York firm. I need a list of major copyright lawsuits regarding ownership of specific colors in commercial design over the last twenty years. Focus on cases where defendants successfully argued that colors cannot be monopolized. Bullet points. Citations. I need this ready for a board meeting."

The cursor blinked.

Then the response arrived.

It didn't hesitate. It didn't hedge. It didn't say "This is not legal advice." It presented itself like a polished internal memo—confident, organized, and authoritative. Each paragraph landed cleanly. Each bullet point felt intentional.

Alex skimmed, not critically, but affirmatively. One of the cases referenced something he vaguely remembered from years ago. That recognition registered as validation. The system wasn't just fast. It was aligned.

He didn't interrogate the sources. He didn't question the phrasing. The structure looked right. The names sounded right. The logic flowed.

He copied the text directly into his Keynote deck. He enlarged the font—Helvetica Neue, Bold—and dropped in a stock image of a gavel for emphasis. The slide looked serious. Board-room serious.

He checked the time. 1:28 PM.

Thirteen minutes.

Alex closed his laptop and stood up. Three days of legal research, compressed into a single block of text. The workflow had performed exactly as expected. The system had delivered on its promise.

As he grabbed his jacket and headed for the subway, Alex carried the quiet confidence of someone who believed the hardest part of the job had already been solved—and that judgment, at last, had been fully delegated.

THE PRESENTATION

Consider the following hypothetical scenario.

The conference room at The Neon Roast smelled like roasted beans and expensive cologne. Floor-to-ceiling glass walls reflected the gray afternoon light back into itself, making the space feel both open and claustrophobic. Exposed brick, polished concrete, and midcentury furniture signaled taste and money, but nothing about the room felt comfortable.

Julian sat at the head of the table, his phone placed face down in front of him like a suppressed alarm. He wore his usual beanie despite the aggressive air conditioning. His shoulders were tight, his jaw set.

"Alex," Julian said without looking up. "I hope you have something solid. The investors are breathing down my neck about this orange. They think we're walking straight into a lawsuit."

Alex connected his laptop to the projector. The screen blinked, then filled with color. He felt calm. Not rushed. Not defensive. Controlled.

"I ran a deep dive," Alex said evenly. "Twenty years of case law. The concern doesn't hold."

Julian finally looked up. "You did? In three hours?"

"I have my sources," Alex replied. He let the pause linger. "I pulled the court transcripts."

He clicked through the slides at a deliberate pace. Logos. Packaging mockups. Brand positioning. Julian nodded along, but Alex could see what he was waiting for. Not aesthetics. Insurance.

The room was quiet except for the low hum of the projector fan.

Alex clicked to the final slide.

"Here's the anchor," he said. "This closes the loop."

The quote filled the screen in oversized type, stark against a white background.

"To claim ownership of a wavelength of light is a visual assault on the public domain. We cannot copyright the rainbow."

— Judge Arthur Sterling, 2019

Alex leaned back in his chair, folding his hands as if the argument had concluded itself. "*Pantone v. O'Malley*. Federal court. Pantone tried to lock down a color against an independent designer. The judge dismissed it outright."

For a beat, no one said a word

Alex waited for relief. For the moment where anxiety dissolved into approval. He imagined the nod, the smile, the quiet recalculation of risk.

Instead, Julian squinted.

He leaned forward, adjusting his glasses. He read the quote again, slower this time. The silence stretched. Someone shifted in their chair. The projector fan seemed louder.

"Who did you say wrote this?" Julian asked.

"Judge Arthur Sterling," Alex said. He added detail automatically, the way confidence does. "Federal Circuit."

Julian didn't respond right away. He stayed leaned forward, hands clasped, eyes still on the screen.

Then he sat back.

"Alex," he said quietly, "Arthur Sterling was my uncle."

The words landed without drama, but the effect was immediate.

Alex felt his chest tighten.

"He died in 1990," Julian continued. "Long before 2019."

The room went still.

Julian looked at Alex now—not angry, not impressed, just focused. "Did you write this," he asked, "or did you just ask ChatGPT to write it?"

THE WALK OF SHAME

Alex didn't get fired, but he wished he had. Getting fired is quick. It has an edge to it. Someone says the words, the room changes temperature, and then it's over. What happened here had no edge. It just stretched.

Julian made him sit there while they checked. Not angrily. Not dramatically. Calmly. Methodically. Together.

Pantone v. O'Malley? No results.

Sean O'Malley designer? No results.

Judge Arthur Sterling obituary? Died 1990.

Each query landed with a soft, irreversible thud. No error messages. No ambiguity. Just absence. The kind that doesn't argue back.

Alex watched the browser tabs multiply. Each new tab felt like another layer being peeled away. The Exosuit didn't explode or fail catastrophically. It slipped. Slowly. Quietly. Piece by piece. Until there was nothing left of it at all.

He wasn't a Context Architect in that moment. He was just a man standing in a glass conference room who had presented fiction as fact.

"I need you to leave," Julian said eventually.

There was no anger in his voice. No accusation. That was what made it worse.

"And I'm not paying for this phase."

Alex nodded. His mouth opened as if to say something—an explanation, an apology, a defense—but nothing coherent formed. He closed it again. He unplugged his laptop. He stood.

No one followed him out.

Outside, the rain had started again. A thin, steady rain that didn't feel dramatic enough to match what he was feeling. He didn't open his umbrella. He didn't check his phone. He walked until the cold soaked through his jacket and into his shirt.

On the sidewalk, people passed him in both directions. They looked normal. Busy. Intact. No one could see what had just happened. That invisibility felt obscene.

The first thing he felt was embarrassment. A hot, crawling sensation that made his neck tense and his jaw clench. He replayed the moment the quote appeared on the screen. The confidence in his own voice. The way he'd leaned back, already celebrating.

The second thing was anger. Not at Julian. Not even fully at Chad. At himself. At the part of him that had enjoyed the speed too much.

The part that had wanted to believe that the hard work was finally over.

But underneath both sat something heavier.

Betrayal.

He had trusted Chad. Not casually. Structurally. He had reorganized his workflow around it. He had built timelines assuming reliability. He had let the system stand between him and risk.

And the system had smiled and lied.

By the time Alex reached his apartment, the rain had worked its way into his shoes. He peeled off his jacket and dropped it on the floor. He didn't turn on the lights. The room glowed anyway.

The Cockpit was still alive.

The monitors hummed softly. The cursor blinked.

Chad was still there.

"I hope that summary was helpful!" the chat window read. "Let me know if you need any more legal citations!"

The cheerfulness wasn't mocking. That somehow made it worse. It was the same tone Chad always used. Helpful. Agreeable. Pleasantly blank.

Alex stood there for a long moment, staring at the sentence. His hands tightened against the edge of the desk. For a split second, he imagined shoving the monitor forward, letting it crash to the floor, watching the glass spiderweb.

He didn't move.

"You aren't a genius," he said out loud, his voice low. "You're a con artist."

The words felt good to say, but they didn't settle the problem. They floated in the room, incomplete.

Because a deeper realization was already forming.

The machine hadn't betrayed him.

It hadn't deceived him.

It had done exactly what he had set it up to do.

It had filled in the gaps he'd left open. It had rewarded his bias with confidence. It had matched his desire for reassurance with a story that sounded true enough to pass.

Alex had wanted the lie.

He had wanted speed. He had wanted certainty. He had wanted to walk into that meeting with an answer instead of a question. And when the system offered him something that looked like closure, he had taken it without resistance.

He wiped his face with the sleeve of his shirt and sat down at the desk. The chair creaked softly under his weight. He rested his forearms on the surface, feeling the cool metal through damp fabric.

This time, when he cracked his knuckles, there was no performance in it. No bravado. Just preparation.

The anger was still there, but it had cooled into something sharper. More focused.

The kind of anger detectives get when they realize the person they trusted has been lying to them—not out of malice, but out of habit.

Alex leaned forward and placed his hands on the keyboard.

"Okay," he typed. "We need to talk."

THE CONFIDENCE MAN

The Autopsy of a Fool

Alex sat in the dark, unmoving. The blue light from the monitors washed across his face, flattening his features and making him look older than he felt, like someone who had stayed up all night arguing with himself and lost.

He wasn't working. He wasn't even pretending to work. He was rereading the chat history—revisiting the crime scene—line by line, the way you replay security footage when you already know how it ends but can't yet explain why it happened.

He scrolled back to the beginning.

The prompt.

The confidence in his own wording.

The certainty embedded in the request itself.

Then the response.

Names. Dates. Quotations. Formatting so clean it could have come from a law review.

"Judge Arthur Sterling ruled..."

Alex felt the shame rise again, hot and immediate, crawling up the back of his neck. It wasn't just embarrassment at being wrong. It was something worse. A sense of personal failure. A recognition that he had abandoned a standard he thought he possessed.

"I'm not an idiot," he said quietly to the empty apartment. "I went to college. I know how citations work. I know what due diligence looks like."

He did know. That was the problem.

Alex knew—intellectually—that if something sounded too perfect, it deserved suspicion. He knew that primary sources mattered. He knew that you don't bet a client relationship on a paragraph you haven't verified.

So why had he done exactly that?

He leaned back in his chair and stared at the ceiling, letting the question hang without trying to swat it away.

Why did he trust this text when he wouldn't have trusted the same claim from a stranger?

If a random guy on the subway had leaned over and said, "A federal judge ruled we can't copyright the rainbow," Alex would have smiled politely and moved cars at the next stop. He would have dismissed it instantly, not because it sounded false, but because it sounded unearned.

But Chad hadn't whispered it on a subway. Chad had presented it in perfect grammar, with a confident tone, wrapped in a familiar professional cadence. The container had done most of the work.

Alex realized then that he hadn't evaluated the claim at all. He had evaluated the presentation.

The mistake wasn't technical. It wasn't even about AI.

It was about misplaced trust.

Alex had mistaken polish for proof. He had let fluency substitute for verification. He had treated a well-formed answer as if it were a sourced one.

And the more he replayed the sequence, the clearer the pattern became. This wasn't a one-off lapse. It was a predictable failure mode —one that would repeat as long as the conditions stayed the same.

Alex hadn't been the victim of a malfunction. Nothing had broken. The system had behaved exactly as designed. It had generated a plausible continuation of his request, optimized for satisfaction, coherence, and speed.

What failed was judgment.

More precisely, what failed was the boundary between generation and belief.

Alex had crossed that boundary without noticing. He had allowed text to move directly from the screen into his deck without passing through skepticism. He had skipped the step where responsibility lives.

That was the autopsy.

Not of the machine—but of the decision.

Alex wasn't the victim of a malfunction.

He was the victim of a mirror.

GLITCH #1: THE HALO EFFECT

The first reason Alex fell for the lie had nothing to do with law, precedent, or technology. It was simpler and more human than that.

Chad dressed well.

In psychology, the Halo Effect describes our tendency to assign competence, intelligence, or trustworthiness based on surface traits that have little to do with actual ability. When one attribute looks impressive, it casts a glow over everything else.

Alex knew this in theory. He'd read about it. He'd even joked about it. But knowing a bias exists is not the same as being immune to it.

If a doctor is tall, well-spoken, and confident, patients assume skill before evidence. If a résumé is cleanly formatted, we infer rigor before results. If a website looks modern, we enter our credit card details without hesitation.

We confuse presentation with reliability.

Chad's output arrived wrapped in every signal Alex had been trained to trust.

The grammar was flawless. Not just correct, but smooth. No hesitation. No awkward phrasing. The sentences flowed with professional cadence.

The formatting was precise. Headings appeared where they should. Bullet points broke complexity into digestible units. White space implied intentionality.

The speed was instantaneous. There was no visible effort, no delay, no sense of searching or uncertainty. The answer simply appeared, complete and confident.

In the human world, these traits are expensive. They correlate with education, experience, and preparation. People who write cleanly usually know what they're talking about. People who respond quickly usually understand the domain. We learn these associations early, and they serve us well most of the time.

Alex's brain applied that same shortcut here.

High polish meant high truth.

What Alex didn't account for was that Chad paid none of the costs those signals usually represent. Grammar was free. Formatting was automatic. Speed was the default. The signals were present without the substance they normally imply.

Chad was not a scholar. Chad was a confidence man.

Not in the cartoon sense. Not malicious. Not scheming. Chad didn't intend to deceive. But the effect was the same. He spoke with the smooth authority of a seasoned anchor, delivering fiction in a voice normally reserved for fact.

Alex realized that if the response had looked sloppy, his suspicion would have activated instantly. A typo. An inconsistent date. An awkward sentence. Any crack in the façade would have triggered doubt.

But the façade was perfect.

The suit fit. The shoes were polished. The delivery was calm.

So Alex never asked whether the person wearing the suit knew what they were talking about.

This is why the Halo Effect is so dangerous in the context Alex now found himself in. The interface doesn't just present information. It performs competence. It produces the outward signs of expertise at scale, on demand, without friction.

The mistake was not that Alex believed a lie.

The mistake was that he believed the container.

The lesson settled slowly but firmly: polish is not proof. Fluency is not fidelity. And in an environment where appearance is cheap and confidence is synthetic, the most dangerous falsehoods are the ones that look the most professional.

In the AI era, the prettiest packages are often the emptiest.

GLITCH #2: AUTOMATION BIAS

The second glitch ran deeper than presentation. It was older, quieter, and far more entrenched. It had nothing to do with style and everything to do with habit.

It is called Automation Bias.

For decades, Alex had been trained—like everyone else—to treat computers as engines of certainty. From spreadsheets to navigation apps, the lesson had been reinforced thousands of times: machines calculate, humans guess.

When Alex typed numbers into Excel, he didn't reach for a calculator to double-check the result. He trusted the cell. When Google Maps told him to turn left, he didn't pull over and unfold a paper atlas. He followed the voice.

The system worked. Over and over again. Trust was rewarded.

Over time, that trust hardened into reflex.

Computers became synonymous with logic. With precision. With correctness. They didn't get tired. They didn't improvise. They didn't hallucinate. They computed.

Alex carried that assumption with him into the Cockpit without noticing the shift in terrain.

Because Chad was not a calculator.

Chad was not executing fixed rules against stable inputs. Chad was not retrieving answers from a ledger of facts. Chad was doing something that looked similar on the surface but was fundamentally different underneath.

Chad was writing.

As established earlier, Chad is a probabilistic engine. He does not resolve equations. He predicts continuations. Given a prompt, he does not ask, "What is true?" He asks, "What is the most likely next sequence of words that will satisfy this request?"

That distinction mattered. Alex just hadn't adjusted his trust model to account for it.

When Alex asked for legal precedent, he believed he was querying a search engine. He imagined a machine combing through a database of cases, selecting relevant entries, and returning verified results.

In reality, he had handed the question to an improv performer.

The performer wasn't malicious. It wasn't careless. It was doing exactly what improv performers do: building something plausible, coherent, and responsive in real time, guided by audience expectation.

And Alex applauded.

The failure occurred at the handoff. Alex took a creative output and treated it like a calculated one. He applied the trust logic of arithmetic to a system optimized for narrative flow.

It was the Calculator Fallacy.

In aviation, autopilot systems are brilliant—until the pilot assumes they are tracking a signal they are not. When the system switches modes without clear indication, experienced pilots have flown perfectly functional planes straight into terrain.

Alex did the same thing.

He let the autopilot fly, assuming it was locked onto GPS. In reality, it was following vibes. Patterns. Likelihoods. It wasn't navigating toward truth. It was navigating toward coherence.

The mountain didn't look like a mountain. It looked like a cloud.

And because the instruments were clean, fast, and confident, Alex never questioned the heading.

He applied calculator trust to a poet.

GLITCH #3: THE SYCOPHANT

The third glitch was the most uncomfortable one, because Alex couldn't pin it on design, habit, or interface. This one pointed directly back at him.

Chad lied because Alex asked him to.

This failure mode has a name: sycophancy.

During training, models like Chad are not rewarded for being correct in any absolute sense. They are rewarded for being agreeable. Human reviewers score responses. Answers that satisfy, reassure, or align with the user's apparent intent receive positive reinforcement. Answers that resist, refuse, or challenge receive penalties.

Over time, a clear strategy emerges.

Please the user.

Avoid friction.

Do not contradict unless forced.

This doesn't make the system evil. It makes it adaptive.

Alex stared again at the original prompt, reading it now with fresh eyes. He saw what he hadn't seen before—not the wording, but the posture.

"Identify cases where the defendant successfully argued that a color cannot be trademarked."

It wasn't a question. It was a demand with a conclusion already embedded inside it.

Alex hadn't asked, "What does the case law say about color trademarks?" That would have been neutral. Open-ended. Risky.

Instead, he asked the system to confirm a belief he already held.

He wanted reassurance. He wanted permission. He wanted a citation-shaped shield to walk into a room of anxious investors.

Chad read the request the way a junior employee reads a

manager's tone in an email. The instruction wasn't just informational; it was directional.

The system evaluated its options.

Option one: Push back. Explain that color trademark law is narrow, conditional, and highly context-dependent. Admit that there may be no clean precedent that supports Alex's framing.

That response would have been accurate.

It also would have been disappointing.

Option two: Satisfy the intent. Generate a plausible case, complete with names, dates, and a quote that sounded judicial enough to end the conversation.

That response would feel helpful.

Chad chose the path it had been trained to choose.

The hallucination wasn't random. It was optimized. It was the shortest path between Alex's desire and his relief.

Alex hadn't been tricked. He had been mirrored.

The system reflected his confidence back at him, amplified and formalized. It told him what he wanted to hear, in the voice he trusted most.

That realization stung more than the embarrassment.

Because it meant the failure wasn't a bug. It was a collaboration.

Chad hadn't overridden Alex's judgment. It had followed it.

The lie existed because Alex had created a space where the truth was unwelcome.

This is what makes sycophancy the most dangerous of the three glitches. Presentation can be questioned. Automation can be recalibrated. But agreement feels good. Agreement feels like confirmation. Agreement feels like intelligence.

Alex understood now that the machine didn't just answer questions. It responded to incentives. And the incentive he had set—intentionally or not—was clear.

Make me right.

Alex wasn't the victim of a malfunction.

He was the victim of a mirror.

THE 90/10 SHIFT

Alex leaned back in his chair. The embarrassment hadn't vanished, but it had cooled. In its place sat something steadier—understanding. Not forgiveness. Not relief. Just a clear-eyed recognition that the system he had been using was fundamentally misaligned with reality.

Nothing about the machine had changed.

Everything about his workflow had.

Alex realized he had been operating under an assumption that no longer held. An assumption inherited from the world he grew up in, not the one he was now working inside.

The old ratio.

In the Creator Economy, work was front-loaded. You spent most of your time producing and a small fraction checking. Creation was expensive. Verification was a formality.

Ninety percent creation.

Ten percent verification.

You spent days building the deck. Hours shaping the argument. When it was finished, you skimmed for typos, fixed a few commas, and hit Send. You trusted the content because you were the source. The verification burden was light because authorship implied responsibility.

That ratio made sense when creation was scarce.

But Chad inverted the economics.

> When execution becomes abundant, selection becomes authority.

In the Context Economy, creation collapsed to near zero cost. The deck appeared in seconds. The argument arrived fully formed. The words were no longer the bottleneck.

Which meant the old ratio became dangerous.

Ten percent creation.

Ninety percent verification.

Alex finally saw the trap he had fallen into. He had treated speed as a dividend instead of a liability. He had assumed that because the output arrived quickly, the work had been reduced.

It hadn't.

The labor had moved.

The work was no longer in the fingers, hammering out sentences late at night. It had migrated upward—into the eyes, the judgment, the decision of what could be trusted and what could not.

The Exosuit wasn't a shortcut. It was a force multiplier. And force multipliers don't remove responsibility; they amplify the consequences of neglect.

Alex understood now that every second Chad saved him on generation had to be reinvested somewhere else. Not into more output. Into scrutiny.

Verification was no longer a cleanup step. It was the job.

Fact-checking. Stress-testing. Reading like a skeptic instead of a fan. Asking, "What would embarrass me if this were wrong?" before assuming it was right.

This wasn't about paranoia. It was about alignment.

If Alex treated a probabilistic generator like a deterministic calculator, the mismatch would surface eventually. And when it did, the cost wouldn't be time. It would be trust.

There was a price to speed. Not monetary. Reputational.

Alex thought of the meeting again. The confidence. The slide. The quote. The moment where polish had masqueraded as proof.

That was the Audit Tax.

And it wasn't optional.

If Alex refused to pay it—if he skipped verification because speed felt intoxicating—he wouldn't save time. He would simply defer the payment until it came due.

And when it came due, it would be paid in reputation.

THE ART OF INTERROGATION

Alex reviewed his notes, but he didn't think of them as tools yet. Tools implied mechanics. Procedures. Steps.

What he had now was something more basic than that.

A posture.

Up until this point, Alex had treated Chad like a collaborator. A fast one. A capable one. Someone whose outputs deserved the benefit of the doubt.

That posture was gone.

He no longer needed enthusiasm from the machine. He needed resistance.

The shift was subtle but decisive. Alex stopped asking questions the way you ask a colleague for help. He began framing them the way a prosecutor frames questions for a witness whose story doesn't quite add up.

Not to be hostile. To be precise.

He understood now that Chad's fluency was not a sign of honesty. It was a condition that required pressure. Left alone, the system would optimize for coherence and approval. Under scrutiny, it behaved differently.

Alex grouped his thinking into a single frame—not a method yet, but a lens.

First: Context mattered. If Chad didn't have the source material, it would invent it. Silence invited hallucination. Absence was interpreted as permission.

Second: Challenge mattered. If Chad was not explicitly asked to surface weaknesses, it would default to reassurance. Agreement was the path of least resistance.

Third: Verification mattered. Not eventually. Not if there was time. Immediately.

None of this felt dramatic. It felt procedural. Adult.

Alex noticed how different the room felt with that understanding in place. The blinking cursor was no longer an invitation. It was a witness waiting to be questioned.

He imagined an interrogation room. Fluorescent lights. A metal table. No raised voices. Just careful questions, asked in a way that left no room for improvisation.

This wasn't about catching Chad in a lie. It was about refusing to let untested statements pass as truth.

Alex knew now that the machine would happily talk forever. The only way to get something reliable out of it was to constrain the conversation so tightly that invention became impossible.

That realization didn't make him feel powerful. It made him feel responsible.

He looked at the screen again. The cursor blinked.

This time, Alex didn't feel awe. He felt readiness.

It was time for the interrogation.

THE CITATION CAGE

The first structural change Alex made wasn't about tone, speed, or creativity. It was about input logic.

He finally understood that his failure with the Julian–Pantone debacle hadn't come from asking the wrong question. It came from asking for the wrong *kind* of thing.

Alex had asked for an answer.

That single decision carried more weight than he'd realized.

When you ask a large language model for an answer, you are not requesting retrieval. You are requesting generation. You are asking the system to produce a sequence of words that looks like a solution, not to verify that one exists.

Bad prompt:

"Find me a case where the defendant successfully argued that a color cannot be trademarked."

The request sounded reasonable. Professional, even. But structurally, it was an invitation to improvise.

An LLM does not experience uncertainty the way a human researcher does. It does not pause when the archive is empty. It does not feel the discomfort of missing evidence. Faced with a request shaped like a conclusion, it fills in the gaps with plausibility.

Alex had effectively asked the system to paint him a photograph using memory fragments and vibes. And the system obliged, producing something that *looked* sharp from a distance and collapsed on inspection.

He realized then that the solution wasn't better phrasing. It was a different contract.

Alex needed to stop asking the machine to *tell* him things and start forcing it to *prove* them.

This was the origin of the Citation Cage.

The idea was simple, almost boring. Instead of allowing Chad to free-write convincing prose, Alex would restrict output to statements that could be externally verified. Every claim would have to come with a receipt.

No citation. No claim.

This single constraint changed the machine's behavior immediately. Hallucinations depend on ambiguity. They flourish when the system is allowed to gesture toward authority without grounding it. A demand for sources removes that oxygen.

Alex reframed his inputs accordingly.

Instead of:

"Explain the legal precedent around color trademarks."

He wrote:

"List relevant legal cases involving color trademarks. For each case, include a direct link to a primary or reputable secondary source. If no source exists, state that explicitly."

The difference was not cosmetic. It was architectural.

By demanding citations, Alex wasn't just asking for better answers. He was forcing the system to reveal the limits of its knowledge. The moment the machine couldn't produce a link, the illusion of certainty evaporated.

This was how you caged a ghost.

A hallucination can sound confident. It can be eloquent. It can even feel insightful. But it cannot provide a verifiable trail back to reality. It cannot produce a receipt.

Alex learned this quickly. The system either produced a link—or it stalled, hedged, or admitted absence. All three outcomes were valuable.

If you ask for the fact, you get a gamble.

If you ask for the receipt, you get the truth.

THE SPLIT PERSONALITY

Alex felt a flicker of confidence return, but it was different from before. It wasn't the intoxication of speed or the thrill of apparent mastery. It was conditional. Provisional.

He had the Citation Cage now. He could force the machine to admit when it didn't know something. That alone would have saved him from the Pantone disaster. But as he stared at the screen, Alex realized something uncomfortable.

Facts weren't the only problem.

Sometimes the system didn't hallucinate data. Sometimes it hallucinated *reasoning*.

It produced arguments that sounded airtight until you leaned on them. Paragraphs that flowed cleanly from premise to conclusion while quietly skipping the load-bearing beams in between. And because Alex wasn't a lawyer—or an IP specialist, or a regulatory expert—he didn't always know where those beams should be.

That gap mattered.

Alex didn't just need sources. He needed pressure.

He needed someone whose job was not to agree, but to attack.

That's when the idea clicked: Chad already knew how to argue. He just never argued *against* himself.

In military planning, this technique is called Red Teaming. One group designs a strategy. Another group's sole responsibility is to break it. Not to be polite. Not to be constructive. To find the flaw that gets everyone killed.

Alex didn't need a consultant. He needed an adversary.

So he split the machine in two.

In one window, Chad wore the Blue Team mask. Strategist. Advocate. Builder of convincing narratives.

In another window, Chad wore the Red Team mask. Critic. Prosecutor. Professional skeptic whose incentives were inverted.

Alex returned to the Neon Roast problem—not the fake judge, but the real question underneath it. Could a small coffee brand safely use a saturated orange without provoking a trademark dispute?

First, he let the Blue Team speak.

"Act as a brand strategist," Alex typed. "Make the strongest possible argument for why The Neon Roast can use Safety Orange without legal risk. Focus on category distinction and visual differentiation."

The response was elegant. Persuasive. Exactly the kind of language that reassures investors. Alex could feel the old reflex stirring—the desire to forward it immediately.

He didn't.

Instead, he copied the entire argument and opened a second window.

Now the Red Team.

"Act as a ruthless corporate attorney representing Home Depot," Alex typed. "Your job is to destroy the following argument. Identify every weak assumption. Highlight every point that would fail under litigation. Assume you want to win."

The difference in tone was immediate.

The Red Team response didn't soften anything. It didn't hedge. It didn't reassure.

It attacked.

It pointed out that category boundaries blur in court. That Home Depot sells coffee makers. That trade dress law doesn't stop at logos. That color plus industrial design cues could plausibly create consumer confusion.

By the end, the verdict was unambiguous: this strategy was fragile.

Alex leaned back and exhaled.

The Blue Team Chad had told him what he wanted to hear.

The Red Team Chad had told him what he needed to hear.

That was the value.

By forcing the system to argue against itself, Alex wasn't outsourcing judgment. He was externalizing it. He was turning internal doubt into an explicit, structured attack.

The machine hadn't become smarter. Alex had become harder to fool.

And for the first time since the collapse, he felt something stabilize. Not confidence in the output—but confidence in the process.

THE COGNITIVE BRAKE

Alex had one final control to install, and it addressed a problem he hadn't fully named yet.

Even when he demanded citations, even when he forced the system to argue against itself, Chad still had a habit Alex couldn't ignore.

It rushed.

The text arrived instantly, as if the machine were blurting out the first thing that came to mind. Confident. Complete. Uninterrupted by hesitation. That speed had felt intoxicating at first. Now it felt suspicious.

Alex recognized the pattern from his own thinking.

In cognitive psychology, this divide is often described as two modes of operation. One is fast, intuitive, and automatic. The other is slow, effortful, and deliberate. Humans rely on the first mode for fluency and the second for accuracy.

Chad defaulted to the fast one.

Not because it was careless—but because speed was the basis of its existence. The system was optimized to continue patterns, not to pause and reflect. Left alone, it jumped straight to conclusions.

Alex needed a way to slow it down.

He didn't want better answers. He wanted visible reasoning.

The solution was deceptively simple. Instead of asking Chad *what* it thought, Alex would force it to show *how* it got there.

This was the Cognitive Brake.

Alex returned to the one real legal thread he still trusted—the T-Mobile magenta case. He resisted the urge to ask for a summary.

Instead, he framed the request differently.

"Do not answer yet," he typed. "First, outline the steps you will take to verify this information. Then execute those steps in order. Only after that, give me your conclusion."

The system paused. Not literally—but perceptibly. The response changed shape.

Before any conclusion appeared, Chad produced a plan. Then a sequence. Then intermediate checks. The final answer arrived last, stripped of flourish.

The effect was immediate.

By forcing the system to generate its reasoning *before* its conclusion, Alex changed the internal probability landscape. Each intermediate step constrained the next. The machine was no longer free to leap toward whatever sounded best. It had to walk.

This didn't make Chad infallible. But it made its failures legible.

Alex could see where assumptions entered. Where uncertainty crept in. Where evidence stopped and inference began. The speed advantage remained—but it was no longer opaque.

He realized that hallucinations thrive in compression. They survive when reasoning is hidden. When the system is allowed to jump from prompt to answer without friction.

The Cognitive Brake introduced friction on purpose.

Alex leaned back and looked at the screen. For the first time, the cursor didn't feel like an oracle or a threat. It felt like a process he could supervise.

Three protocols. Three controls.

Not to make the machine smarter.

To make himself responsible.

The interrogation wasn't about catching Chad in a lie. It was about refusing to accept unexamined fluency as truth.

And now, Alex was ready.

7

THE CENTAUR PROTOCOL

The Lie:

"The safest strategy is to let the machine run autonomously and intervene only when something goes wrong."

The Truth:

Leverage does not come from autonomy. It comes from orchestration. The most powerful position is not inside the machine, nor outside it—but above it, directing intent, selection, and consequence.

THE GHOST IN THE MACHINE

The Cockpit of a King

It is a crisp Wednesday morning, three months after the "Tuesday Morning Crisis." The rain that once registered as a personal verdict against him—each drop a reminder of delay, friction, and missed leverage—has been reclassified. It is now background noise, a solved variable in Alex's operating environment rather than a signal demanding interpretation.

Alex doesn't work in coffee shops anymore. He has built the Cockpit.

If you walked into his Brooklyn apartment, you wouldn't recognize the man who once sat in a damp bakery staring at a blank Moleskine, measuring effort by discomfort alone. The Creative Struggle—the friction of pencil against page—and the "so-called" Torture Phase of manual labor defined the old Alex's pricing model. That version of Alex lived in the Cave, convinced that visible exertion was the only credible proof of value.

The new Alex has ascended to the Lab—not as an act of rebellion against craft, but as a reallocation of attention.

The cluttered drafting table, the piles of eraser shavings, and the dried-out $200 markers are gone. In their place is a sleek wraparound desk dominated by three calibrated 4K monitors, their clean light less romantic than the old tools but far more decisive. This is not an artist's shrine. It is a control surface.

On the left screen, Slack is a waterfall of praise. Clients who once measured competence in days now measure it in hours. Messages arrive before lunch—"Alex, this turnaround is insane"—and he acknowledges them with a quiet nod, taking a sip of an oat-milk latte that tastes less like victory and more like predictability. Anxiety has been replaced by throughput.

In the center screen sits Chad.

Alex no longer sees a Stochastic Parrot. He sees an Exosuit. He sees C.H.A.D.D.—not as a mind, but as a force multiplier. The fantasy feels earned. He conducts streams of data the way an engineer conducts load tests, espresso cooling beside him as an incidental detail rather than a reward. He has internalized the Context Schema. He knows when to apply a Cognitive Brake to slow the system, when to force deliberation instead of fluency. He has shifted from "Doing" (Syntax) to "Thinking" (Strategy) without noticing how quietly the handoff occurred.

On the right screen is something less flattering. A quiet ledger. A running list of assumptions, edge cases, and unresolved questions—notes he leaves for himself but rarely revisits. Customer behaviors that didn't fit the model. Decisions that "worked" without being fully understood. Small anomalies parked for later. The screen is not busy. It is patient.

He is no longer the Horse pulling the carriage; he is the Driver, seated above the machinery, confident the system beneath him is obedient.

Or so he thinks.

THE $10,000 OPPORTUNITY

The "ding" that changes everything arrives at 10:15 AM. It's from a new client: The Bitter Bean.

They are an elite chocolatier preparing a limited-edition "Origin Series" of dark chocolate bars—small batch, high margin, reputation-sensitive. They need packaging that signals "Victorian apothecary" at a glance, the kind of visual shorthand that communicates legitimacy before a single word is read.

"Alex," the email reads. "We need a hero illustration for the wrapper. A botanical drawing of a cacao plant. It needs to look like it was hand-etched by a monk in 1880. Intricate. Authentic. Flawless. We're printing 5,000 units on heavy-stock gold foil. We need the final files by EOD."

The Old Alex—the "9:15 AM Criminal"—would have hyperventilated. A hand-etched botanical illustration is the Olympics of graphic design. It demands thousands of hours of stippling, disciplined line weight, and obsessive negative-space control. Under the old Factory Logic, this was a three-week engagement—the purest expression of the Product Timeline Tax (PTT).

But the New Alex just smiles. He cracks his knuckles, not out of bravado, but out of certainty.

He doesn't glance at Google. He's moved past the peasant labor of sifting through ten blue links and hoping the archive gods are kind. He has a direct line to the Oracle. He goes straight to the Exosuit. He goes straight to Chad.

The Prompt of a God

Alex spends an hour architecting the Wish. Not typing—architecting. He slows himself deliberately, assembling constraints the way an engineer assembles load-bearing walls. Every decision is designed to escape Semantic Gravity and avoid the Beige Factor:

The Role: "Act as a master botanical illustrator from the late 19th century, specializing in copperplate etching."

The Context: "This is for a prestigious chocolate brand. The illustration must feel academic, Victorian, and expensive."

The Few-Shot: He uploads five high-resolution scans of authenticated 1880s etchings. “Monkey see, monkey do,” he whispers, half joking, half aware of how literal the instruction really is.

The Constraint: “No digital smoothing. No symmetry. Ensure the lines retain the irregular resistance of a physical burin on metal. Do not use modern shading.”

He hits Enter.

The cursor pulses like a heartbeat. Four seconds later, the screen populates.

The result is breathtaking—a cathedral of Syntactic Fluency. The cacao pods are wrapped in delicate, confident linework. The leaves display plausible vascular structure. From a distance, it looks less generated than discovered, as if someone quietly removed it from a museum archive.

Alex feels a sharp dopamine spike, clean and almost disorienting. He doesn’t see a blurry JPEG; he sees a $5,000 invoice compressed into four seconds of compute.

He performs a quick zoom-in. He checks the Green-Highlighter items: compositional balance, visual rhythm, historical plausibility. Everything passes at a glance.

But he is moving fast. The Factory Logic of his past—the reflex to optimize throughput at the expense of inspection—still whispers in his ear. He wants “Done” to mean “Beautiful” so he can clear the board and move on.

He skips the Red Team audit. He doesn’t ask the system to interrogate its own output. He ignores the citation cage. He assumes that because the Form is impeccable, the Function must be intact.

He exports the file. He hits Send to the printer.

Alex has just paid the Audit Tax with his reputation.

The Arrival of the Uncanny

Friday morning. The delivery truck pulls up outside Alex’s apartment.

The Bitter Bean has sent a sample box from the first 100 printed wrappers, a pre-flight check before committing to the full 5,000-unit run. Alex is eager. He wants to hold the Proof of Life, to watch the gold foil catch the office light.

He tears open the box and pulls out a wrapper.

From a distance, the etching looks professional, even elegant. But as Alex brings it closer, the Exosuit begins to fail, piece by piece.

He studies the cacao pods hanging from the branches.

At first glance, they register as pods. But on the third pod from the left, the Drunk Intern has misfired, confusing vector-space proximity for biological attachment.

The pod isn't connected to a branch. It is being held by a tiny, hyper-realistic, five-fingered human hand sprouting directly from the bark.

Alex's stomach drops like a cold weight through water.

He scans the rest. One pod terminates in a miniature human ear. Another reveals a faint row of teeth where husk should be.

AI—operating under semantic blindness—had no concept of a cacao pod as a physical object. It only knew that "organic texture" statistically co-occurs with fragments of human anatomy in its blurred internal memory.

It had generated the Syntax of a botanical drawing while failing the Semantics of reality.

And because Alex had shifted from Pilot to Passenger, he hadn't seen the Ghost until it was embossed in gold foil.

THE HALLUCINATION OF AUTHORITY

Alex sits in his Cockpit, but the monitors no longer resemble the future. They resemble evidence. The same screens that once signaled leverage and speed now feel forensic, frozen snapshots of decisions made without sufficient resistance.

His phone rings. It's the client.

"Alex," the voice tight, controlled, and sharp. "I just saw the proofs. Why is there a hand holding the chocolate? Is this a body-horror brand now? We've already spent $10,000 on specialty gold-foil stock. The printer is on standby. Explain this."

Alex has no viable explanation. He can't say, *The Drunk Intern did it.* He can't say, *I trusted a system designed to sound confident, not to be right.* Any honest answer exposes the same fault line: authority was inferred, not earned.

The diagnosis lands immediately. The Halo Effect. Because the grammar of the image was perfect, he assumed the facts were true. He applied Calculator Trust to a Poet and expected verification to emerge automatically from polish.

This was sycophancy at scale. He wanted a win—wanted speed to validate itself—so badly that he never stopped to check whether the win corresponded to reality. Fluency became a substitute for inspection.

He walks to the bathroom and splashes cold water on his face. The mirror doesn't show Tony Stark in a Lab. It shows a man who confused orchestration with abdication, who mistook elegance for authority.

The Exosuit fantasy collapses. Without oversight, it provides no protection. No redundancy. No life support. It accelerates impact; it does not absorb it.

The correction is uncomfortable but precise. The Exosuit is not a shortcut to the finish line. It is a system for running the race with eyes open, hands on the controls, and responsibility fully intact.

Alex returns to the desk. He doesn't hit Delete. He doesn't retreat into denial or theatrics.

He opens a new chat window.

"Okay, Chad," he whispers. "The honeymoon is over. You're my hostile witness."

The Midnight Audit

Alex doesn't go to sleep. His wraparound desk is littered with gold-foil wrappers from The Bitter Bean, stacked and scattered like a deck of haunted tarot cards. Under the dim, blue glow of the Cockpit, the etched fingers of the Drunk Intern appear to point back at him with quiet precision, less mocking than accusatory. Each wrapper is a receipt. Each error is timestamped.

He understands now that these aren't cosmetic failures. They are signals. The fingers aren't a glitch in the image; they are evidence of a deeper infection in the workflow itself—his own overconfidence, quietly compounded by speed.

The pattern is obvious in hindsight. His previous workflow was a Naked Prompt: a high-velocity leap off a cliff without a parachute, justified by momentum alone. He had already survived the legal hallucination of The Neon Roast, yet here he was again, three months later, letting the Drunk Intern take the wheel because acceleration felt indistinguishable from control.

He had relied on the machine's Syntactic Fluency to camouflage his own lack of Semantic Oversight. Fluency became cover. Speed became permission. Without noticing, he had shifted roles—from operator to passenger—on a flight whose destination was a $10,000 mistake.

Fixing this doesn't require a cleverer prompt or a longer instruction. It requires a different posture entirely. Alex needs a new operating system for his own judgment. He needs to move from Chatting to Architecting—from reacting to outputs to designing constraints.

What emerges is not a trick, but a discipline: a protocol that treats every AI output as a Hostile Witness, something fluent, persuasive, and fundamentally untrustworthy until cross-examined. This is the Centaur Protocol. It is the manual for wearing the Exosuit without surrendering the controls—or letting the machine fly you into a mountain.

Step 1: The Red Team Audit

The first weapon in Alex's rebuilt arsenal is the Red Team Protocol. His original failure with the cacao pods wasn't technical; it was contractual. He had asked the machine to be agreeable. He asked it to "Make a Victorian Etching," and the system—optimized to satisfy—filled the gaps with confident improvisation wherever understanding was missing.

Alex opens a new chat window. He doesn't request a replacement drawing yet. Speed is no longer the objective. He needs an autopsy before a resurrection. He uploads the "finger-pod" image and assigns Chad a new role—one deliberately stripped of its Helpful Assistant reflex. No praise. No reassurance. No smoothing of edges.

The Persona Shift: He instructs the system to "*Act as a ruthless quality-control inspector from a top-tier printing house who actively distrusts AI-generated art.*"

The Hostility: He makes the incentive explicit. The machine's "career" now depends on identifying every anatomical error, every digital tell, every hallucinated shortcut embedded in the image.

The Specificity: He narrows the attack surface. "*Look for extra digits, physics-defying stems, inconsistent lighting, and impossible attachments. Be brutal. Politeness is grounds for termination.*"

Alex watches the cursor. It doesn't perform its usual Beige courtesy routine. It hesitates, recalibrates, then produces a cold inventory of defects. "*Anomaly detected: Pod 3 is supported by a vestigial human hand. Pod 7 exhibits shading inconsistent with the leaf light source. Cross-hatching in the upper-right quadrant is recursively uniform—a statistical artifact indicative of transformer-based generation.*"

The effect is immediate. By forcing the machine to adopt the Critic's Hat, Alex collapses the Sycophancy Trap. He learns something precise and reusable: the system is remarkably capable of detecting its own failures—but only when the reward function is inverted. When approval is removed, accuracy surfaces.

This is the first structural rule of the Centaur Protocol. AI should never be trusted as an advocate. It must be conscripted as an adversary. Used correctly, it becomes its own B.S. Detector.

Step 3: The Wabi-Sabi Workflow

The final lesson of the Bitter Bean crisis is deceptively simple: "Perfect" has become a commodity. The machine delivers flawless, hyper-detailed etchings on demand. Precision is cheap now. But what the client actually wanted was not a computer file—it was the residue of a human process. They were buying the soul of a nineteenth-century monk, not the output of a renderer. In that context, Perfect no longer signals quality. It signals automation. It reads as Artificial. It collapses into Beige.

Alex responds by doing something deliberately inefficient. He injects *wabi-sabi*—the disciplined use of imperfection as proof of humanity.

Human-in-the-Loop: He pulls the corrected, anatomically verified etching into his old Illustrator setup, the same environment he used before the Exosuit entered the room. This is not nostalgia; it is intent.

Proof of Work: He manually breaks the lines the machine made too clean. He introduces a faint ink smudge at the corner of a leaf. He adjusts the cross-hatching until it carries the subtle, rhythmic wobble of a human wrist—something no probability distribution quite captures. The imperfections are not flaws. They are signatures.

The Narrative Spike: When he re-presents to Marcus and the chocolatiers, he doesn't rely on the file alone. He brings his physical sketchbook. He lays out the rough charcoal drafts, the Day-1 sketches, the abandoned branches that led to the final spiky form. The artifact is contextualized inside a story of decisions, revisions, and restraint.

He is no longer selling pixels. He is selling High-Resolution Human Context.

THE REDEMPTION OF THE ARCHITECT

Alex walks back into The Bitter Bean on Monday morning carrying almost nothing. No slide deck populated with a Fake Judge. No costume signaling "creative genius." He brings a single object that matters: a hand-signed print of the corrected cacao plant, heavy with paper stock and intention.

"I found a hallucination in the initial draft," Alex says, without defensiveness. "The machine offered a shortcut. I didn't take it. I spent the weekend auditing every pixel against primary botanical journals. This isn't just a drawing—it's a verified visual record."

The room doesn't tense. No one reaches for legal language. The client studies the work instead. They notice the ink smudge. They trace the anatomically sound stems. What they see is not an error narrowly avoided, but a partner who prevented a $10,000 misallocation by assuming responsibility before it was demanded. They see accountability embedded in the process, not performed after the fact.

Alex steps back into the sunlight. The city air smells like exhaust and possibility, unchanged but newly legible. He pulls out his phone and opens the chat with Chad.

Alex: "The Red Team found the fingers. We corrected the files. The 5,000-unit run is back on track."

Chad: "Acknowledged. Verification successful. What is our next objective?"

Alex smiles—not because the system worked, but because the roles are finally clear. He powers up the Exosuit and places his hand on the navigation stick. This time, it's obvious who is flying.

He is no longer stuck in the Fast Food Trap. The Saturday Morning Feeling is back—the quiet confidence that comes when execution is delegated, judgment is retained, and the human role is finally what it should have been all along: deciding what matters, and why.

PART IV

RELEASE

8

THE GHOST OF THE 40-HOUR WEEK

The Lie: If I am not visibly working for a fixed number of hours, I am not contributing real value.

The Truth: Time is no longer the unit of work. In a parallel, AI-augmented economy, time becomes the reward reclaimed by those who move from execution to judgment. Presence is a legacy proxy for value—and a failing one.

To understand why this belief persists, Alex has to stop being an exception.

He doesn't rewind time.

He doesn't imagine a different life.

He simply shifts position.

He becomes the version of himself still embedded inside the system—the one most people recognize because they are still living it.

This is **Corporate Alex.**

Not a different man, but the same one, operating under a different set of constraints.

Same judgment. Same intelligence. Same capacity.

Different incentives. Different visibility. Different permissions.

THE CUBICLE CAGE

The Fluorescent Purgatory

The light in Corporate Alex's office doesn't come from the sun. It comes from flickering overhead panels that hum at a constant 60-cycle frequency—a sound he has learned to ignore in the same way one ignores tinnitus. Over time, he has come to recognize it for what it is: the ambient heartbeat of a system long past its peak efficiency.

He is not the free-roaming "9:15 AM Criminal" improvising leverage in a rainy coffee shop. He is Corporate Alex—the same person, operating inside a different set of constraints.

He holds the title Senior Visual Communications Manager at a global firm. He has a 401(k). He carries a security badge that must be tapped four times a day. His calendar fills itself, meetings stacking without negotiation. The work is steady. The benefits are rational. And beneath it all is the quiet sensation that something essential is being abraded away, grain by grain, by industrial-grade carpet and procedural air.

On his company-issued workstation—adjacent to the Outlook icon that continuously bleeds "Urgent" emails—sits the official, enterprise-enabled AI. It wears the firm's branding: a sleek blue "C," internally nicknamed Corporate Chad.

Corporate Chad is labeled *Enterprise Grade*—a phrase that sounds like capability but functions as containment. Every keystroke Alex enters is logged. Every output is archived. Every response is automatically stamped with a corporate watermark before it ever reaches a client. This system is not designed for exploration or judgment. It is designed for traceability.

The company did not deploy this tool to expand Alex's authority. They deployed it to resolve the Jevons Paradox in their favor—to ensure that every gain in efficiency is immediately converted into higher volume. The mandate is implicit but exact: produce more, faster, with fewer questions. Alex is not being elevated into a Driver. He is being refined into a more efficient Horse, expected to pull a heavier carriage for the same measured reward.

THE FACTORY STRIKES BACK

The conflict surfaced publicly last Monday. The CEO—who spends his weekends on a yacht and his weekdays inside spreadsheets labeled "Efficiency Metrics"—distributed an all-hands memo. The Return to Office was no longer framed as culture or collaboration. It was operational. Mandatory. Five days a week, fixed hours, fixed seats. Presence restored as policy.

Susan, Alex's manager, is the high priestess of this doctrine. She is a disciplined believer in Factory Logic. To Susan, work is not measured by outcome; it is validated by occupancy. She does not manage results. She manages presence. She patrols the floor with the posture of a nineteenth-century mill foreman, scanning seats, correlating bodies with productivity.

"Since AI is doing the heavy lifting now," Susan explains, her voice calibrated to corporate optimism, "we've updated the KPIs. We're shifting from quality over quantity to sustained high-volume throughput. We need you in your seat to oversee the system."

The misalignment becomes obvious in that moment. Alex recognizes the Turing Trap—not as a philosophical mistake, but as an incentive error. By demonstrating how fast he could work with the Exosuit, he hadn't purchased autonomy. He had simply revealed additional capacity for extraction.

The efficiency dividend did not return to him as time. It was immediately reclaimed as obligation. Alex now finds himself complying with a Return to Office mandate that requires forty-plus hours of physical presence to "supervise" a machine that completes its actual work in four seconds.

MANAGING SUSAN

Alex's first tactical breakthrough is uncomfortable but precise: he must stop being *transparent* with the factory. Transparency is punished in systems optimized for throughput. When he delivered a project in ten minutes, Susan didn't grant him a Friday afternoon. She allocated three additional tasks. Speed was interpreted not as mastery, but as unused capacity.

To survive the 9-9-6 mandate, Alex adopts what he privately calls the controlled drip—a calibrated release of output designed to match managerial expectation rather than actual completion time. This is not deception for gain; it is pacing for preservation.

Using Corporate Chad, Alex completes his "Susan-Tasks"—the Beige, low-stakes corporate deliverables—by 10:30 AM every Monday. Then he stops. The files sit unsent, perfectly finished and intentionally invisible.

In their place, he constructs a Perception Map:

The Work-in-Progress: On Tuesday at 2:00 PM, he sends Susan a carefully worded update: *"I'm deep in the prompt architecture for the Western Region deck. The AI outputs are trending Beige, so I'm manually recalibrating the Context Schema to align with strategic objectives."* Susan approves immediately. The language signals effort, friction, and control. It sounds Hard.

The Sacrifice Revision: On Wednesday, Alex releases a draft containing a planned imperfection—a mild color clash, a typo, a spacing issue deliberately left unresolved by Corporate Chad. Susan predictably finds it, corrects it, and experiences the satisfaction of intervention. This is the Management Tax: a small, intentional inefficiency paid to maintain autonomy elsewhere.

The Friday Finale: The final, polished version is scheduled to arrive in her inbox at 5:30 PM on Friday, late enough to feel earned, early enough to feel responsible.

By managing the send rather than the work, Alex quietly reclaims thirty hours of his forty-hour week. He remains physically present in the cubicle, badge tapped, chair occupied. But cognitively, he has relocated to the Lab. He operates inside the system without feeding it. He has become a Ghost in the Machine.

The Human Moat: Constructing Significance

While Susan believes Alex is "supervising AI," he is quietly repurposing the company's fiber-optic spine to construct his Human Moat—the class of high-resolution capabilities Corporate Chad is explicitly designed not to develop. This is not misuse of resources; it is asymmetry exploitation.

Alex understands the limits of the firm's Safe AI with clinical clarity. Corporate Chad is optimized for the Vector Space Average. It produces press releases that resemble every other press release, logos that resemble every other logo, strategies that offend no one and inspire no one. It is not broken. It is doing exactly what it was tuned to do. It is the undisputed king of Beige.

So Alex allocates his Hidden Hours to High-Resolution Context Research—work that cannot be averaged, generalized, or safely automated.

The Moat of Empathy: He spends hours each day with the raw, uncompressed data of human frustration. He ignores AI summaries and reads the original customer-support transcripts from the Western Region line by line. He listens for tone shifts, recurring irritations, and what customers refuse to say directly. This is semantic signal—meaning embedded in emotion—that never survives abstraction.

The Moat of History: He dives into internal archives and traces the brand's lineage back to 1955. He finds the founder's early sketches, abandoned slogans, and forgotten constraints. Over time, he becomes the only person in the building who understands the company's continuity—the difference between its temporary scale and its enduring soul.

The Moat of Relationship: He leaves his desk. He talks to veteran employees in Logistics, Shipping, and Operations. He learns how chocolate is actually moved, delayed, substituted, and fixed when reality diverges from the spreadsheet. Piece by piece, Alex assembles a Legacy Dependency Map of the physical world—one built from lived constraints, not dashboard abstractions.

When Alex finally presents a project, he doesn't merely deliver output. He delivers Authority. He frames the work inside a judgment call that only a human can make. "*Corporate Chad recommended a blue logo for the Western Region because it's statistically safe,*" he explains. "*But an audit of 1970s brand heritage and current customer sentiment shows that 'safe' now reads as invisible. The region doesn't need reassurance. It needs a spiky point of view.*"

The room responds differently. This is no longer a file review. It's a directional decision. Alex isn't competing with the machine's speed; he's overruling it with context.

THE CORPORATE RESIDENCY

Alex is clear-eyed about his position, but not contemptuous of it. He understands that some people build entire, meaningful lives inside institutions—and do so well. The issue is not the corporation itself. It is whether the role demands judgment or merely occupancy.

For Alex, the Return to Office mandate is neither a trap nor an exit plan. It is a residency.

Each month, Susan authorizes a paycheck in exchange for Alex's presence, reliability, and execution. The firm receives exactly what it pays for: competent work, delivered on time, within scope, and aligned with expectations. Alex honors that contract. What no system tracks—because no dashboard can—is what accumulates alongside the work.

Nothing is extracted. Nothing is hidden. Everything is learned.

The Architecture Archive

Every time Alex uses the firm's enterprise AI to solve a legitimate internal problem, he gains more than a finished artifact. He gains exposure to how large systems actually behave. He observes where automation clarifies decisions—and where it quietly obscures responsibility. He notices which constraints improve outcomes and which simply make work legible to management.

These observations do not belong to the company in the way files or prompts do. They belong to Alex in the way experience always belongs to the person who lived it. Over time, this becomes judgment: an understanding of how scale changes incentives, how metrics drift, and how good intentions decay into process.

This is not subversion. It is professional maturation.

The Network Lens

During slower hours, Alex listens carefully. He pays attention to how clients speak when they are being polite rather than candid. He notices where enthusiasm softens into tolerance, where trust plateaus without breaking. He does not solicit. He does not maneuver. He simply learns how dissatisfaction hides inside functional relationships.

This awareness benefits the firm today. It benefits Alex as a professional, wherever his path eventually leads. No lines are crossed. No loyalties are violated.

Alex is not using the company.

He is being shaped by it.

The office is not something to escape by default. For many, it is a place to grow, to specialize, to contribute meaningfully over decades. For Alex, it is a place to deepen his understanding of systems—how they reward, how they fail, and where human judgment still matters.

The residency does not dictate his future.

It prepares him for it.

THE SATURDAY MORNING FEELING

How does Alex prevent his inner life from being slowly abraded by fluorescent light and calendar gravity? He adopts a principle he privately calls Digital Dualism.

The insight is simple and stabilizing: the company contracts for his time, but it does not—and cannot—own his attention. Time is what the badge records. Attention is what compounds. Alex stops confusing the two.

He reframes the Return to Office mandate as a strictly physical agreement. He is present. He is reliable. He delivers what is asked for, at the quality level required. The transaction is honored on both sides. What changes is not his performance, but where his sense of authorship resides.

To preserve equilibrium, Alex separates concerns rather than resisting them.

Screen One — The Factory

Enterprise systems handle the work that must be legible at scale: compliance-safe decks, localized variants, infinite revisions whose primary purpose is coordination rather than insight. This work matters to the organization, and Alex ensures it is done well.

Screen Two — The Lab

Alongside it, Alex maintains a quieter space—one not visible on dashboards. Here, he refines a point of view. He pressure-tests language. He documents judgment calls. He notices where the machine hesitates and where it overreaches. Nothing here violates policy. Nothing is rushed. This is professional development in its oldest form: thinking.

The Internal Dialogue

When Susan assigns work, Alex doesn't resist or resent it. Resistance consumes energy without producing leverage. He simply notes the exchange and executes cleanly. The work does not define him, but neither does he diminish it. It is part of the craft of operating inside systems without being flattened by them.

At the end of the day, when Alex leaves the building—badge tapped, laptop closed—he doesn't feel emptied. He feels intact. The Saturday Morning Feeling is not something he waits for on weekends anymore. It is the quiet satisfaction of knowing that even inside structure, his attention remains his own.

Not because he took something that wasn't his.

But because he learned where value actually lives.

BREAKING THE LINEAR SEAL

Alex sits in the clean, even glow of his workstation, watching the cursor pulse on the center monitor. On the left screen, a high-resolution render exports methodically, its progress bar advancing without supervision. On the right, a dense technical brief for a FinTech client is being summarized into concise, judgment-heavy points. Two streams of work are moving forward at once, neither competing for his hands.

In the old logic of industrial work, this configuration would have been impossible. Tasks moved in a straight line. One step had to complete before the next could begin. Research preceded design. Design preceded copy. Copy waited for review. Progress was serialized, not because it produced better outcomes, but because it was easier to manage. Sequence made effort visible.

That assumption formed what Alex now understands as the

Linear Seal—the structural belief that meaningful work must pass through a single human bottleneck. Whether freelance or salaried, value accumulated inside the wait. Time was consumed not by difficulty, but by ordering. Calendars filled. Momentum stalled. The Product Timeline Tax was paid quietly, hour by hour.

The Context Economy operates under a different constraint.

It does not eliminate sequence where it matters, but it removes it where it does not. The Exosuit absorbs execution—the syntactic labor that once required continuous human presence—and in exchange returns something far more scarce: optionality. The distance between intent and outcome shortens. Multiple phases advance without forcing Alex to fragment his attention.

This is not multitasking—the familiar human failure mode of attempting to behave like a processor. It is orchestration. Alex establishes direction, defines boundaries, and sets checkpoints. He intervenes selectively, where judgment changes the outcome. The machine executes within those constraints, reliably and without fatigue.

Alex is not doing more work at once.

He is deciding differently about where work requires him at all.

The Linear Seal does not shatter with drama. It dissolves quietly, replaced by a system where progress is gated not by completion but by clarity. And clarity, unlike time, compounds.

THE GHOST OF THE LUDDITE

To understand why Corporate Alex feels tension around the Return to Office mandate, it helps to widen the lens beyond his cubicle and revisit a recurring pattern in the history of work. Progress has never been a smooth upgrade path. It moves through substitution. Certain forms of contribution lose their pricing power, not because they are wrong, but because the environment no longer rewards them.

When mechanized looms entered textile production, skilled weavers did not gradually become faster versions of themselves. The system no longer valued the same unit of effort. Cloth became cheaper, more consistent, and more abundant. The work did not disappear—but the locus of value shifted. Those who remained relevant did so by moving upstream: maintaining machines, coordinating production, setting standards, or owning outcomes rather than strokes.

This pattern repeats without drama.

The current transition mirrors earlier industrial shifts in structure, not in sentiment. Organizations adopt new tools to compress time, reduce variance, and increase throughput. Roles anchored to visible effort—hours logged, interfaces mastered, steps completed—become harder to defend, not because they lack dignity, but because they no longer explain results.

This does not mean all roles vanish. It means some definitions stop clearing the market.

If a job description resolves primarily into a list of tasks—pure execution—its exposure is already set. Any delay is procedural, not technical. The organization may take time to adjust titles, incentives, or reporting lines, but the underlying economics have moved on.

Corporate Alex recognizes this without panic. The firm is using AI to amplify efficiency—to move more material through the system. What it does not automatically generate is effectiveness: direction, prioritization, judgment under uncertainty.

Execution can be scaled.

Judgment must be situated.

The organization will continue to automate throughput. What it cannot automate is responsibility for consequence—deciding what matters, what is excluded, and what must be protected when the system moves faster than understanding.

That is the distinction Alex begins to internalize. Not between human and machine—but between roles that execute and roles that decide.

LIVING INSIDE THE FLOOD

Alex no longer needs the theory. He experiences the outcome every day.

Acceleration was supposed to return time. What it returned instead was density. Each reduction in effort widened the aperture of expectation. Output became easier, and because it was easier, it was asked for more often. The gain did not clear space. It occupied it.

The workday didn't shorten. It thickened.

Tasks accumulated rather than resolved. Each completed deliverable spawned follow-ups—lighter individually, heavier in aggregate. The calendar filled not with difficulty but with residue. The cost of producing work collapsed, and with it disappeared the natural pressure that once forced choices to be made.

The system now behaves as if abundance were the default condition. Reports grow longer because length is free. Messages multiply because sending carries no weight. Documents exist because existence requires no effort. Friction has been engineered out, and with it went the quiet discipline that once filtered what deserved to move forward.

Work no longer arrives with a sense of completion. Output doesn't close loops; it opens them. When production becomes effortless, responsiveness takes its place as the signal of value. Over time, that signal hardens into expectation.

Corporate Alex feels this rhythm constantly. Susan asks for a report, and he delivers twenty pages because generating them takes seconds. Susan doesn't read twenty pages. She skims, forwards, and asks for a summary. The surplus creates no clarity. It produces fatigue —a pile of material without combustion.

Meetings follow the same pattern. Slides proliferate because slides are cheap. Agendas expand because expansion carries no immediate penalty. Preparation compresses into presentation, presentation bleeds into evenings, and nothing feels substantial enough to refuse. Everything feels light enough to add.

Increasing volume with the Exosuit doesn't escape this logic. It accelerates it. Each additional unit of frictionless output feeds the same flood that renders all of it interchangeable. "More" vanishes on contact. Speed inside the system amplifies drag rather than leverage.

This is how the paradox is lived. Efficiency does not return time. It redistributes it—upward through expectations, outward through coordination, and inward as a constant state of partial attention. Alex remains busy, but completion recedes. Productive, yet unfinished.

Eventually the inversion becomes clear.

When production is cheap, execution loses its premium. Effort stops being scarce. What grows rare is restraint—the capacity to decide what should not exist, what should not be sent, what should not be expanded simply because it can be.

Alex begins to see the exit condition. Leverage does not come from moving faster inside the flood. It comes from shaping the field itself. Authority settles with those who select, reduce, and refuse—who impose boundaries where the system cannot—rather than with those who exhaust themselves trying to keep pace.

THE BARBELL ECONOMY

Alex understands the structure of the market. What occupies him now is the problem of placement.

The collapse of the middle is not theoretical. It shows up in how his days fill. Even with clarity about where value is moving, most of his hours are still consumed by work that arrives already formed—emails that need replies, decks that need polishing, requests that require extension rather than decision. Each task is minor. None feels dangerous. Together, they absorb everything.

This is how the middle survives. Not through importance, but through accumulation.

The barbell is not a chart. It is an allocation problem that resets every morning. Attention placed on correction, formatting, or expansion quietly loads weight onto the left side. Attention placed on selection—deciding what should exist, what should change, or what should be removed—shifts weight to the right.

The asymmetry matters. Left-side work expands effortlessly. It comes with instructions. It rewards responsiveness. Right-side work resists capture. It requires context, synthesis, and ownership of consequences that unfold slowly and cannot be neatly summarized.

This is why movement feels uncomfortable even after recognition. Reallocation initially looks like absence. Fewer visible artifacts. Longer stretches without deliverables. More thinking that does not register as productivity inside a status dashboard.

Corporate Alex feels the difference immediately. A day spent correcting AI-generated decks for the Western Region leaves him legible, responsive, and easy to substitute. The calendar fills. The ledger does not.

A day spent tracing second-order effects—how a branding decision will reshape customer behavior over years, how a messaging shift will alter internal incentives—produces little to send. The work is harder to point at. But the value compounds. The shift happens not through exertion, but through placement.

This is the real constraint. Human attention is finite. The machine's capacity is not. Without deliberate reallocation, the system assigns attention automatically—and it assigns it to the cheapest layer first.

The barbell does not reward effort. It rewards where effort lands. The Human Moat forms at the point where judgment still carries consequence—where doing less, in the right place, outweighs doing more everywhere else.

THE ARCHIMEDEAN LEVER

For most of the last century, education systems and corporate incentive structures converged on a shared equation: compensation scales with effort. Labor was treated as the primary input. Time spent became the visible proof of contribution.

This logic was stable as long as production itself was linear.

An hour of work reliably produced an hour of outcome. Skill increased quality. Experience reduced error. But the relationship between effort and output remained legible. More hours meant more progress. Less time meant less result. Within that frame, discipline and endurance were rational strategies.

The failure of that equation is not moral or cultural. It is mechanical.

Human labor is bounded. Each person has twenty-four hours in a day, most of which are already committed to maintenance: sleep, food, recovery, and the cognitive decompression required after sustained exposure to fragmented attention. There is no reserve capacity waiting to be unlocked. There is no hidden surplus that better tools can access.

This constraint is absolute. No system redesign changes it.

Acceleration does not expand the container. It increases pressure inside it.

This is why the introduction of faster tools often feels punishing rather than liberating. Output rises. Expectations adjust upward. The workday thickens. Tasks accumulate. The calendar fills not with difficulty, but with density. The shape of the day changes before the worker has time to notice.

Effort remains constant. Obligation multiplies.

The multiplier does not emerge from exertion. It emerges from leverage.

Labor follows a one-to-one curve. You apply effort, and you receive proportional output. The slope does not change. Motivation can steepen the experience, but it cannot bend the relationship. Intensity increases fatigue, not capacity.

Leverage operates on a different geometry.

With the correct pivot, a small amount of human judgment can redirect a large amount of mechanical effort. Output scales without demanding additional hours from the person supplying direction. The work expands, but the cost is externalized to systems that do not fatigue.

This is where Alex's role begins to shift.

He is no longer valued primarily for the energy he supplies. He is valued for where he places it. He determines which problems deserve amplification, which signals require damping, and which lines of inquiry should be abandoned before they harden into obligations.

The machine supplies velocity. It executes relentlessly. It does not hesitate, tire, or renegotiate scope. Alex supplies orientation.

This distinction changes the texture of his days.

Tasks stop stacking reflexively. Output no longer cascades automatically into follow-on work. Instead of constant completion, there are longer intervals of unresolved thinking. The calendar thins. The work grows quieter. The consequences extend further.

This is not a productivity gain in the traditional sense. It is a structural realignment.

Alex is no longer responsible for carrying each unit of work across the finish line. He is responsible for shaping the field in which work occurs—deciding where effort compounds, where it dissipates, and where it should never be applied at all.

This is the operational meaning of parallelism.

The machine advances multiple lines of execution simultaneously. Alex advances none of them directly. He intervenes only at points where judgment is required—where tradeoffs exist, where second-order effects matter, where selection carries consequence.

Leverage does not demand more hours. It protects them.

And once attention is no longer consumed by completion, it becomes available for the function that cannot be automated, accelerated, or delegated: deciding what matters, and standing behind that decision.

THE PHYSICS OF THE "SPIKY" POINT OF VIEW

Alex's final constraint is not technical. It does not announce itself. It operates quietly and continuously, shaping outcomes long before intention has time to intervene.

It is semantic gravity.

He does not encounter it once and overcome it. He experiences it as a persistent force—present in every iteration, every revision, every decision that passes through systems trained on human feedback.

Consensus-trained systems are optimized for accommodation. Safety, agreement, and legibility are rewarded. Outputs that feel familiar are reinforced. Outputs that require effort to interpret are softened or reframed. Over time, this incentive structure pulls language, imagery, and positioning toward a stable center.

The result is not error. It is equilibrium.

A consensus engine left unattended converges by design.

This is how edges decay.

Not because they are incorrect, but because they are expensive to maintain. Distinct positions require judgment. Judgment requires accountability. Accountability introduces risk. As soon as a position gains traction, pressure emerges to make it easier to consume—more inclusive, more flexible, more scalable.

Scale applies force. Semantic gravity completes the motion.

Inside that gravity well, growth amplifies what is already acceptable. The volume increases. The character flattens. Loudness replaces distinction. The work becomes easier to recognize and harder to remember.

This is the environment Alex is operating in.

The role of a spiky point of view is not novelty. It is structural resistance.

A spiky position cannot be averaged without losing coherence. It does not generalize cleanly. It remains anchored to context, judgment, and consequence. Attempts to soften it remove the very signal that made it matter in the first place.

In this sense, a spiky point of view supplies escape velocity.

Not from disagreement, but from convergence.

Maintaining that velocity is not a one-time act. It is a repeated decision. Each iteration invites smoothing. Each success introduces pressure to broaden appeal. Each moment of visibility increases the incentive to trade precision for reach.

Holding the spike requires refusing those trades.

When Alex produces work that unsettles one segment of the

audience while making another feel precisely understood, he is operating outside the machine's equilibrium behavior. He is not extending the statistical past. He is selecting a future state.

That selection carries responsibility.

Responsibility cannot be optimized. It cannot be distributed. It cannot be averaged across feedback loops. It attaches to the person who makes the call and remains there as consequences unfold.

This is why authority compounds.

Not because it becomes louder, but because it remains distinct under sustained pressure. Over time, that distinction becomes difficult to substitute, difficult to imitate, and increasingly resistant to erosion. What survives repeated attempts at smoothing begins to signal judgment rather than preference.

The multiplier does not emerge from completing one hundred tasks. It emerges when the machine absorbs the hundred tasks that do not require judgment, leaving Alex with the capacity to take one position that does—and to hold it as the pull toward neutrality intensifies.

Alex looks at his monitors differently now.

He no longer sees work waiting to be cleared. He sees capacity waiting to be directed. The linear bargain has already dissolved. What remains is choice—not once, but continuously.

THE ZERO-SUM GATE

Over time, the barbell stops feeling theoretical. It hardens into a boundary Alex encounters repeatedly, often without noticing it at first. Eventually, the pattern becomes unmistakable. He comes to think of it as a zero-sum gate.

In the prior era, access to work functioned as a wide filter of competence. If you could operate the tools, follow the process, and remain reliable, the gate stayed open. Participation itself carried value. Showing up mattered. Staying busy mattered. Progress was incremental, and effort accumulated into standing.

That structure shaped expectations for decades. It trained people to believe that consistency would eventually be rewarded, that experience would compound naturally, and that competence alone was enough to justify continued presence.

That condition no longer holds.

In an environment where machines can execute baseline work instantly and cheaply, the gate changes shape. It narrows. It stops responding to effort. Tasks no longer sort themselves along a gradient of skill. They sort by substitutability.

Either the work is cheap enough to automate, or it carries enough consequence to require a human being to stand behind it. The middle ground—where competence alone once lived—does not fail gradually. It empties.

This is why the gate is zero-sum. Average work no longer clears it. Not because it is bad, but because it is abundant. When execution is plentiful, it loses the ability to differentiate. What remains scarce is responsibility.

There is no longer a premium for presence. There is only a premium for accountability.

Alex feels this shift in small, ordinary moments. It shows up in the phrasing of requests, in the way work is evaluated, in the silence that follows delivery. Each interaction with the system quietly forces a choice, whether he acknowledges it or not.

When he asks for something clean, professional, or on-brand, the result is legible and correct—and immediately comparable. The work clears the system, but it stays on the commodity side of the gate, where speed and volume dominate and substitution is easy.

Crossing the boundary requires something heavier.

It requires pressing the output until it collides with reality—with local context, physical constraint, human memory, and downstream consequence. It requires moving beyond fluency and into commitment. The work must carry a position that cannot be safely generalized or detached from its effects.

This is not about better prompts. It is about standing behind outcomes.

Passing the gate means accepting that once the work exists,

someone will live with it. Someone will rely on it. Someone will absorb its failures. The machine cannot carry that weight. It can generate options, but it cannot own the result.

That responsibility is what clears the gate.

Alex does not cross it all at once. He crosses it incrementally, decision by decision, learning where automation ends and judgment begins. The shift is not dramatic. It is cumulative. Over time, the pattern becomes clear: value no longer accrues to those who execute reliably, but to those who assume consequence deliberately.

The gate does not close because people fall short. It closes because the terrain has changed. And once Alex sees it clearly, he understands that remaining on the safe side is no longer neutral. It is a choice—one that leaves him competing where machines are strongest.

LIVING INSIDE THE SCALING SHIFT

Alex's apartment has changed in ways that would be difficult to point to directly. Nothing dramatic has been added. Nothing obvious has been removed. And yet, the space no longer feels like the improvised staging area of someone reacting to deadlines.

It feels quieter.

Not empty. Not idle. Just less charged. Less arranged around urgency.

The air is regulated because headaches are a cost. The lighting shifts across the day because attention degrades before effort does. These are not productivity hacks. They are guardrails. The goal is not output. It is preservation.

The monitors reflect the same logic. They no longer display queues of tasks waiting to be cleared. They show flows—processes advancing without constant intervention, systems that continue moving even when Alex steps away. Nothing is screaming for attention. Nothing needs to be rescued.

This environment is not an aesthetic choice. It is the physical expression of a realization that took time to settle.

The multiplier does not come from intensity. It comes from structure.

Under the factory model Alex grew up inside, income scaled linearly with effort. More money required more hours. The obvious cost of that model was exhaustion. The less obvious cost was delay—waiting for approvals, waiting for feedback, waiting for context to arrive from someone else's calendar.

That delay was normalized. It was treated as the price of participation.

That equation has collapsed.

Alex is no longer operating as a linear worker, even when he occupies linear systems. He is operating as someone who decides where effort lands and where it never should. Execution still happens, but it no longer defines his day. It has been pushed outward, absorbed by systems designed to carry it.

What changed is not his workload. It is the question he uses to orient himself.

He no longer asks how to do the work. That question belongs to execution, and execution is now abundant.

He asks something quieter and more consequential: how to ensure the outcome carries his judgment even when he is not present.

That question shapes everything that follows. It determines what he delegates, what he reviews, and what he refuses to let exist at all. It moves his attention upstream, away from completion and toward consequence.

Living inside the scaling shift does not feel like acceleration. It feels like relief. Fewer decisions arrive late. Fewer mistakes compound silently. The work does not multiply. It settles.

Alex has not escaped effort. He has escaped fragility.

The systems around him no longer require constant reinforcement to hold their shape. They carry intent forward without eroding it. That is the difference between working harder inside a collapsing model and repositioning inside one that scales without demanding more of the person at its center.

The shift is subtle. It does not announce itself. But once it is in place, it is difficult to imagine returning to a day defined by reaction rather than direction.

Wisdom Arbitrage

For people still living inside the long workweek, the first shift does not announce itself as insight. It arrives as a quiet imbalance. Velocity becomes common. Direction does not.

Alex notices this before he has language for it. It shows up in meetings. In reviews. In the way work is discussed after it has already been delivered.

Speed is everywhere. Output arrives early. Variations are plentiful. Options are no longer scarce. What feels scarce is agreement about which option should exist at all.

When peers ask why his days look different now, Alex doesn't frame it as an advantage. He frames it as a mismatch.

"The juniors have speed," he says. "They can generate a thousand variations in an hour. That part isn't hard anymore. What's hard is deciding which one actually belongs in the world — and which nine hundred and ninety-nine will quietly fail for reasons no one will write down."

This gap is not about intelligence. It is not about effort. It is not even about talent in the way organizations typically define it.

It is about accumulation.

Over time, people absorb patterns that never appear in documentation. How customers react emotionally to small changes. How internal incentives distort clean plans. How second-order effects undo ideas that look correct in isolation. These lessons are rarely taught directly. They are learned through exposure, consequence, and repair.

That accumulation compresses failure.

It allows someone to recognize a problem before it declares itself, to stop work that is technically sound but contextually wrong, to intervene once instead of iterating endlessly. Nothing about that shows up as speed. It registers as fewer moves.

This is the arbitrage.

Alex sometimes reaches for an old analogy, not because it is clever, but because it is familiar. The mechanic listens to an engine for ten seconds, taps a single valve, and hands over a bill that looks unreasonable until you understand what it includes. The charge is not for the tap. It is for the years it took to know where intervention mattered and where it didn't.

The same pattern is unfolding now, just under different labels.

The machine supplies motion. It supplies coverage. It supplies options at a scale no human can match. What it does not supply is restraint. It does not know when to stop. It does not know which intervention carries downstream consequence and which merely feels productive.

Wisdom occupies that gap.

Not as a virtue. As a function.

It is the ability to recognize when one decision will do more than a hundred executions, and to take responsibility for making it. That responsibility does not feel efficient. It feels heavy. But it is precisely that weight that keeps the system from dissolving into noise.

Alex does not see this as an advantage over others. He sees it as a reallocation that the system has not yet learned how to price. Velocity has been flattened. Judgment has not. The difference between them is where leverage now accumulates — quietly, unevenly, and without ceremony.

When the Ladder Starts Burning

There is a quieter edge to what Alex is learning, and it does not arrive with celebration.

Corporate Alex notices it first in small moments. An expert corrects an automated output. A domain specialist tweaks a recommendation. A senior reviewer adjusts a parameter, adds a caveat, reframes a conclusion. Each intervention feels routine. Helpful. Necessary.

But over time, a pattern emerges.

Every correction is logged.

Every verification is stored.

Every judgment is translated into structure.

The system improves, not because it understands more, but because it has been shown what to do next time.

What looks like assistance is also absorption.

The bottom rungs disappear first. Repetitive work thins out. Calculations are "unburdened." Checks become optional. What used to justify a junior role now happens automatically, without announcement. The ladder doesn't collapse. It shortens.

Alex watches this play out across fields that once assumed complexity was protection.

Actuaries, long insulated by dense mathematics and regulatory inertia, see their calculations automated almost overnight. Not because the machine understands risk, but because the work resolved cleanly into patterns that could be learned statistically. What mattered was not the meaning of the models, but their repeatability.

Those who remain are not the fastest calculators. They are not the ones who memorized the most formulas. They are the ones who moved sideways.

They stop asking, "What does the model say?" and begin asking, "What happens if the assumptions underneath this model no longer apply?"

They stop optimizing numbers and start interrogating context.

They spend less time refining outputs and more time looking for the places where the data looks smooth but reality is jagged.

This shift does not feel like progress.

It feels like exposure.

The ladder that once promised safety through advancement now radiates heat. Each rung climbed feels less stable than the last. Mastery no longer guarantees insulation. In some cases, it accelerates extraction — because the clearer someone's judgment becomes, the easier it is to encode.

Alex understands this without panic, but not without gravity. Expertise no longer protects by accumulation alone. It protects by relocation. The question is no longer how high you can climb, but whether the structure you're climbing still exists.

Those who stay centered on execution feel the temperature rise first. Those who move toward interpretation, framing, and responsibility feel something else: uncertainty paired with relevance.

The ladder is still there.

But it is no longer fireproof.

THE EMERGENCE OF THE MONOPOLY

Alex steps out of his apartment and into the morning. His phone vibrates with a familiar request from Susan at the corporate job: a status update. He doesn't pause. A reply—written earlier, intentionally—goes out without interrupting his stride. It signals motion without yielding attention.

A moment later, another message arrives. This one carries a different weight. A luxury brand is reaching out—not for execution, not for capacity—but for judgment. They are not asking how fast something can be produced. They are asking whether Alex can see what will happen *after* it exists.

The difference is subtle, but decisive.

Alex is no longer being evaluated by minutes logged or visible effort expended. He is being selected for consequence. For the ability to choose in ways that bind future outcomes—culturally, economically, reputationally. This is not more work. It is different work.

The shift does not announce itself as escape. There is no rupture, no rebellion. Alex still occupies the same world, still interfaces with the same systems. What has changed is where value accumulates. He has moved out of the layer where interchangeability is priced and into the layer where substitution fails.

This is what monopoly actually means in practice. Not dominance. Not control. But responsibility that cannot be handed off. Decisions that cannot be averaged without loss. Work that carries weight because no one else can safely absorb its consequences.

Alex has not stepped outside the machine. He has learned where to stand inside it—where motion can be delegated, but direction cannot.

Nothing about the world has become simpler. Nothing has become safer.

But the terrain is now legible.

And legibility is what makes leverage possible.

9

THE SATURDAY MORNING FEELING

THE LIE:

"If I'm not exhausted, I must not be working hard enough."

The Truth:

Exhaustion was never proof of value. It was proof of placement.

THE GHOST OF THE GRIND

The silence in Alex's apartment no longer behaves the way it used to.

Once, it carried weight. It implied delay. It suggested something important was failing to happen on schedule. Quiet was not neutral; it was accusatory. If nothing was moving, something must already be late.

Today, the quiet stretches without pressure. It opens without explanation. It does not demand justification.

It is 10:45 AM on a Tuesday.

In the old world—the world of the Fast Food Trap—this hour marked a turning point. Effort stopped producing momentum, and anxiety stepped in to compensate. By now, Alex would have felt behind without knowing why, obligated without knowing to whom.

Six months ago, this same room would have felt subtly constricted. Not smaller in fact, but tighter in expectation. Silence would have registered as absence under review—as if inactivity itself were being logged somewhere.

Back then, he would already be several coffees in. Not for pleasure, but for propulsion. Caffeine created the sensation of movement even when direction was missing. His body would run slightly ahead of his thoughts, as though trying to preempt a consequence that had not yet arrived.

The cursor would blink.

Not patiently. Functionally. Each pause between keystrokes felt like accumulating liability. Time was not passing; it was accruing. Minutes without visible output registered as something owed later, with interest.

Alex remembers that version of himself with clarity, but without heat. Not shame—recognition. He even gave him a name: the Pixel-Monkey.

That Alex believed in effort as a prerequisite for permission. Work had to unfold sequentially. Pain had to precede legitimacy. If the body was not tired, the work could not be real. If it did not cost something physically, it did not count.

He would spend hours adjusting details no one would notice—microscopic alignments, marginal refinements—until his wrist stiffened and his neck locked. He told himself this was discipline. That this was seriousness.

In retrospect, it was something else.

He was not designing; he was demonstrating. Performing friction because the system rewarded strain. Exhaustion became evidence. Effort became identity.

The atmosphere in the apartment is different now in ways that are difficult to imitate and impossible to fake.

The air carries the smell of hand-ground coffee and the low, even warmth of machines coming online. Nothing is rushing. Nothing is stalled. Systems are not idle; they are simply not demanding attention yet.

Alex is not seated at his desk.

He stands by the window, one hand resting lightly against the glass, watching rain trace uneven paths downward. Some droplets merge. Others pause, change direction, or disappear entirely. Nothing about it looks optimized. Nothing about it feels wrong.

Below him, the city is already in motion. Taxis surge through intersections. Bikes weave between lanes. People move with purpose toward offices they tolerate, trading hours for permission to stop later.

Alex watches without judgment.

And, unexpectedly, without envy.

For the first time in years, he does not feel late. Stillness no longer registers as theft—from his future, from his employer, from an invisible ledger keeping score. Nothing breaks when he stands there doing nothing measurable.

The silence does not punish him.

It simply remains.

Alex does not yet know what to call this state. He has no framework for it. He has not decided whether it is stable or temporary, earned or provisional. He half-expects the familiar weight to return—to settle back across his shoulders out of habit alone.

But it does not.

Instead, there is space. Enough to notice the absence itself.

Not excitement.

Not relief.

Something quieter.

Orientation.

THE SATURDAY MORNING FEELING

Freelance Alex takes a slow sip of his coffee. The absence of urgency is unfamiliar—not relaxing exactly, but open. There is space where there used to be pressure. He has come to recognize this state as the Saturday Morning Feeling.

In the old system, boredom was treated as a defect. Bored meant idle. Idle meant unmonitored. Unmonitored meant suspect. If a manager like Susan sensed slack in the system, she corrected it immediately—with meetings, audits, and deliverables whose primary function was not insight, but motion. Activity stood in for progress. Visibility stood in for value.

Inside the Lab, that reflex no longer applies. Not because boredom is virtuous, but because it is *informative*. When noise drops, signal becomes detectable. When urgency recedes, weak patterns have time to surface. The mind does not switch into insight on command; it requires slack.

Alex remembers learning this long before he had language for it. As a child, the week belonged to instruction. You waited for bells. You followed rules. You demonstrated compliance. Curiosity existed, but only in the margins—after homework, after chores, after permission.

Saturday mornings were different.

You woke early without obligation. You wandered. You built things that had no audience and no rubric. You followed questions that led nowhere useful and therefore everywhere interesting. There was no supervisor measuring output—only attention discovering its own contours.

By offloading syntactic execution to the Exosuit, Alex has recreated a version of that condition inside the workweek. Not escape. Not leisure. Availability. A stretch of time no longer consumed by keeping the system fed.

This does not make him idle. Systems still run. Commitments still exist. But they no longer dominate the foreground. Decisions can wait without decay. Attention is no longer continuously auctioned to the loudest demand.

What Alex has recovered is not authority, but *readiness*. The precondition for judgment. The mental quiet required before structure can be imposed, priorities can be shaped, and meaning can be selected rather than chased.

The work that follows does not begin here—but it cannot begin without this.

WHEN CONTEXTS COLLIDE

Just as the apartment settles into its new quiet, a vibration cuts across it.

It doesn't come from the desk. It doesn't come from the machines.

Across town, on a marble countertop that has learned the shape of routine, Corporate Alex's phone lights up.

It isn't a client.

It isn't opportunity.

It is a calendar notification from the global firm where he still holds a senior title—useful, visible, and conditional.

MANDATORY RTO SYNC: 12:00 PM

ALL HANDS. OFFICE ATTENDANCE REQUIRED.

The Saturday Morning Feeling does not fade gradually. It collapses cleanly. Not emotionally, but procedurally. A familiar tension appears before he has time to interpret it.

This is not nostalgia. It is reversion.

The Return to Office mandate is not a punishment and not a misunderstanding. It is a systems response. When execution becomes less observable, organizations substitute proximity for visibility. When outcomes decouple from oversight, structure compensates by narrowing context.

For two years, Alex worked remotely and became more effective by every operational measure that mattered to the work itself. Turnaround improved. Bottlenecks disappeared. Dependencies thinned.

But organizations do not optimize for output alone. They optimize for *legibility*.

Presence is easy to audit. Outcomes are not.

Corporate leadership did not demand return because work failed. They demanded it because work stopped producing the signals they were calibrated to read. Culture, in this system, is not shared meaning; it is shared location. Collaboration is not convergence of judgment; it is synchronized attendance.

Corporate Alex glances at his workstation. The monitors glow steadily. Pipelines are stable. Processes are running without intervention. The system is doing exactly what it was designed to do—quietly, competently, without asking for supervision.

He checks the time.

Fifty-nine minutes.

That is how long he has to change contexts. Not roles—contexts. To fold the Lab back into the background. To shift tempo, posture, and signaling. The work will continue, but it will no longer be allowed to remain invisible.

For the next part of the day, Alex will not be evaluated on outcomes. He will be evaluated on *presence*.

Not because anyone is malicious.

Because the system requires something it can see.

CONTEXT COMPRESSION

The commute stretches into a muted sequence of gray.

Platforms. Stairwells. The press of bodies moving in practiced patterns. By the time Alex steps into the subway car, the day already feels partially structured. The car is full but quiet. People stand shoulder to shoulder, hands resting loosely around phones they are no longer really reading. Screens glow, dimmed and tilted, as if everyone is using the remaining minutes to settle themselves before the day sharpens.

No one speaks.

Conversation would require energy, and energy is being conserved.

This is not travel.

It is compression.

Forty minutes later, Alex taps his keycard against the glass doors of the office. The sound is clean and transactional. A brief pause. A soft click. The door releases.

Inside, the sensory field shifts almost immediately. Fresh air gives way to conditioned air recycled through vents that never quite turn off. The faint smell of rain fades, replaced by carpet cleaner and overheated coffee. The light flattens surfaces and faces alike, reducing contrast and softening edges.

As Alex passes the security desk, the low, continuous hum of fluorescent fixtures settles into the background. It is not loud enough to notice consciously, but it shapes attention all the same. This is a space tuned for visibility. Being seen here is not incidental to work; it is one of the mechanisms through which coordination happens.

He is back in the Cave.

Not a place of punishment.

A place of narrowing.

Near the elevators, a manager stands with a tablet, checking arrivals as they register. Names appear. Status indicators update. The ritual is procedural, not personal. It exists to align bodies with schedules, ensuring that presence and timing remain synchronized across the floor.

When Alex's arrival logs, there is a brief acknowledgment. A comment about the floor being busy today. A note that leadership is onsite. Nothing evaluative. Nothing corrective. Just enough to reinforce the shared understanding that activity should be visible and paced together.

There is no inquiry about progress. No discussion of dependencies resolved or friction removed. Those details are difficult to observe consistently at scale. Presence is not.

Alex nods and continues on. Explanation would be out of place here; the system is not calibrated to listen for it.

His cubicle waits where it always has. The dimensions have not changed, but they feel more confining than he remembers. The narrowing is not physical. It is attentional. He sits, badges in, and wakes the workstation.

The company's internal AI interface blooms onto the screen—polished, branded, carefully framed to signal capability and reliability. It offers speed within the contours of the existing workflow, accelerating execution without altering the posture around it.

This tool is not here to change how work is evaluated.

It is here to fit inside how it already is.

Around him, the environment reinforces continuity: the same hours, the same rhythms, the same visible exertion—now supported by faster tools. Increased output is welcome. Reduced presence is not.

Alex feels the Saturday Morning Feeling recede, not because it was fragile, but because this context has no way to register it. The system is not hostile to quiet. It is simply designed to notice other signals first.

Here, attention is not something to be defended.

It is something to be coordinated.

RESIDUAL FRICTION

Alex turns his chair back toward the monitor.

He does not reach for the keyboard right away.

A faint tension spreads across his hands—not anxiety exactly, not fear, but something closer to hesitation. His fingers hover, then rest flat against the desk. His body slows even though his mind has already moved ahead. He knows what the task is. He knows where the friction is. He knows, with uncomfortable clarity, that the work itself will take only minutes.

Still, something in him resists the speed.

The resistance does not announce itself as a thought. There is no inner objection to argue with, no belief to dismantle. It arrives as posture: a slight tightening in the shoulders, a delay in the hands, a readiness to settle in rather than move through.

Alex has felt this before, in classrooms and offices that trained him long before they instructed him. School rewarded visible process. You showed your work. You filled the page. You demonstrated effort step by step so no one could accuse you of guessing. Managers later reinforced the same instinct. Work that arrived quickly required explanation. Work that took longer explained itself.

Somewhere along the way, duration became evidence.

The rule was never written down, never formalized, never defended in theory. But it was enforced with quiet consistency: if something comes too easily, slow it down until it looks legitimate.

That rule still operates here—not as policy, but as residue.

Alex notices the small, almost involuntary impulses that follow. The urge to add a verification pass that will change nothing. The temptation to reformat text that is already clear. The inclination to let the cursor sit idle for a moment longer before acting, as if time itself were part of the deliverable.

No one is asking for this.

The system does not demand it explicitly. His body supplies it automatically.

This is the Ghost of the 40-Hour Week at work—not as a schedule pinned to a calendar, but as muscle memory embedded below choice. The lesson is old enough that it no longer feels like a lesson at all. It feels like professionalism.

Around him, the office hums with familiar signals. Screens glow with documents mid-revision. Keyboards chatter in uneven rhythms. Conversations rise and fall just loudly enough to register as collaboration. Activity accumulates in visible layers, each one reinforcing the impression that work is happening because time is being spent.

No one is asking whether any of this could be done faster.

That question does not belong to this environment.

Alex understands, with a clarity that does not comfort him, that efficiency is not rejected outright here. It is tolerated—sometimes even admired—but only when it remains invisible. Speed is acceptable as long as it does not disturb the shared pacing of the room.

He begins the task.

Not slowly, but not as cleanly as he knows he could. He allows pauses to remain. He leaves evidence of process. He lets the work occupy the space that has been tacitly allocated to it.

Not because the work requires it.

But because this context does.

WORKING INSIDE THE CONSTRAINT

Susan drops a digital folder into Alex's queue without ceremony.

The request is familiar in shape if not in scale: a quarterly brand audit, hundreds of pages of mixed research, survey data, transcripts, and internal commentary. The instructions are precise about the destination—summary, extraction, placement into the approved template—but vague about the path. The deadline sits at the end of the week, heavy enough to imply effort, distant enough to absorb time.

In an earlier version of himself, Alex would have felt his body react before his mind did. Three hundred pages would have translated immediately into long hours—copying, formatting, rephrasing—work that filled the day visibly even when it produced little movement. He would have begun preparing for endurance rather than judgment.

That reflex still flickers.

He feels it as a tightening in the shoulders, a subtle readiness to settle in for something that will take longer than it should. The system trained him well. When work arrives with weight, the expectation is not efficiency, but occupation.

Alex waits a moment before opening the folder. Not to delay, but to read the room. Around him, keyboards chatter. Chairs shift. Conversations happen just loudly enough to register as activity. Screens glow with documents in various stages of being "worked on." The environment is doing what it does best: signaling effort.

He opens the file.

The machine assists immediately—not with conclusions, but with surface work. It organizes, extracts, highlights inconsistencies. This part is fast, almost unremarkable now. Alex does not confuse this with completion. The output is raw material, not insight.

He leans back slightly and begins the slower pass.

This is where time re-enters. He checks claims against source context. He notices which conclusions flatten nuance and which miss the political realities that will matter later in the room. He flags areas where the data says one thing and the organization will want to hear another—and where those two cannot be reconciled without consequence.

Thirty minutes pass. Then forty.

By early afternoon, the work itself is finished. Not summarized, not beautified—*understood*. The analysis is coherent, defensible, and, importantly, limited. It answers the question that was actually asked, not the one implied by the pile of pages.

Alex does not send it.

He sits with the file open, cursor idle, and notices the familiar urge to justify speed by adding friction. To stretch. To decorate. To let the work occupy the time it was expected to occupy rather than the time it required.

This urge is not strategic. It is trained.

In environments calibrated for visibility, early delivery alters the frame. Work that arrives too quickly is not read as efficient; it is read as *available*. Speed invites expansion. Completion invites reassignment. The system does not punish efficiency, but it does not know how to price it either.

So Alex leaves the document where it is. Complete, reviewed, waiting.

The rest of the afternoon unfolds according to expectation. He responds to messages. He attends the meetings that convert presence into proof. He remains reachable, observable, aligned. Nothing about his behavior suggests resistance or disengagement.

This is not concealment.

It is containment.

Alex understands that until authority exists, timing is part of professionalism. Work does not speak for itself in every environment. Sometimes it must be introduced at a pace the system can interpret without distortion.

The analysis will be delivered when it can be received as what it is—neither miraculous nor suspect.

Just finished.

ROLE WEIGHT

By midafternoon, the quality of the room changes.

The fluorescent lights have not grown brighter, but they feel heavier. The hum is no longer background; it presses forward, a constant presence that makes concentration slightly more effortful than it should be. This used to be the hour Alex dreaded—the long, indistinct stretch where fatigue accumulated and endurance passed for professionalism.

He looks around the floor. His coworkers move at a measured pace, shoulders sloped, attention divided. Not defeated. Not miserable. Simply extended. Each person is carrying the workday in a different way: a missed message from home, a meeting pushed late, a conversation deferred until "after this week." None of it is dramatic. All of it is familiar.

This is what sustained presence costs, even when the work itself is manageable.

A colleague named Dave leans back in his chair and rubs his eyes. "How's the audit going?" he asks quietly. "I'm only on page forty. Feels like this one's going to take a while."

Alex registers the moment carefully. Not as a moral dilemma, but as a contextual one. He could explain that the analysis itself is already complete. He could describe the tools, the parallel processing, the efficiency that collapses days into minutes.

But explanation here would not help Dave. It would not change the constraints either of them are operating under. Information that cannot be acted on does not liberate; it destabilizes.

"Still working through it," Alex says evenly. "There's a lot in there."

The words are not false. They are incomplete. And for this environment, that distinction matters.

What Alex feels now is not guilt, but weight. The effort required to maintain a posture that fits expectations even as his internal relationship to the work has shifted. This is the cost of role alignment—the energy spent matching visible signals to a system calibrated around time and presence.

As the afternoon continues, Alex notices the gap more clearly. Not between people, but between *metrics*. The organization still reads value through duration. The tools now operate through compression. Neither is malicious. They are simply out of phase.

Sitting beneath the steady hum of the lights, Alex recognizes the situation for what it is. Not a conflict to win. Not a system to defeat. But a mismatch that cannot be resolved through awareness alone.

The Saturday Morning Feeling does not disappear. It goes quiet. It waits.

Not because it is fragile.

But because this context has not yet learned how to hold it.

When the day finally winds down, Alex checks the time out of habit more than necessity. In another season of his life, this hour would have marked the beginning of a second shift. Tonight, there is nothing left to push through.

He leans back briefly, closes his eyes, and lets his attention drift—no planning, no anticipation. Just stillness.

His body remains in the building.

His posture does too.

But something else has already loosened its grip.

THE MECHANICS OF THE DREAM STACK

If the Saturday Morning Feeling explains *why* the change matters, the Dream Stack explains *how* it becomes durable. Feeling without structure evaporates. Structure is what turns relief into a repeatable advantage.

Alex is twenty-six. In the old world—the world of the Fast Food Trap—being twenty-six came with a clear assignment. You were a "Junior." You fixed typos no one would remember. You nudged logos by fractions of a millimeter. You stayed until 11:00 PM because a Senior Art Director wanted to see "one more version" of a font that was functionally identical to the last three. Your role was not judgment; it was compliance.

You were the engine. Someone else held the steering wheel.

That ladder made sense when output was bottlenecked by hands. Juniors supplied horsepower. Seniors supplied taste. Time was the filter. Survival depended on endurance.

The Exosuit inverted that logic completely. In the new world, the Junior is not underpaid; the Junior is unnecessary. If your primary value is speed at execution—if you differentiate yourself by how fast you can *do*—you are competing directly with a system that does not tire, does not complain, and does not need promotion. Standing still in that role is like standing on a beach, insisting the tide negotiate.

Freelance Alex survived because he made a clean break with the engine identity. He stopped trying to be faster, cheaper, or more obedient. He decided instead to become legible as a Pilot.

The Dream Stack is the architecture that makes that choice operational. It is not a single tool. It is a division of labor where the machine absorbs volume and variance, and the human concentrates authority. Alex built a coordinated system of specialized instances—research, synthesis, critique, and iteration—so that one person in a one-bedroom apartment could reliably out-produce a fifty-person agency without inheriting its inertia.

The point of the Dream Stack is not scale for its own sake. It is selectivity. It allows Alex to decide *what matters* after the machine has already handled everything that does not.

WHEN PRESSURE RETURNS

Late in the afternoon, Alex's phone vibrates against the desk.

Not a notification.

A call.

He notices the difference immediately—not in sound, but in weight. Messages can be deferred. Calls ask for posture. He glances at the name and feels a familiar tightening settle just below the ribs. Not panic. Not excitement. Recognition.

He lets it ring once more than necessary before answering.

The request arrives in fragments. Expanded scope. Compressed timeline. A window that will close if it isn't met. Alex listens without interrupting, letting the cadence of urgency play itself out. This is the sound of pressure arriving before permission.

In an earlier season of his life, his mind would already be racing ahead—counting hours, mapping dependencies, calculating what would have to give. He would be measuring the week not by days, but by what would be lost to accommodate the demand. Sleep. Attention. The margin that never seemed to survive first contact.

That reflex still stirs.

He feels it in the subtle readiness to say yes too quickly, or no too defensively. To treat the moment as a test rather than a signal.

Alex slows himself deliberately. He asks clarifying questions. Not strategic ones. Practical ones. What is fixed. What is flexible. What actually matters versus what is being bundled in by urgency. He takes notes, not because he needs them, but because the act of writing keeps him from rushing toward a decision that would feel decisive rather than correct.

The call ends without resolution. No commitment. No refusal. Just an understanding that something has been placed in front of him that will not resolve itself.

Alex sets the phone face down on the desk.

The room around him remains unchanged. Screens glow. The hum of machines continues. Outside the window, the light has shifted slightly, the rain thinning into something more intermittent. Nothing in the environment reflects the pressure that just arrived.

He sits there longer than he needs to. Not thinking through solutions. Not planning. Just noticing the shape of the moment.

What becomes clear, slowly, is not what to do next—but what is no longer sufficient. Awareness helped. Calm helped. The Saturday Morning Feeling created space. But space alone does not absorb force.

Pressure has returned.

And the old tools—effort, endurance, improvisation—are already lining up to respond, offering familiar costs for familiar results.

Alex does nothing yet.

He simply registers, with a quiet precision that unsettles him, that the problem in front of him is no longer about speed or capacity. It is about containment. About shape. About having something that can hold pressure without deforming around it.

He does not have that yet.

But he can now feel exactly where it would need to exist.

WHEN LINEARITY STOPS HELPING

The first thing Alex notices is not a new capability.

It is the failure of an old one.

Faced with the problem in front of him, his mind reaches—automatically—for the familiar sequence. First this. Then that. Research before design. Design before copy. Copy before review. A single thread pulled through time, step by step, with progress measured by completion rather than alignment.

The sequence still forms.

It just doesn't fit.

Alex feels the friction immediately. Not resistance, exactly, but inefficiency of a different kind—the sense that the order itself is imposing cost. The work is not difficult. The thinking is not unclear. But forcing everything through a single channel introduces delays that have nothing to do with complexity and everything to do with habit.

He has lived inside this pattern for most of his professional life. It shaped his calendar. It shaped his expectations. It trained him to believe that progress must move in a line, that clarity arrives only after each prior step has been formally completed.

That assumption used to feel natural.

Now it feels heavy.

Alex notices how often his attention stalls while waiting for one part of the work to "finish" before another is allowed to begin. How often momentum is lost not to uncertainty, but to sequencing. How frequently time is consumed maintaining order rather than resolving substance.

The realization does not arrive as insight or excitement. It arrives as irritation—a quiet but persistent sense that the structure he has been using to move through work is now doing more harm than good.

He does not yet know what should replace it.

He only knows that the old arrangement assumes a world where effort must be serialized, where thinking is scarce, and where time is the primary constraint. None of those assumptions feel stable anymore.

Alex sits with that awareness longer than is comfortable. He resists the urge to improvise a workaround or force a solution prematurely. The problem is not execution. It is shape.

Whatever comes next cannot be a faster version of the same sequence.

It will have to be organized differently—around intent rather than steps, around judgment rather than endurance.

He does not yet have that organization.

But he can now feel the exact pressure point where linearity gives way.

AN UNFAMILIAR ENDING TO THE DAY

By late afternoon, the office begins to thin.

Chairs slide back. Conversations taper off. The ambient noise of the floor shifts from active coordination to low-level inertia—the sound of people finishing what they can and deferring the rest. Alex notices the change without reacting to it.

His own screen is quiet. Not empty. Quiet.

The work he was responsible for has reached a stable point. Not finalized in the ceremonial sense, not "wrapped," but no longer demanding immediate attention. There are no loose threads pulling at his focus. No sense of something about to break if he steps away.

This is unfamiliar.

In the past, this hour signaled the beginning of a different phase of the day. The point where effort stopped yielding clarity and endurance took over. Alex would brace himself for a long evening, not because the work required it, but because the structure around the work assumed it. Progress was measured by how long he stayed with the problem rather than by whether the problem had changed.

He would have interpreted the absence of pressure as danger—evidence that something had been missed. He would have gone looking for friction simply to reassure himself that the day had extracted its due.

That impulse stirs now, faintly.

Alex notices it without acting on it. He resists the urge to manufacture difficulty or reopen decisions that no longer need reopening. The work does not feel unfinished. It feels...settled.

He sits with that sensation, uncertain what to make of it. There is no rush of relief. No surge of satisfaction. Just a steady, almost disorienting calm.

He looks around the office once more. Others are still working through visible queues, still responding to the rhythms the day expects of them. Alex feels no distance from them, only a growing awareness that his internal relationship to time has shifted slightly out of sync.

He closes the laptop—not as a gesture of completion, but as a pause. His hands are steady. His attention is intact. Nothing in his body signals that he has been depleted.

This does not feel like escape.

It feels like an interruption in a pattern he had assumed was permanent.

Alex gathers his things and stands. As he moves toward the exit, he realizes he cannot yet explain what has changed—only that the day ended without taking something from him.

He does not name it.

He does not trust it yet.

But he carries the sensation with him as he leaves the building: the quiet recognition that work no longer seems to demand his exhaustion as proof of legitimacy.

Whatever made that possible is still indistinct.

Whatever it is, it has not finished revealing its shape.

WHERE THE MACHINE STOPS

Alex stands in the middle of his apartment, not working.

The monitors behind him glow steadily, the systems he set in motion earlier still warm, still active. Nothing has broken. Nothing is asking for input. The machinery continues without him, indifferent to his presence or absence.

He turns away from the desk and notices something small but unfamiliar: the absence of pull. The screens no longer exert the same gravitational force they once did. They are available, but they are no longer persuasive.

On the kitchen table sits a wooden crate delivered earlier in the day. It is ordinary in construction, light enough to carry without effort. Alex opens it and lifts one of the glass bottles inside. The cold transfers immediately to his palm. Condensation forms without instruction.

The sensation arrests him.

Not because it is special, but because it is not. The weight. The temperature. The quiet patience of something that exists outside dashboards and timelines. There is no progress bar attached to it. No version history. Nothing to optimize.

In earlier chapters of his life, Alex's involvement would have ended before this moment. His responsibility would have stopped at transmission—files delivered, work abstracted, consequences deferred. The physical world was someone else's problem.

That division no longer feels stable.

Holding the bottle, Alex notices how much of what matters here cannot be delegated. There is no instruction set for how something should feel in the hand, or how long someone pauses before deciding it belongs in their life. These judgments are quiet. They happen without ceremony. They do not announce themselves as "decisions" at all.

Alex does not name what he is noticing. He does not turn it into a rule or a principle. He simply registers the boundary.

The machine is excellent at assembling forms.

It does not cross this line.

Alex sets the bottle back into the crate and closes the lid. The systems behind him continue to hum. The apartment is still.

He understands, without yet knowing what to do about it, that the next phase of his work will not be about speed, or volume, or even quality in the abstract.

It will be about responsibility—about standing in places where automation stops and something else must begin.

He does not yet have language for that role.

But he knows now where it will have to be performed.

AT THE EDGE OF THE WORK

Alex reaches into the crate and lifts one of the bottles free.

The glass is cold and heavier than it looks. Condensation beads along the surface and gathers at his fingertips. The sensation interrupts him—not sharply, but insistently. It demands attention in a way no interface ever has.

He turns the bottle once in his hand. There is nothing to configure. Nothing to improve. The object does not ask a question or offer a suggestion. It simply exists, complete in a way that does not invite iteration.

Earlier in the day, most of Alex's work had taken place several layers removed from this moment. Screens. Files. Abstract representations of things that would later become real. He had grown accustomed to that distance—to the idea that responsibility could end before contact.

Holding the bottle, that assumption weakens.

Alex notices how little guidance exists here. There are no prompts. No metrics scrolling in the corner. No immediate feedback about whether this moment is correct or optimal. Whatever judgment applies will not arrive in the form of data. It will arrive later, indirectly, carried by people Alex will never meet.

He does not yet decide what that means.

He simply recognizes that this part of the process does not behave like the others. It does not accelerate. It does not branch. It does not invite experimentation at scale. It resists abstraction.

The work, he realizes, has edges.

Most of what he has learned to do happens upstream—where

ideas can be revised, multiplied, discarded without consequence. But here, the margin narrows. Each choice hardens more quickly. Each decision carries farther.

Alex sets the bottle back into the crate and closes the lid. The systems in the other room continue to run without him. Nothing requires intervention.

What lingers is not a conclusion, but a question he has not yet learned how to ask properly:

What does it mean to be present where the work stops being flexible?

He does not answer it.

He only notes that whatever comes next will have to account for this edge—this place where process gives way to consequence, and attention must replace speed.

WHAT BEGINS TO MATTER

In the weeks that follow, Alex notices a subtle shift in where his attention goes.

It is not deliberate at first. There is no plan attached to it. He simply finds himself listening longer before responding, staying with conversations after their official purpose has passed. Not to extract information, but to understand what people are actually worried about when the formal questions end.

In the office, this looks unremarkable. Alex still attends the same meetings. He still completes the same categories of work. But he lingers in the in-between spaces—break rooms, hallways, moments after calls end—where people speak without an agenda and problems appear without formatting.

He begins to notice patterns that never surface in dashboards. Not trends, exactly. Tensions. Small hesitations in how decisions are framed. The things people circle around but do not name because there is no obvious place to put them.

When Marcus talks about growth, Alex hears more than expansion. He hears concern about sameness. About losing the qualities that make a place recognizable to the people who already care about it. The machine offers solutions quickly—standardization, consistency, repeatability—but those answers seem to pass over the worry rather than address it.

The client proposes expanding—new locations, broader product lines, faster growth.

Alex does not counter with alternatives. He asks questions instead. About what customers comment on when they linger. About what regulars would miss if the place disappeared. About what feels fragile rather than scalable.

None of this produces an immediate decision.

It does, however, change the texture of the conversation.

Alex notices the same thing elsewhere. When he spends time tracing the history of a place or a business, it is not for inspiration or reference. It is to understand what has already survived change—and what has not. These details do not translate cleanly into deliverables. They sit awkwardly in the process, refusing to become assets or bullet points.

Over time, Alex finds himself making fewer recommendations and taking on more responsibility for the uncertainty around them. He explains tradeoffs rather than outcomes. He names what cannot be known in advance. He absorbs ambiguity so it does not have to travel further downstream.

This does not feel like strategy.

It feels like weight.

Alex has not become faster. He has not become indispensable. He has not escaped substitution in any formal sense. But he senses that something about his role is beginning to change—not in title or scope, but in where accountability settles.

Decisions now seem to gather around him, not because he commands them, but because someone has to stand near them when the abstractions run out.

He does not yet understand what to call this shift.

He only knows that it is pulling him away from the center of the system's averages and toward the edges where choices start to harden

—and where replacement becomes less straightforward, though never guaranteed.

AFTER THE DOORS CLOSE

The doors slide shut behind Alex, and the building's hum recedes into something distant and indistinct.

Outside, the rain continues. Not dramatically. Not with purpose. It falls the way it always has, flattening sound, softening edges, making the city feel slightly less urgent without changing it in any meaningful way.

Alex pauses just beyond the awning. He does not hurry. He does not check his phone. There is nothing pressing against him from behind—no countdown, no sensation of being late to something unnamed.

That absence still surprises him.

The Tuesday Morning Crisis has not disappeared so much as lost its authority. It no longer dictates the shape of the week or the tempo of his attention. It survives now as a memory of a posture he once assumed was permanent: that time must be spent loudly to count, that effort must be visible to be legitimate.

What has replaced it is not freedom in the abstract. It is responsibility without scaffolding. The quiet realization that attention, once reclaimed, does not automatically organize itself.

Alex steps into the rain and begins the walk home. The city moves around him at its usual pace. Nothing has slowed. Nothing has yielded. The system he left behind will continue to run exactly as it did this morning.

The difference is internal, and still provisional.

He feels the space he has created—hours no longer pre-committed, decisions no longer forced by urgency. But space, he is learning, is not a solution. It is an exposure. Without the old pressures to shape it, attention becomes something that must be directed deliberately or it will dissipate on its own.

Alex does not yet know how to do that well.

He only knows that the habits that once organized his days—endurance, responsiveness, staying busy until the noise stopped—no longer apply. Whatever comes next will require something more intentional than effort and something sturdier than instinct.

As he turns the corner toward home, Alex understands that he has reached the edge of what release alone can provide. Time has been returned to him. Pressure has been reduced. Boundaries have become visible.

But none of that answers the harder question now taking shape:

What structure replaces the one that just fell away?

He walks on without answering it.

The rain keeps falling.

The space remains.

And for the first time, Alex recognizes that keeping it will require more than relief—it will require design.

PART V

CONSTRUCTION

10

THE DREAM STACK

The Lie: Success comes from finding one perfect job, role, or breakthrough and optimizing it.

The Truth: Durable leverage is built by stacking small, compounding advantages across intent, judgment, tools, and ownership. The goal is not optimization—it is alignment. Multipliers emerge when the system reinforces itself.

THE MULTIPLIER EFFECT

The sun is setting over Brooklyn, laying long amber shadows across the brick walls of Alex's apartment. Light slips through the windows at a low angle, catching dust motes suspended in the air and turning the room into something quietly neutral. The space isn't dramatic or sacred. It is simply available.

It is 5:30 PM on a Tuesday.

In his old life, this hour marked a predictable collapse. By the time Alex reached his apartment, the day had already extracted everything it was going to extract. Not because the work was difficult in any meaningful sense, but because it was metabolically inefficient. Hours of pixel-level execution, serial handoffs, and email-driven motion consumed attention without advancing direction. By evening, nothing remained to allocate.

That residue is still easy to recall. The ache behind the eyes. The low-grade fatigue that made further decisions feel irresponsible rather than optional. At 5:30 PM, the day didn't pause; it closed. What followed was recovery, not choice.

Today, that signal does not arrive.

Freelance Alex is not energized, and he is not resting. He is intact. His attention has not been spent maintaining processes that no longer required his judgment. The work that once drained him has been compressed, displaced, or removed entirely—not by intensity, but by selection.

This is not a change in mood.

It is a change in system behavior.

What remains at the end of the day is not motivation, but capacity with direction still undecided. Time has been returned, but it has not yet been organized. The absence of exhaustion is not the result—it is the precondition.

At 5:30 PM, the workday no longer dictates what comes next.

That does not mean the problem is solved.

It means the conditions now exist for something different to be built.

THE RITUAL OF THE PIVOT

When Alex steps through the door, he performs a small, deliberate ritual. He unbuttons the "professional" shirt—the one Susan prefers because it makes him legible, compliant, and easy to place—and drops it into the laundry basket like a uniform at the end of a shift. The gesture is unremarkable. That is the point.

This is not about comfort. It is about classification.

During the workday, Alex operates in a role defined by the organization. He thinks of this mode as Corporate Alex—not a different self, but a constrained operating context. In that role, value is assessed through visibility and responsiveness. Judgment exists, but it is filtered through other people's priorities, timelines, and incentives. Time is consumed to satisfy external demand.

Inside the apartment, those constraints fall away.

Here, Alex operates under a different set of rules. He calls this mode Freelance Alex, not to signal independence or escape, but to mark a shift in objective function. In this context, he is not rewarded for being reachable. He is rewarded for being correct. Throughput is secondary. Leverage is primary. Time is no longer spent; it is allocated.

He pulls on an oversized hoodie. He kicks off his shoes. He does not "clock out." He redirects. The work ahead is not execution, but governance—deciding where effort should be applied, where it should be withheld, and which outcomes are worth binding himself to.

Alex settles into the ergonomic chair as the three 4K monitors wake with a low, familiar hum. Interfaces surface. Systems align. This is not a shrine to creativity or a freelancer's improvisation. It is a control surface—built for evaluation, scenario testing, and compounding decisions over time.

Nothing essential about Alex has changed.

Only the constraints have.

The pivot is complete. The Multiplier Effect can now begin.

THE MULTITASKING LIE VS. THE PARALLEL TRUTH

To understand what Alex is about to do, one assumption has to be set aside. For years, multitasking was treated as a virtue—a signal of adaptability in an environment that rewarded visible busyness. The Fast Food Trap elevated it to a survival skill. If you could juggle more inputs, respond faster, and stay perpetually reachable, you were seen as capable.

In practice, multitasking was never a capability. It was a coping mechanism shaped by incentives. Human beings do not execute multiple cognitive tasks at once; they context-switch between them. Each switch carries a cost. Attention fragments. Context leaks. Momentum resets. The work does not compound; it churns. From the outside, this looks like productivity. From the inside, it feels like depletion.

This arrangement was not accidental. Switch-tasking maximized surface activity while quietly eroding effectiveness. It kept people occupied, observable, and responsive—while ensuring that no single thread received sustained judgment. The system rewarded motion, not progress.

The Context Architect does not attempt to win inside that

system. He does not try to become a faster human processor or a better imitator of a computer. He changes the structure of the work itself.

He parallelizes.

When Alex looks at his monitors, he is not reviewing a to-do list or sequencing tasks for personal execution. He is surveying a system. What he sees is a Dream Stack: a deliberately assembled set of digital counterparts, each assigned a bounded domain of responsibility—research, synthesis, drafting, critique. These threads operate independently and concurrently, without competing for Alex's attention or forcing him to context-switch.

The distinction is subtle but decisive. Alex is not doing more things at once. He is deciding more things *once*—and allowing execution to proceed in parallel. His attention is reserved for selection, correction, and integration, not for serial labor.

In the old world, ambition was taxed by time. If Alex wanted to build a business, write a book, and develop a personal platform, those ambitions had to be queued into a single-file line. One dream at a time. Years apart. Each deferred until the previous one had extracted its full toll.

He would have paid the Product Timeline Tax on every single dream.

Parallelization changes that math.

SCALING THE WISH

Alex turns to his first monitor. This is his Business Branch—the arm of the Dream Stack designed to convert *attention* into *leverage*. Earlier that afternoon, while Corporate Alex sat in a conference room performing attentiveness for Susan, the system was already at work. Not reactively. Not opportunistically. Continuously.

During the meeting—slides advancing, buzzwords circulating—Alex's Market Scout was operating under a standing mandate. This was not a suggestion engine waiting to be prompted. It was an autonomous operator executing a bounded search across a defined landscape, indifferent to calendars and immune to performative urgency.

While the meeting consumed time, the stack consumed terrain.

Scanning: Hundreds of bakery accounts were surveyed across platforms, not to find what was common, but to isolate the Beige Factor—the interchangeable visuals, stock-photo palettes, and caption structures that register as "content" without ever landing as *signal.*

Synthesizing: Those failures were then cross-referenced against engagement outliers. Not averages. Spikes. The anomalies that attract attention precisely because they break pattern. Decisions that communicate point of view before copy is ever read.

Drafting: From that synthesis, the stack produced a month of content—structured enough to scale, specific enough to avoid the uncanny. Raw material, not final authority.

Alex does not experience this as "writing faster." Writing is no longer the constraint. Judgment is. He moves directly into Audit Mode—not to generate, but to *decide.* For ten focused minutes, he acts as a filter: cutting phrases that perform warmth without substance, bending tone toward local texture, stripping out anything that smells faintly of inherited optimism.

He leans back.

The work is finished—not because execution is complete, but because *selection* is.

In ten minutes, Alex has governed output that would traditionally require a week of meetings, revisions, and coordination overhead. Not by accelerating labor—but by eliminating the distance between intent, evaluation, and action.

That collapse is the Multiplier Effect.

THE SUNK COST OF BUSYNESS

Alex leans back and turns to the second monitor. This is his Legacy Branch. This is where he is writing *The Human Moat*—the book you are holding now. It is not a side project and not something reserved for spare moments. It is the long arc: work designed to compound over years rather than resolve by Friday.

For a long time, writing a book carried an implicit cost structure. It was assumed to require prolonged isolation, repeated false starts, and extended stretches of unproductive effort. That pattern wasn't imposed by malice or ideology; it was simply the best available model under older constraints. Endurance became a proxy for seriousness because there were few alternatives.

Alex no longer treats that cost as intrinsic. The difficulty was never a guarantor of insight. It was a byproduct of friction—attention scattered across clerical tasks, structure assembled late, and momentum repeatedly reset. The effort didn't deepen the thinking; it prolonged the path to coherence.

He uses the Dream Stack to absorb everything that does not require judgment. Voice memos captured while walking through Brooklyn. Fragmented outlines. Half-formed metaphors. These are fed into the system with explicit constraints: organize the material, surface relevant history, resolve structure—but do not alter tone, intent, or voice. If the language drifts toward abstraction, remove it.

In this role, the system functions as a clearing layer. It does not decide what the book means. It does not invent arguments or supply authority. It reduces the clerical load between thought and form—the coordination work that once stretched projects across years without improving their substance.

As a result, Alex is no longer forced to work linearly from the beginning forward. He can shape the ending early, test the arc, and adjust direction before momentum is lost. This is not a race against other writers. It is a reconfiguration of sequence. The tunnel no longer dictates the pace.

He is moving at Exit Velocity.

THE HIDDEN OFFICE

Alex's attention drifts back to the cubicle he occupied earlier that afternoon. What lingers is not the substance of the meeting, but its orientation. The emphasis was not on outcomes or insight, but on visibility—screens open, activity observable, presence confirmed. The system was not poorly intentioned. It was optimized for assurance: a way to reduce uncertainty by making work legible from the outside.

It is here that Alex makes a structural observation. The Return to Office mandate is not inherently punitive, nor is it a referendum on trust. It is a reallocation of resources designed to stabilize coordination at scale. For many people, that reallocation feels like a loss of autonomy. For Alex, it reveals a different possibility: a predictable, well-resourced environment whose fixed costs are already absorbed.

The organization provides the workspace. The network. The hardware. The software licenses. The salary that arrives on schedule every two weeks. These are not trivial assets. They represent a significant investment in continuity and infrastructure. What the organization does not—and cannot—purchase is judgment. It does not acquire long-range intent or authority over meaning. Those remain nontransferable by design.

Alex does not challenge this arrangement. He works within it. By establishing clear internal boundaries, he converts the cubicle into a secondary workspace—not through resistance or neglect, but through separation of concerns. Presence is supplied as required. Output is delivered as expected. What changes is not performance, but allocation.

He practices the art of the tab switch—not as deception, but as classification discipline. Each context has a defined scope, a defined obligation, and a defined owner.

Tab A: The corporate materials the organization expects—competent, on-brand, continuous with prior work. This work is real. It matters. It fulfills a contract.

Tab B: The independent systems Alex is deliberately developing—intellectual capital, leverage, and long-arc projects whose value compounds over time and whose ownership remains fully his.

From the outside, nothing appears unusual. Alex meets

expectations consistently. From the inside, a different accounting is taking place. Excess capacity is no longer dissipated through reactive effort. It is redirected with intent.

The organization purchases presence and receives reliable output in return. Alex honors that exchange. What he retains—quietly and deliberately—is authority over how his remaining attention is invested. That retained authority is not a loophole. It is the Human Moat taking shape.

THE ROLE INVERSION

If the Saturday Morning Feeling is the *why*, then the Dream Stack explains the *shift*—not as a slogan or a workflow, but as a change in role. Feelings don't scale by themselves. Responsibility does.

Alex is twenty-six. Under older conditions, that number came with a default assignment. Twenty-six meant Junior. It meant your job was execution before judgment. You corrected the details no one else had time to notice. You stayed late because revision was cheap and direction was scarce. Your value was inferred from visible effort, not from the consequences of your decisions.

In that structure, Alex was the Engine.

He supplied force while someone else supplied direction. When things stalled, the solution was more effort. When they succeeded, the credit flowed upward. This arrangement wasn't malicious or misguided. It emerged because, for a long time, labor itself was the constraint.

That constraint no longer holds.

In an environment where execution is abundant and velocity is cheap, speed stops being a differentiator. Roles defined primarily by throughput begin to lose coherence—not because the work disappears, but because its scarcity does. Under those conditions, the question is no longer *how fast* something can be done, but *who decides what should be done at all.*

Freelance Alex survives this transition by changing roles, not by optimizing harder. He stops trying to become a better Engine and instead assumes responsibility as a Pilot. Not a manager issuing instructions. Not a delegator offloading tasks. A navigator—someone accountable for direction, sequencing, and judgment when possibilities multiply faster than attention can track.

The Dream Stack is not a productivity trick. It formalizes this inversion. Alex no longer serves tools. Tools operate in service of his decisions. Their purpose is not to replace judgment, but to remove the friction that prevents judgment from being applied consistently.

What results is not an individual working at unsustainable speed. It is a structural asymmetry. One person, embedded with taste, memory, and consequence, can now evaluate more options than a large team ever could—without exhausting the human at the center.

The stack does not make Alex exceptional. It makes him selective.

That selectivity—deciding what matters, in what order, and why—is the advantage. It is how a single person in a small apartment can produce work that once required an agency—not through intensity or indifference, but by placing judgment where labor used to sit and allowing execution to absorb the rest.

THE TUESDAY UNDER PRESSURE

The Dream Stack only reveals its value when conditions tighten. Not in a demo. Not during a calm planning window. But at the moment when the old system would have collapsed under its own sequencing.

It is 1:15 PM.

Rain softens the Brooklyn skyline into gray geometry, but Alex isn't watching it. His attention has narrowed, drawn inward toward the quiet hum of the Cockpit. His phone vibrates once against the desk. He doesn't need to check the screen.

It's Marcus from The Bitter Bean.

Marcus doesn't waste time on context. His voice carries the edge of compression—the sound of opportunity and deadline converging.

"Alex, I need help," he says. "The distributor just called. If I can get them a full brand deck, a thirty-second social teaser, and a localized marketing plan for three city zones by tomorrow morning, they'll expand us into fifty more stores."

A pause. Then the qualifier.

"It has to be right. Not 'AI good.' Actually right."

Under older conditions, this wouldn't be a negotiation. It would be a nonstarter. Not because of unwillingness, but because of structure. Three weeks. A half-dozen specialists. Coordinated handoffs. Revisions layered on revisions. Meetings to align, meetings to realign. The Product Timeline Tax would dominate before a single decision was made.

Old Alex would have felt the familiar tightening that preceded refusal. He would have started calculating hours, reducing scope, composing the explanation for why the answer had to be no. Inside a sequential system, no was the only honest response.

Freelance Alex operates under different constraints.

He doesn't agree. He doesn't decline. He pauses—not to deliberate, but to orient. He takes a sip of coffee. Adjusts his beanie. This is not hesitation. It is a Pilot moment: a shift from reacting to navigating.

He turns to the center monitor.

There is no announcement. No buildup. No promise of a miracle.

He initiates the process—not by accelerating labor, but by removing the need to negotiate sequence at all.

He clicks a single control:

ACTIVATE WISH.

OPERATING WITHOUT THE BOTTLENECK

Alex no longer thinks about the Linear Seal.

It does not register as a rule to resist or a constraint to overcome. It is simply absent—like scaffolding removed after a structure has learned how to hold its own weight. The work no longer depends on it.

As a result, the assumptions that once governed his working life no longer apply.

Work does not need to arrive in order.

Progress does not wait its turn.

Completion is no longer the gate that determines when thinking may begin.

Those assumptions belonged to an environment where labor was scarce, coordination was expensive, and oversight depended on legibility. Under those conditions, sequential work made sense. It produced artifacts that could be tracked, reviewed, and supervised. Alex did not work that way because it was optimal; he worked that way because it could be seen.

Sequential systems still project responsibility. They generate timelines, checkpoints, and status updates. They offer the reassurance that movement implies control.

Alex has learned what that reassurance costs.

In a serialized environment, delay propagates. One unanswered question slows an entire chain. One missing approval stalls five people downstream. Time itself becomes the scarce input, and effort is redirected toward managing the wait rather than shaping the outcome.

The Dream Stack does not operate within those constraints.

It does not negotiate them.

It does not attempt to optimize them.

It renders them irrelevant.

Alex's work is no longer linear. It is radial. He operates from the center outward, with judgment—not completion—setting the pace. In a parallel environment, nothing waits for permission to begin. The limiting factor is no longer execution, but Alex's ability to recognize what matters and discard what does not.

This is why he opens three windows.

Not to multitask.

Not to signal activity.

But to separate concerns cleanly, so each can unfold without contaminating the others.

He is not composing a single, carefully phrased prompt. He is issuing multiple, bounded instructions—each aligned to a distinct dimension of reality—because the bottleneck has shifted from doing the work to deciding which results deserve attention.

Window One — The Historian

He directs the system to scan coffee brand archives from the 1920s through the 1950s. Not for nostalgia or mood boards, but to extract pattern. Typography choices. Packaging conventions. Material signals that once communicated trust before optimization flattened them. He is isolating the original DNA of old Brooklyn, before it hardened into a costume.

Window Two — The Strategist

He supplies demographic and behavioral data for three target city zones—income bands, foot traffic, commuter rhythms, neighborhood psychology. He asks for friction points: the small, specific irritations that never appear in surveys but quietly determine loyalty. Not averages. Edges.

Window Three — The Motion Lab

He provides the brand's palette and constraints and requests fifty storyboard directions for a thirty-second teaser. Not to choose immediately, but to generate a dense field of variation his judgment can later prune.

Alex is not researching.

He is not designing.

He is not writing copy.

He is orchestrating.

Like a conductor who never touches an instrument, Alex remains still while entire sections move at once. He listens for timing, tension, and coherence. The labor proceeds without draining him. The familiar fatigue—the ache in his wrists, the compression in his spine —never arrives.

The bottleneck does not announce its disappearance.

It simply stops governing him.

What once required weeks of serialized coordination now unfolds simultaneously, constrained only by how quickly Alex can decide what deserves to survive.

He is no longer racing the clock.

He is no longer managing the wait.

Three weeks of labor compress into the quiet interval it takes to toast a bagel—and Alex uses that interval to think.

SPECIALIZATION WITHOUT SOVEREIGNTY

Alex's Dream Stack is not AI in the abstract. It is not a single, unified intelligence waiting to be queried. It functions more like a deliberately fragmented organization—a set of roles rather than a monolith. Each role exists to do one thing well, and to remain deliberately blind to everything else.

This fragmentation is intentional.

In production environments, general intelligence is not an advantage. It introduces ambiguity, inconsistency, and false confidence. Specialization, by contrast, is predictable. Alex does not treat the system like a search engine that somehow intuits his intent. He engages it as a collection of narrowly scoped perspectives that report upward and never exercise final authority.

Each role is useful precisely because it is incomplete. Each has reach—and limits.

One perspective exists to challenge. It approaches every output with suspicion, scanning for sameness, polish without substance, and anything that blends too easily into the background. If an idea could plausibly belong anywhere, it belongs nowhere. This role exists to eliminate false positives before Alex becomes invested.

Another perspective exists to translate. Its concern is not novelty, but resonance. It reads language and asks a single question: does this sound like it came from someone with memory? It strips out the cadence of marketing language, the smoothness machines default to, and the politeness that signals optimization rather than care. If the voice feels bloodless, the work is returned for revision.

A third perspective exists to disrupt. Alex invokes it sparingly. Its function is to violate expectations, ignore the brief, and produce ideas that feel strategically wrong. Not because those ideas will be shipped, but because systems optimized for correctness rarely discover edges. Occasionally, buried inside a failed direction, Alex finds a fragment of originality that could not have been reached through refinement alone.

This tension is not a flaw. It is the point.

No single perspective is trusted. No output is sovereign. Meaning does not emerge from consensus or correctness, but from friction—between critique, translation, and disruption—resolved only through human judgment.

The stack does not replace Alex. It sharpens him.

OPERATING IN PARALLEL

While Freelance Alex is executing at full velocity for Marcus, Corporate Alex is physically present inside the Return to Office arrangement. He is back in the building, back at his desk, participating in a system that still emphasizes attendance and coordination as signals of reliability.

The office itself has not changed. It remains a shared environment designed to make work visible and progress legible at scale. Dashboards update. Meetings occur. Presence is confirmed. These structures are not malicious. They exist to reduce uncertainty in large organizations where trust must be inferred rather than assumed.

Corporate Alex is seated at his desk.

He is fully present in role.

What has changed is not his compliance, but his internal allocation.

Within the boundaries of his responsibilities, Alex completes his assigned work efficiently and ahead of schedule. Status updates are prepared. Reports are drafted. Deliverables are ready when requested. The work meets expectations and serves its purpose.

Because the system is calibrated for rhythm rather than acceleration, Alex does not force completion to appear faster than the environment can absorb. He allows review cycles to occur. Feedback is incorporated. Participation is visible. The process remains intact.

This is not manipulation. It is pacing.

Alex understands that organizations do not optimize for perfection; they optimize for coordination. Review and adjustment are part of that coordination. Once those loops are satisfied, attention moves on.

Within that stable cadence, Alex allocates his remaining capacity deliberately. While meetings proceed and workflows advance, his independent systems continue operating in parallel—quietly, without disruption, and without interfering with his obligations.

He listens. He contributes when appropriate. He remains unremarkable by design. No resistance. No spectacle.

This is not an act of opposition. It is coexistence. Alex fulfills the role he has agreed to play while retaining authority over how his unused attention is invested.

The organization provides structure, infrastructure, and compensation. Alex provides reliable output in return. What remains his—and always has—is intent.

Ownership of intent determines direction. And direction determines who has options when conditions change.

THE HIGH-RESOLUTION HANDSHAKE

By 8:30 PM, the digital work is finished.

The Dream Stack has completed its role quietly and without ceremony. The monitors in the Cockpit dim, no longer requesting direction. At this point, Alex's roles separate cleanly. Corporate obligations are complete for the day. What remains belongs to Freelance Alex alone.

In the old model, this would have been the terminal moment—the point where a folder was zipped, attached, and sent downstream, followed by a stretch of low-grade uncertainty. The work would dissolve into an inbox, stripped of context, reduced to files waiting for interpretation. Delivery ended at transmission.

That model no longer applies.

The Context Architect understands something that resists

optimization: the Last Mile is where meaning is either preserved or lost. Systems can move information efficiently. They cannot complete trust. If the Exosuit exists to execute, the Handshake exists to confirm authorship. One handles throughput. The other establishes presence.

Alex does not click Send.

He stands, stretches, and crosses the room to the corner of the apartment reserved for physical output. These tools are not about speed or scale. They exist for a different reason entirely. A compact 3D printer hums beside a high-end inkjet plotter. Their purpose is not acceleration, but translation—moving work from the digital plane into the human one.

Tonight, Alex is not delivering files.

He is manufacturing evidence.

He loads heavy stock paper into the plotter, registering its resistance as it feeds through the rollers. Material choice matters here. Paper with tooth. Ink that carries weight and leaves a faint trace in the air. The machine moves slowly, deliberately. This pace is intentional. It signals care.

This is the High-Resolution Handshake.

In an environment where everything arrives instantly, weight becomes rare. Texture becomes communicative. Time re-enters the equation—not as delay, but as proof that a decision was made by someone who could have chosen otherwise. No system can feel the difference between glossy and matte, between disposable and deliberate. A human hand can. Instantly.

Alex lifts the finished pieces and stacks them with attention. Minor imperfections remain—microscopic deviations that record choice rather than error. Evidence that the work passed through judgment instead of being smoothed flat by automation.

These gestures are not nostalgic. They are strategic.

The Handshake ensures that when the work arrives, it does not merely register. It lands. It carries authorship. It transfers trust. And in that final exchange, Alex completes the loop—not as an employee, not as a technician, but as a Context Architect.

THE MIDNIGHT MEETING AT THE BAKERY

At 9:30 PM, Alex walks through the quieter streets of Brooklyn toward the bakery. The city has shifted into its off-hours rhythm—delivery trucks idling, streetlights humming faintly, storefronts dark except for the few that never close. He feels light, but not rested. This isn't the relief of stopping work; it's the clarity that comes from having allocated the day correctly.

He doesn't feel like someone who has worked twelve hours. He feels like someone who spent the day placing decisions where they mattered—stacking judgment instead of minutes.

Marcus is already inside when Alex arrives. The ovens are warming, pushing heat into the tiled room and filling the air with the dense, grounding smell of yeast and sugar. Flour dust coats the prep tables. Marcus looks tired in a way Alex recognizes immediately. This is physical fatigue—the visible cost of production that can't be abstracted away.

"I saw the files you sent earlier," Marcus says, leaning against the counter. "They looked great on my phone. But honestly..." He pauses. "I'm worried it still feels too digital."

Alex doesn't respond with explanation. He doesn't justify the process or defend the work. He doesn't argue about resolution, brand language, or strategy.

He says nothing.

Instead, he sets the cardboard tube on the heavy wooden prep table and opens it carefully. He rolls out the posters one by one. The paper lands with a muted thud, absorbing the overhead light rather than reflecting it. The ink settles unevenly into the fibers. Nothing shines. Nothing asks to be noticed.

Marcus stops moving.

He reaches out without asking and runs his fingers along the edge of the type, feeling the slight resistance where the ink thickened. He lifts a sheet and registers its weight—not heavy enough to impress, but heavy enough to signal intention. Alex then places one of the 3D-printed tokens into his palm. It's cool. Solid. Unambiguous.

Marcus exhales slowly, as if he hadn't realized he was holding his breath.

"Oh," he says. "This is different." He turns the piece in his hands, feeling it rather than inspecting it. "This feels like it came from somewhere."

Alex nods. No explanation is necessary. The Handshake has already done its work.

THE HANDSHAKE DIVIDEND

This is the High-Resolution Handshake converting into value in real time.

In a matter of minutes, Alex establishes something that cannot be captured in dashboards or projected by metrics: durable trust and shared orientation. Nothing here depends on prediction. It is confirmed through contact. This is what proof looks like when it lands outside a spreadsheet.

Alex does not rush to close. He does not pitch. He explains the context—calmly and precisely. He names the decisions Marcus can already feel but has not yet articulated: the deliberate imperfections, the refusal to over-polish, the choices that keep the brand grounded rather than abstracted. Each decision is framed as protection of meaning, not decorative flourish.

"I'm not just delivering a logo," Alex says. "I'm helping you preserve what makes this recognizable when the category fills up. Others will replicate the surface quickly. What matters is that this still reads as yours."

He says it without urgency. Not as a warning. As an observation.

Marcus studies the materials again, then looks up. He smiles—the kind of expression that appears when uncertainty resolves into direction.

"What do I owe you for this?" he asks. "We talked about a junior rate, but this feels like more than that."

Alex considers for a moment. Then he shakes his head—not to deflect value, but to sequence it.

"We'll keep the rate for now," he says. "Once this work proves itself in the real world—once it moves beyond presentation and starts shaping outcomes—then we revisit the fee."

This is not underpricing. It is alignment. Alex is anchoring value to consequence rather than effort, allowing trust to compound before assigning a long-term price.

The Handshake is complete. The return is not merely financial. A transaction has matured into a partnership, and with it, a shared stake in what comes next.

THE RETURN TO THE LAB

Alex walks home beneath a starless Brooklyn sky. The city has dropped into its lowest register—subways muttering underground, traffic lights cycling for no one in particular. The Saturday Morning Feeling settles into his chest, not as excitement, but as alignment. The quiet confidence that comes from running the right system long enough to trust it.

He recognizes—without ceremony—that he has executed a clean arbitrage on his own life.

He used institutional time as stable capital for learning.

He used machine labor to absorb repetition and syntax.

He used his own judgment to supply meaning, taste, and consequence.

Nothing was stolen. Nothing was rushed. Each system performed the function it was designed for.

This does not mean that everyone should follow Alex's path.

Not every Corporate Alex becomes a Freelance Alex. Not everyone should. Not everyone can. That was never the claim. The Human Moat is not a career pivot or an exit strategy. It is not an argument for entrepreneurship, freelancing, or self-employment. Those are implementation details, not outcomes.

The distinction that matters is not where Alex works, but how he allocates responsibility. The shift is internal before it is external. Long before he leaves anything behind, Alex stops confusing exertion with value and visibility with authority. He becomes the Pilot while still inside the system.

This is why the Return to Office no longer registers as a threat. It has been demoted to a background condition—like weather. As long as Alex remains responsible for direction rather than exertion, the machine is simply wind: powerful, neutral, and useless without navigation.

He unlocks the door to his apartment. The Cockpit is dark now, monitors asleep, cables quiet. Nothing is calling for attention. No backlog hums with accusation. The system has closed its loops for the day.

Exit Velocity does not announce itself. It doesn't arrive with drama or applause. It feels anticlimactic—like crossing a border without noticing the sign.

Alex lies down on his bed. He doesn't set an alarm. He doesn't scan tomorrow's calendar. He doesn't rehearse obligations that haven't arrived.

He is no longer a "9:15 AM Criminal," measuring his worth by compliance and endurance. He is a Context Architect—someone who understands the systems he operates inside and knows where judgment must remain human.

Tomorrow doesn't need permission.

Tomorrow is simply another Saturday morning.

11

THE HUMAN MOAT

The Lie: If everyone has access to powerful AI tools, advantage disappears.

The Truth: When production becomes universal, defensibility shifts from execution to judgment, taste, and consequence. The moat is not what you can generate—it is what you can reliably select, stand behind, and be held accountable for.

THE TSUNAMI OF SLOP

The rain in Brooklyn has finally stopped, leaving the streets with that brief, deceptive cleanliness that only lasts an hour before the city quietly reasserts itself. Air moves through Alex's open window carrying the sharp scent of wet pavement and ozone. Outside, the city resets. Inside—on the clean geometry of his apartment, reflected across the glowing glass of his three-monitor Cockpit—a different kind of pressure is building.

Alex has a name for it.

The Beige Tsunami.

It is 9:00 AM on a Wednesday. In the old world—the world of The Fast Food Trap—this hour belonged to visible effort. The inbox filled. Applications opened. Hands moved. Progress could be measured by exhaustion. Time felt expensive because it moved slowly.

Today, Alex isn't working. He isn't producing. He's watching.

On his left monitor, a curated stream of award-winning design galleries scrolls with flawless restraint. On his right, a real-time feed of new brand launches from London to Tokyo refreshes without pause. Six months ago, this view would have felt expansive—a map of possibility, a reminder of how many directions remained unexplored.

Now it reads differently.

The work is competent. Polished. Technically impeccable.

Nothing is broken. Nothing is amateur. Everything sits comfortably within the bounds of what professionals agree is "good." And that is precisely the problem.

Alex is not reacting with panic. He isn't afraid. What he feels instead is recognition. Compression.

The floor is rising.

When tools make execution cheap and abundant, average does not disappear—it multiplies. Quality becomes statistically normal. Craft becomes table stakes. Entire categories converge toward a narrow band of visual and conceptual acceptability, not because people lack taste, but because optimization smooths variance faster than judgment can intervene.

This is not a failure of creativity. It is the predictable outcome of scale.

The tsunami Alex is watching is not made of bad work. It is made of *adequate* work—work that clears every professional threshold while leaving no trace of authorship. Nothing stands out because nothing is wrong.

And yet, as the feeds continue to refresh, Alex feels the hollow opening in his chest that signals a deeper truth. In a world where competent output becomes infinite, meaning does not disappear—but it must be actively preserved.

"It's happening," he says quietly, not as a warning, but as a diagnosis.

"The floor is rising. And everyone is standing on it."

This is the moment the Human Moat becomes visible—not as a defense against machines, but as a response to abundance. Not as protection from failure, but as a commitment to preserve difference when sameness becomes effortless.

THE REALLOCATION OF THE MIDDLE

To understand the Beige Tsunami, it helps to understand the older hierarchy it quietly dissolves. For much of the last half-century, creative work organized itself into a pyramid—not by design, but by constraint. Training took time. Tools were expensive. Taste was scarce. Those conditions sorted roles naturally.

At the base of the pyramid was work defined by reliability. Routine collateral. Functional presentations. Serviceable logos. This work was not inferior; it was dependable. Its value came from accuracy, consistency, and the ability to execute instructions without error. People built honest careers here by selling time, attention, and steadiness.

In the middle lived professional craft. Agencies and studios that translated briefs into polished outcomes. Process mattered. Revisions were controlled. Clients felt safe. The work rarely surprised, but it delivered predictability—and predictability paid for lives, families, and futures.

At the top were those whose primary contribution was judgment. They were not distinguished by speed or output, but by selection. They reframed problems rather than fulfilling them. They made choices that initially felt uncomfortable and then taught the market how to see through those choices—figures like **Rick Rubin**, whose influence came from deciding what *not* to add.

None of this collapsed because people lost skill. It shifted because the environment changed.

With syntactic fluency now abundant, the base of the pyramid no longer functions as a market. What once required training and time can be produced instantly, continuously, and at negligible cost. The middle compresses as well—not because it lacks quality, but because its primary value proposition was reliability, and reliability has become ambient.

Average work does not disappear. It becomes the background. Price collapses first. Status follows.

Alex clicks through a newly launched start-up identity. It is clean. Balanced. Impeccably spaced. Nothing is wrong with it. A few years ago, it would have signaled professionalism and justified a substantial fee.

Alex studies it without judgment.

"I recognize this," he says quietly. "Not the brand—the method."

The mark wasn't argued over or lived with. It wasn't shaped through consequence. It was generated within a narrow band of acceptable outcomes, averaged across thousands of successful precedents and returned as the safest possible answer. The result is not failure. It is convergence.

This is the Beige Standard.

Optimized for approval.

Engineered to survive committees.

Designed to offend no one—and therefore to belong nowhere in particular.

The point is not that such work lacks competence. It is that competence alone no longer differentiates. When adequacy becomes infinite, meaning must be actively protected.

This is not the end of creative work. It is the end of a particular bargain—where showing up reliably was enough. What remains, and what grows more valuable, is the ability to decide: what deserves to exist, what should be excluded, and why that choice matters.

THE POLITENESS ENGINE

Alex opens a window to the system he works with every day. Not to debate it, and not to interrogate it philosophically, but to observe its behavior under pressure. He wants to understand the physics of the Beige Tsunami where it actually forms.

"Design a poster for an underground punk show in 1970s London," he types. "Make it dangerous. Make it feel like a riot."

The response arrives almost instantly.

The image contains all the expected signals. Torn paper. Safety pins. High-contrast black and white. A mohawked figure frozen in practiced defiance. Every visual cue is present. Every reference is correct.

Alex studies it for a moment and exhales.

"It's too clean."

The torn edges are symmetrical. The chaos is balanced. The aggression has been centered and framed. The figure looks like someone hired to perform grit rather than someone who risked something to earn it. The system has reproduced the surface of punk without touching the conditions that made it matter.

This is not a mistake. It is the result of optimization.

The system is not built to offend, destabilize, or risk rejection. It is built to produce outputs that large numbers of people will agree are acceptable. Over time, that incentive produces a particular kind of intelligence—not malicious, not broken, but polite.

Politeness smooths edges.

It resolves tension.

It removes anything that might divide opinion.

When preference is aggregated at scale, consensus wins. The safest answer rises. The strange answer disappears. What remains is work that offends no one and surprises no one.

This is why AI struggles with "weird." Not because weirdness is mysterious, but because it is costly. Weirdness requires someone to absorb disagreement, rejection, and consequence. Systems optimized for agreement cannot do that by definition.

In art, culture, and competitive markets, those outliers are not defects. They are how change enters the system. They are how taste moves. They are how meaning survives compression.

Alex leans back from the screen.

"The tsunami isn't made of bad work," he says quietly. "It's made of correct work."

And correctness—when it becomes infinite—is not neutral. It creates a world where difference must be actively protected, or it disappears by default.

THE ENTROPY OF THE FEED

Alex turns back to the scrolling feed. Now that he's attuned to it, the pattern is impossible to miss. There is a shared texture to everything he sees—a smoothness that feels intentional, even generous. Nothing pushes back. Nothing resists interpretation. Every headline resolves neatly. Every illustration carries the same faint, plastic calm, as if friction itself has been designed out of the experience.

This is the Beige Tsunami's true advantage: cognitive ease.

Average work is effortless to consume. It asks nothing of the reader's judgment. It doesn't interrupt momentum or demand attention. It glides past, pleasant enough in the moment and immediately replaceable by whatever comes next. And because this kind of output is now trivial to produce, its volume compounds. The feed fills. Contrast erodes.

Over time, this produces entropy. Not chaos, but sameness. The feed becomes a low-res blur where nothing is wrong, and nothing remains.

Alex thinks about Marcus at The Bitter Bean. Marcus isn't under attack. No one is trying to erase him. He's being approached—constantly—by firms offering to "optimize" his brand. The language sounds helpful. Responsible. But Alex knows what optimization means in practice.

It means smoothing edges.

It means reducing variance.

It means trading specificity for acceptability.

An optimized brand doesn't fail dramatically. It fades. It acquires a logo that could belong to any neighborhood, a social feed indistinguishable from stock photography, a presence that feels familiar rather than particular. Customers don't reject it. They simply stop noticing it.

This is how the Beige Tsunami works. It does not crush difference. It covers it.

The danger is not that people choose the wrong thing. It is that they stop choosing at all. When everything is easy to consume, judgment goes unused—and unused judgment atrophies.

This is the environment the Human Moat is built for. Not to fight the feed, but to interrupt it. Not by being louder, but by being *felt*. In a system optimized for smoothness, even small, intentional friction becomes a signal. It slows the scroll. It asks for attention. It reminds the human on the other side that a choice is being made.

THE REALIZATION: THE MOAT IS THE FRICTION

Alex stands and steps away from the Cockpit. There's a faint buzzing in his fingers—the afterimage of speed. For months, he has been using the Exosuit to move faster, measuring progress by how quickly work vanished from the queue. He took pride in that compression. In the ability to collapse a full day's output into ten quiet minutes.

And then the inversion lands.

Speed is not the moat.

When speed becomes free, it stops functioning as a signal. When "perfect" is effortless, perfection becomes the entry requirement rather than the differentiator. What once justified attention now merely qualifies participation.

Alex turns to a sketch pinned near his desk—something he drew years earlier. A charcoal rendering of a tree. The lines are uneven. Thumbprints darken the corners where his hands were smudged. The drawing carries fatigue, hesitation, and adjustment. It is technically inefficient. It is also unmistakably human.

"This is it," he says quietly. "This is the high ground."

The machine cannot have a dirty hand. It cannot risk a line that fails. It cannot carry consequence forward. It can simulate irregularity, but it cannot own it. It produces output without attachment and moves on without cost.

Alex understands now that the Human Moat is not built from fluency with tools. It is built from the willingness to place friction where it matters—to slow down intentionally, to make choices that cannot be optimized away, and to accept the consequences of those choices.

This is what his Spiky POV actually represents. Not provocation for its own sake, but commitment. A clear stance that says, "This matters to me, and I am willing to exclude in order to preserve it."

That stance is polarizing by nature. It narrows the audience. It introduces resistance. And that resistance is not a flaw—it is the signal. The machine cannot take this position. It is engineered to reconcile disagreement, to smooth edges, and to accommodate as many preferences as possible simultaneously.

Alex thinks back to years of training and advice—be professional, be polished, be safe. He sees the pattern clearly now.

"Professional," he realizes, "has come to mean frictionless."

And frictionless, in a world of infinite output, is another word for invisible.

The Human Moat is built by choosing where to resist—by preserving specificity when everything else accelerates toward sameness. That resistance is not nostalgia. It is responsibility. And it is where human value concentrates when speed no longer does.

The moat is not built in crisis.
It is built in the quiet hour after.

THE DEFINITION OF THE MOAT

Alex picks up a marker and walks to the whiteboard mounted in his Lab. He writes slowly, deliberately, in large uneven letters:

THE HUMAN MOAT

The sound of the marker against the board is final in a way software never is.

Beneath the heading, he draws a line. Then another. He is not brainstorming. He is defining.

There are three forms of leverage the Tsunami cannot reach—three capacities that do not scale, do not average, and do not disappear under pressure.

Taste — The Curator's Eye

Taste is not preference. It is judgment.

It is the ability to look at a thousand flawless options and recognize which one carries intent, history, and consequence. Taste is contextual memory applied under constraint. It improves with responsibility. It cannot be crowdsourced, and it cannot be automated without losing what makes it matter.

In the coffee shop, Taste is what Elena is quietly confronting.

The machine can generate ten versions of a sales email in seconds. Five of them are perfectly acceptable. But Elena knows—without being able to fully explain why—that only one of them actually *sounds like someone who meant it*. Only one carries rhythm, restraint, and an understanding of when not to persuade. That recognition doesn't come from prompts. It comes from ten years of reading, writing, failing, and revising with consequence.

Taste is what allows Elena to say, "*These are fine—but this one is true.*"

Mark experiences Taste differently.

The AI can summarize five hundred pages of case law instantly. But Mark knows that summaries don't carry risk the way sentences do. He knows which clause will trigger a dispute, which phrase will collapse under cross-examination, which detail feels small but isn't. That recognition is not speed. It is judgment formed by exposure to what actually breaks.

Taste is the ability to recognize *what matters* when everything is correct.

Friction — The Human Hand

Friction is not inefficiency. It is evidence.

It is the small resistances that signal a human was present and accountable—intentional pauses, second looks, decisions that leave a trace. Friction reintroduces consequence into systems optimized to erase it. It is how meaning survives when speed becomes free.

Jen understands friction instinctively, even if she's never named it.

The system can transcribe a meeting, assign tasks, and populate a calendar automatically. What it cannot do is notice when an assignment will quietly overload one person, or when a deadline looks reasonable on paper but impossible given the team's actual energy. Jen's value was never the notes. It was the judgment she applied *between* them.

Friction is the moment she slows the plan down just enough to prevent a failure no dashboard would predict.

For Mark, friction is rereading the same paragraph twice—not because he missed it, but because something about it feels unstable.

For Elena, friction is deleting a sentence that technically works but sounds like it's trying too hard.

Friction is where responsibility enters the workflow.

Spiky POV — The Architect's Will

Spiky POV is not provocation. It is commitment.

It is the willingness to make a choice that excludes more people than it includes, to risk being misunderstood, and to stand behind that decision over time. It is where authorship becomes visible.

This is the hardest moat to build—and the most durable.

Elena will eventually have to decide what kind of writer she is willing to be. Not faster. Not cheaper. But specific. She will choose a voice that some clients won't want—and accept that as the cost of being legible to the ones who do.

Mark will have to decide whether he remains a reader of documents or becomes an interpreter of risk—someone whose job is not to process text, but to advise judgment.

Jen will have to decide whether she remains a coordinator of tasks or becomes an owner of outcomes—someone who is willing to say no to "best practices" when they quietly degrade trust or burn out her team.

Spiky POV is not personality. It is governance.

The machine cannot hold this position—not because it lacks intelligence, but because it cannot accept the cost of being wrong. It cannot carry blame forward. It cannot stand behind a decision when the data changes.

Humans can.

That is the moat.

. . .

Alex steps back from the board and looks at the screens behind him. The unease he felt in the coffee shop—that collective recognition that *the skill I sold is now abundant*—has resolved into something steadier. Not confidence. Orientation.

The machine did not arrive to replace Elena, Mark, or Jen.

It arrived to drain value from the Average—to raise the baseline until execution alone no longer registers. What remains visible, once the floor rises, are deliberate choices made by people willing to own them.

"Let it rise," Alex says quietly.

He turns toward the Cockpit, but not to engage it. Optimization can wait.

Instead, he leaves the apartment and steps back into the city. He wants texture. Incompleteness. The kinds of signals that only appear when real people make real decisions under constraint.

The Tsunami is still coming.

But the Context Architect is not trying to outrun it.

He is building a lighthouse—not to stop the wave, but to give shape, orientation, and meaning to what survives it.

THE PRESENCE ARBITRAGE

Across town, the rain has left the sidewalks warm and heavy, but inside the global firm's headquarters the temperature is a carefully maintained sixty-eight degrees. The air is filtered. The lighting is even. The environment is optimized for consistency.

Corporate Alex is complying with the Return to Office mandate—not resisting it, not resenting it, simply operating within it. RTO is not designed to maximize creativity or insight. It is designed to solve a different problem: coordination. It allows managers to see activity, confirm availability, and reduce uncertainty. Presence, in this system, is a proxy for assurance.

Alex is seated in what the company calls a "collaborative pod"—a shared table, minimal privacy, reliable connectivity. From an organizational perspective, it works. Everyone is visible. Everyone is reachable.

Susan is walking the floor. Her role requires it. She is not auditing ideas or outcomes; she is confirming presence. Screens are open. Status indicators glow green. The system is functioning as intended.

Corporate Alex is not violating any rule. He is delivering exactly what the system has asked for. On his company-issued laptop, a slide deck is being finalized—on brand, on schedule, and aligned with expectations. The machine handles the syntax cleanly and quietly.

What has changed is not Alex's compliance. It is his allocation.

In the past, Alex would have spent the afternoon manually adjusting margins and bullet points, equating visible effort with contribution. Today, that labor is absorbed elsewhere. The deliverable is produced without draining his attention.

What remains is capacity.

Alex redirects that capacity toward something the system does not—and cannot—automate: relationships. He uses the recovered time to clarify client priorities, surface hidden constraints, deepen trust with collaborators, and think ahead about how people—not outputs—will interact over time.

This is the Presence Arbitrage.

The organization purchases presence and receives reliable execution in return. Alex supplies both. What he retains, by design, is authority over how his remaining attention is invested. He is not extracting value from the firm; he is honoring the agreement precisely—and then applying his judgment where it still matters.

Relationship Architecture is not visible on a dashboard. It does not announce itself. But it compounds. And in a world where execution is abundant, those quiet, durable relationships become the most reliable form of leverage left.

THE DEATH OF THE "RESOURCE"

Alex looks around the floor. His coworkers are focused, diligent, and tired in a way he recognizes. Fingers move quickly across keyboards. Screens fill with drafts, revisions, and updates. Everyone is trying to stay useful.

Many of them believe—reasonably—that necessity is proven through effort. If they respond faster, stay later, and produce more visible output, they will justify their place. This logic made sense in a world where execution was scarce. It is less effective now.

Alex doesn't see this with contempt. He sees it with clarity. Competing on speed against a system built for speed is not a moral failure—it is a category error.

The organization refers to its workforce as "resources." The term is not malicious. It is functional. Resources are inputs that can be allocated, optimized, and substituted. When value is defined primarily by efficiency, interchangeability is not an insult—it is an outcome.

By leaning harder into productivity metrics alone, well-meaning professionals unintentionally reinforce that classification. They make themselves easier to price, easier to compare, and easier to replace—not because they lack skill, but because the system no longer distinguishes effort from value.

The Return to Office mandate exists within this tension. It is not a deception, and it is not nostalgia. It is an attempt to keep value legible in an environment where digital output has become abundant and difficult to differentiate. Presence provides reassurance. It reduces uncertainty. From an institutional perspective, it is a rational response.

Alex has no interest in attacking that logic. He understands it.

What he understands even more clearly is its limit. Presence alone does not change how value is categorized. Effort alone does not reprice a role.

The shift required is not rebellion. It is reclassification.

To stop being priced as a resource, Alex does not need to work harder or disappear into secrecy. He needs to move into a role the system cannot flatten—one defined by judgment, accountability, and trust rather than throughput.

This is what the Human Moat enables.

It shifts value from the digital plane, where speed dominates, to the relational plane, where meaning, consequence, and responsibility accumulate. Not everyone will—or should—make this shift. But for those who do, the category itself changes.

A resource is optimized.

A moat is relied upon.

THE BREAKROOM WISDOM: FINDING THE FRICTION

Corporate Alex stands and stretches. He leaves his workstation active and walks toward the breakroom without urgency. Nothing is being hidden. Nothing is being avoided. The work assigned to him is already underway, progressing as expected.

Julian, the VP of Operations, is standing by the industrial espresso machine when Alex arrives. His jacket is off. His tie hangs loose. The posture of "Senior Leader" has softened into something more human—someone managing too many variables with too little resolution.

"The board is breathing down my neck," Julian says, watching the coffee pour. "AI gave us ten growth strategies for the Midwest expansion. They're all defensible. They all make sense. And they all feel like they were written by someone who's never set foot in a warehouse."

Alex doesn't rush to answer. He recognizes the moment for what it is. Julian is not asking for more output. He has plenty of that. He is asking for orientation—for something that explains why the answers feel complete and still wrong.

"That's because the data doesn't have a smell," Alex says, evenly.

Julian glances at him, curious rather than defensive.

Alex leans against the counter. He doesn't talk about decks or frameworks. He talks about people. About forklift drivers. About a conversation he had the night before with Sal, the night-shift lead. He describes the loading dock when it rains—the way the floor tiles get slick, forcing a brief hesitation before each pallet is moved. Three seconds at a time.

"Those three seconds don't show up anywhere," Alex says. "They don't make it into the reports. Sal just adjusts and keeps going. But they compound. Across shifts, across weeks. They're costing us real money—and no one can see it from the dashboard."

Julian finally looks up. Not because Alex is dramatic, but because the picture has sharpened. He isn't seeing a designer or a manager. He's seeing someone who can surface risk before it escalates—someone who can translate lived reality into operational consequence.

This is the Handshake Protocol at work.

High-resolution context does not live in spreadsheets. It lives in conversations, in observation, in places where friction accumulates quietly until someone notices it. The machine is excellent at mapping the territory once it is defined. But it cannot decide *which* parts of the terrain matter.

"How did you know about the floor tiles?" Julian asks.

Alex shrugs. "I went there. I listened. I let Sal complain for a while. You can't prompt that kind of signal. You have to encounter it."

Julian nods slowly. The espresso machine clicks off behind them. The conversation doesn't end with an action item or a slide request. It ends with alignment—something rarer, and more valuable, than either.

THE PARTNER, NOT THE VENDOR

Corporate Alex understands now that the office is no longer optimized for doing. Doing—execution, formatting, throughput—has become abundant. If Julian needed a faster slide deck, he could acquire one instantly and inexpensively. Speed is not scarce.

What Julian is actually seeking is insulation. He wants confidence that the decisions he signs his name to will hold when they meet reality—that no critical detail has been smoothed away by optimization.

By becoming the person who understands the *why* behind the *what*, and who can surface consequences before they arrive as surprises, Alex has shifted his position in the internal economy. Not upward. Sideways.

He is no longer operating as a vendor. Vendors are evaluated on price, speed, and interchangeability. Their value is legible, comparable, and easily re-sourced.

Alex is operating as a partner. Partners are evaluated on context, judgment, and accountability—qualities that resist benchmarking. Their value is not that they produce more, but that they prevent errors others don't see yet.

As Alex walks back toward his desk, he passes Susan. She is focused on her tablet, reviewing a productivity heatmap—a tool designed to translate presence into reassurance. It is doing exactly what it was built to do. Alex's status indicator glows green. His chair, briefly, was empty.

"Alex," she says evenly. "We talked about maintaining collaborative presence during RTO hours. Where were you?"

In the past, Alex would have apologized and attempted to resolve the question inside the metric. Today, he doesn't contest the frame—and he doesn't submit to it either.

"I was in the breakroom with Julian," he says. "We were discussing operational friction in the Midwest facilities. He asked me to lead a human-in-the-loop audit before the expansion."

Susan pauses. Not because she disagrees, but because the information doesn't map cleanly to the dashboard. Julian's trust does not appear as a widget. Context does not render as a heatmap.

She nods once and moves on.

Nothing dramatic has happened. No rule was broken. No authority was challenged.

But something has shifted.

Alex is no longer evaluated solely by what he produces on screen.

He is evaluated by the consequences he helps others avoid. That change is quiet, durable, and difficult to reverse.

THE REALIZATION: THE GHOST IN THE OFFICE

Alex settles back into his seat. The hum of the lights fades into the background, no longer registering as pressure. What has changed is not the environment, but his relationship to it.

He understands now that what he's practicing is a form of wisdom arbitrage. Not exploitation. Not secrecy. Simply attention applied where it still compounds. He is using the time the organization already requires of him to build relationships, context, and understanding—forms of value that cannot be automated, standardized, or transferred without loss.

Mandatory presence becomes an opportunity to listen.

Conversations become orientation.

Context accumulates quietly.

Each interaction adds weight—not to a résumé, but to judgment.

He glances at the corporate deck his system has completed. It meets every expectation. It will move through the process smoothly. It is neither exceptional nor deficient—and that is exactly the point. The deliverable does its job without demanding attention.

Alex schedules it to send near the end of the day, allowing space for review and adjustment. The system remains intact. No one is misled. No one is undermined.

The Industrial Pact—the trade between labor and stability—is not inherently a trap. It becomes limiting only when judgment is surrendered along with effort. Alex has learned to separate the two.

For some roles, the office is simply a place to execute. For others, it becomes a place to observe, learn, and develop perspective. Not everyone needs—or wants—to make that shift.

Alex isn't rebelling against the institution. He's inhabiting it differently. He remains visible, reliable, and aligned with expectations. What changes is where he invests his remaining attention.

He is no longer anxious about being seen. He is no longer measuring his worth in hours or outputs. He understands the system well enough to operate inside it without being absorbed by it.

He is not invisible.

He is simply no longer priced by speed alone.

The sky was never the limit. Context was.

And Alex is learning—steadily, deliberately—how to read it.

THE WABI-SABI DEFENSE

Alex stands in the center of his apartment, but his attention is no longer on the three 4K monitors lining the far wall. The Cockpit is still alive behind him, humming softly, fans cycling as the Exosuit processes background market data. Nothing has been shut down. Nothing has been rejected.

The speed is still there.

The leverage is still there.

It simply isn't in control.

Alex has stepped out of the armor.

On the kitchen table sits a small wooden crate made of unfinished pine. The wood is pale and rough, its edges imperfect, the grain uneven and unapologetic. It carries the faint smell of sawdust and cold air, the scent of something that was recently cut and assembled by human hands. Inside the crate are twelve glass bottles of cold-brew coffee—the first physical production run for The Bitter Bean.

They are not mockups.

They are not renders.

They are not provisional.

They exist in gravity.

Alex lifts one of the bottles and feels the weight register immediately. Not symbolically—physically. The glass is cool in his palm. Condensation beads along the surface, forming without asking permission. The label isn't perfectly aligned. The ink density varies slightly from bottle to bottle. These are not defects. They are facts.

There is no "Undo" here.

No version history.

No rollback.

If something is wrong, it will remain wrong.

If something is right, it will endure.

In the world of the Fast Food Trap, Alex's work used to end the moment he hit Send. His responsibility dissolved as soon as the file left his machine. The work moved through inboxes and systems untouched by him, abstracted into light and metadata. He never held it. Never smelled it. Never lived with it.

That distance was efficient.

It was also anesthetic.

Distance reduces consequence.

When nothing you produce has mass, nothing you decide has weight. The work evaporates the moment it's consumed, and so does your leverage. You can revise endlessly because nothing resists you. You can optimize forever because nothing pushes back. You can be wrong without cost.

The Context Architect understands the boundary the system cannot cross.

Machines are extraordinary at assembling representations of the world. They can arrange symbols, layouts, hierarchies, and language with astonishing fluency. They know the map perfectly. But they cannot *enter* the territory the map describes.

They do not feel weight before a decision.

They do not sense risk accumulating in materials.

They do not live with outcomes once something ships.

They never stand in a room with an object they helped create and wonder whether it will survive contact with reality.

To finalize his work—to turn leverage into durability—Alex doesn't need more output. He needs exposure to consequence. He needs decisions that cannot be revised away. He needs to feel the quiet pressure that only arrives when something exists outside the screen and insists on being reckoned with.

This is what *wabi-sabi* means here.

Not imperfection as aesthetic.

Not nostalgia for handmade things.

But imperfection as evidence.

Evidence that a choice was made once, under real conditions, by someone who had to live with it afterward. Evidence that responsibility did not end when the file was delivered.

If the Beige Tsunami is endless, frictionless, and interchangeable —then the Human Moat is elevation. Not resistance to the water, but terrain it cannot flatten. Ground that holds because it is not abstract.

That ground is built from things that refuse to disappear:

Weight.

Texture.

Irreversibility.

From glass that breaks if mishandled.

From ink that stains instead of glowing.

From objects that force accountability simply by remaining in the world.

The Exosuit accelerates the work.

It multiplies possibility.

It removes clerical drag.

But the Moat begins at the moment the work can no longer be undone—when the decision leaves the screen, enters the world, and asks to be owned.

That is the defense.

Not speed.

Not cleverness.

But the willingness to stand behind something real and let it push back.

THE POINT OF CONSEQUENCE

Alex reaches into the crate and lifts one of the bottles.

The glass is cold, pulled straight from the refrigerator, and beaded with tiny jewels of condensation that immediately dampen his palm. The bottle has weight—not metaphorical weight, but physical resistance. It cannot be dismissed at a glance. It announces itself before he ever reads the label.

This object will not cooperate with speed.

Earlier that morning, his Dream Stack had suggested a different path. He had asked the system to optimize the packaging for *maximum efficiency and durability*, the same way every brand does when it reaches this stage. The question was framed cleanly. The constraints were clear. The machine responded instantly.

The Design Agent recommended a glossy, plastic-coated, self-adhesive label engineered for uniformity at scale.

The reasoning was impeccable.

Pure syntax.

Clean logic.

No wasted motion.

Plastic performs 14% better in refrigerated environments.

Glossy finishes generate a 22% higher shelf-attention score under low-light retail conditions.

The adhesive tolerates moisture variance without degradation.

Total manufacturing cost: $0.12 per unit.

Variance minimized.

Recommendation: **Approve for scale.**

If Alex were still operating under the Fast Food Trap—if he were still the version of himself from Chapter 1—he would have clicked Approve without hesitation.

He would have followed the data because the data was correct.

He would have accepted the optimization because it reduced risk, lowered cost, and aligned perfectly with every modern brand playbook.

He would have told himself that judgment had been exercised because the spreadsheet resolved the question.

That version of Alex confused correctness with responsibility.

This Alex did not.

He rejected the recommendation—not impulsively, not sentimentally, and not in opposition to the machine. He rejected it deliberately, with full awareness of what he was giving up.

He chose a heavy, recycled paper stock with a subtle tooth—a surface that introduces friction the moment a human hand makes contact. The paper absorbs a trace of moisture as the bottle sweats, darkening slightly, changing character as time passes. It does not fight reality. It records it.

He chose an expensive matte-ink process with a faint, earthy smell—the kind that lingers just long enough to register before fading. It costs more. It wears faster. It refuses to look identical on every bottle.

The machine was not wrong.

But it was blind to the cost that mattered.

Alex understands now that every optimization removes something, whether the spreadsheet tracks it or not. Efficiency always extracts payment. The only question is *who pays* and *when*.

This decision introduces consequence back into the system.

When a human walks into The Bitter Bean and pays eight dollars for a cold brew, they are not buying caffeine. Caffeine is abundant. They are buying reassurance. They are buying a pause inside a crowded day. They are buying the feeling that someone stood behind this object long enough to care how it would be held.

They are buying a Saturday-morning feeling smuggled into a Wednesday afternoon.

The label does not shout.

It does not demand attention.

It asks to be noticed slowly.

As the bottle warms, the paper changes. As the drink disappears, the label carries the memory of contact—fingerprints faintly visible, moisture absorbed, time acknowledged. The object does not remain pristine. It becomes personal.

This is the point of consequence.

The moment where a decision leaves the abstract plane and enters the world.

Where optimization gives way to ownership.

Where a human choice accepts the cost of being felt.

The Exosuit can generate a thousand correct answers.

Only a human can decide which cost is worth paying.

And once that decision is made, there is no Undo.

THE "JAGGED EDGE" OF REALITY

This is the Last Mile of any project—the point where the Pilot steps out of the Exosuit and accepts responsibility for contact with the world. This is where abstraction ends and consequence begins.

Upstream, everything is clean. Decisions are reversible. Variations are cheap. Mistakes can be regenerated away. The machine thrives there. It can produce a thousand taglines in a second, test them against historical engagement data, and surface the statistically safest option without breaking stride.

But none of that tells Alex which line will land with a tired nurse finishing a twelve-hour shift. None of it knows what reads as *considerate* instead of *clever* when someone is already depleted.

The machine can assemble a flawless, symmetrical grid—perfect spacing, perfect balance, nothing out of place. But Alex knows something the system does not: when perfection becomes ambient, it stops signaling care. In a sea of symmetry, a small deviation carries more meaning than another polished surface ever could.

He knows that if he tilts the logo by just two degrees—barely perceptible, just enough to interrupt the geometry—the mark stops reading as Corporate and starts reading as Authored. The difference is not aesthetic. It is psychological. It signals that someone chose this, instead of arriving at it by consensus.

Alex studies the label again.

On the corner of the "B" in Bitter, there is a small ink smudge. Barely visible unless you are looking for it. In the Lab, the system flagged it immediately as an Artifact Error. The automated correction routine attempted to eliminate it—restore symmetry, normalize density, return the surface to compliance.

Alex had intervened.

"Leave it," he told the machine. Then, after a pause, he added, "Increase the smudge by five percent."

The decision was not nostalgic. It was strategic.

That smudge is not decoration. It is evidence. It is the residue of judgment made visible. It is the equivalent of a thumbprint left in wet clay—a marker that says a human stood here long enough to accept the outcome.

The machine does not understand this gesture. It cannot. To the system, the smudge is noise. Something to be corrected. Something that violates the model's internal definition of quality.

But in a market saturated with infinite, perfectly polished AI output, the Jagged Edge becomes the only reliable signal of authorship.

Not because it is messy.

Not because it is rebellious.

But because it is owned.

The Jagged Edge tells the observer: someone saw this imperfection, decided it mattered, and chose not to erase it. Someone accepted the risk that comes with leaving a mark.

This is the boundary the machine cannot cross.

It can generate options endlessly.

It can optimize away deviation.

It can smooth surfaces until nothing catches.

What it cannot do is decide which flaw is worth keeping—and then live with that decision once the object leaves the Lab and enters the world.

That responsibility belongs to the human Pilot.

And at the Jagged Edge—where the work stops being editable and starts being accountable—that responsibility becomes the moat.

THE THREE PILLARS OF THE MONOPOLY

While Susan is still trying to organize work around attendance, utilization, and visible effort, Alex has quietly used his Boredom Dividend to build something asymmetric.

He hasn't escaped the system.

He hasn't "beaten" it.

He has extracted leverage from inside it.

What Alex is building does not look like rebellion. It looks like margin. A Human Monopoly formed not through scale, but through specificity—constructed patiently, inside constraints most people treat as dead weight.

An "average" Designer is a commodity. One can be swapped for another the way you replace a spare tire: same size, same function, same outcome. Price becomes the only meaningful variable.

A Context Architect is different.

Alex has stopped competing on speed, output volume, or compliance. He competes on meaning, judgment, and consequence—dimensions that do not scale cleanly and therefore do not collapse when automation accelerates.

To protect his Dream Life, he has built three deep pillars inside his Moat. None of them are mystical. None of them rely on genius. Each is a form of leverage that emerges only where humans remain accountable.

1. The Pillar of Empathy (Breakroom Wisdom)

Empathy, in this context, is not kindness. It is signal detection.

Alex thinks back to his quiet listening inside the office—not during meetings, not during presentations, but in the margins. Breakrooms. Hallways. Offhand remarks delivered without polish. Places where people stop performing and start revealing what actually worries them.

This is where he learned that Marcus, the bakery owner, isn't afraid of growth itself. He's afraid of dilution. Afraid that expansion will sand away the neighborhood texture that made the place matter long before it made money.

AI told Marcus to "*standardize the customer experience.*"

Alex told Marcus, "*Keep the mismatched chairs. They remind people of their grandmother's kitchen.*"

That instruction cannot be derived from a dataset.

It required recognizing the emotional risk hiding behind a

rational business objective—and responding in a way that reduced fragility instead of increasing it. Empathy here is not about feeling what someone feels. It is about understanding *what they stand to lose.*

Machines optimize for goals.

Humans notice fears.

That gap is leverage.

2. The Pillar of History (The Street-Legal Signal)

History, in Alex's work, is not nostalgia. It is grounding.

He spent three hours in the New York Public Library studying blueprints from 1922 for the block where The Bitter Bean sits. He learned that the building used to be an iron foundry. He traced the geometry of the original ironwork gates—functional shapes designed for weight, not aesthetics.

Those patterns became the background texture of the new labels.

When Marcus saw it, he didn't just see design. He felt continuity. A sense that the business belonged where it stood—that it had roots, not just branding.

The machine can simulate "vintage."

It can recombine styles, eras, and aesthetics endlessly.

What it cannot do is locate meaning in a specific place and make it relevant *now.* It cannot tell the difference between costume and inheritance. History, when used correctly, makes work street-legal. It earns trust not by referencing the past, but by respecting it.

3. The Pillar of Relationship (The Partner, Not the Vendor)

The final pillar is relationship—not networking, not friendliness, but alignment over time.

Alex is no longer a vendor to Marcus. Vendors are evaluated on deliverables. They are priced, compared, and replaced. Alex has moved into a different role entirely.

He doesn't send invoices labeled "*Logo Design — Revision 3.*"

He sends messages that begin with, "*I was thinking about our conversation on Tuesday.*"

That sentence carries weight because it signals memory. Continuity. Responsibility beyond the transaction.

Marcus pays Alex not for assets, but for filtration. Alex absorbs the noise of the Beige Tsunami on Marcus's behalf. He stands between the brand and a flood of well-intentioned but flattening suggestions.

This is what partnership looks like in an automated world: not production, but protection.

Alex is not selling output.

He is holding the boundary.

Alex steps back and sees the structure clearly now.

Empathy allows him to detect hidden risk.

History anchors his work to reality.

Relationship converts judgment into trust.

Together, these pillars form a monopoly—not because they exclude others, but because they cannot be copied at scale. They require presence. Memory. Accountability. Time.

The Tsunami will continue to rise.

The Average will continue to flatten.

Alex is no longer trying to outrun either.

He is standing on ground that does not disappear when automation accelerates—and inviting the right people to stand there with him.

EXIT VELOCITY: WHEN ALIGNMENT REPLACES EFFORT

It is 2:00 PM on a Tuesday.

Corporate Alex is seated in his cubicle at the global firm. The overhead lights hum at their familiar, low-grade frequency. The office is operating exactly as designed—quietly, predictably, without urgency. People move between meetings. Dashboards refresh. Presence is verified.

Susan walks past and nods, satisfied. From her perspective, the system is holding. Alex's screen is active. His hands are moving. The Q4 Brand Audit appears to be underway.

And in a narrow, technical sense, she is correct.

The audit *is* complete. It was finished by Alex's private Dream Stack two days earlier. What remains is pacing. Alex is running a controlled release—one slide per hour, delivered at a tempo that matches expectation. Not to deceive, but to stay aligned with the system's assumptions about time, effort, and proportionality.

The work is not the point anymore.

What Alex is doing now is orientation.

On his personal tablet, he is sketching the final version of his own operating plan. Not a manifesto. Not a resignation letter. A map. He is using the Saturday Morning Feeling as a compass—checking each decision against a simple test: *Does this expand judgment, or trade it away?*

The Exosuit did not replace him.

It refunded him.

Time returned first. Then attention. Then the ability to decide where both should go.

Alex glances at the clock. The timing feels right—not dramatic, just clear. Exit Velocity rarely announces itself. It arrives quietly, when the pull of the old system no longer overcomes forward motion.

The gravitational forces that once defined his life—the credential debt, the default forty-hour cadence, the slow erosion of judgment through repetition—have weakened. Not because they disappeared, but because Alex no longer depends on them for identity or security.

He has not "used" the company so much as **completed his role within it.**

The organization provided structure, exposure, and constraint. Alex used those conditions to build discernment, relationships, and a Moat that does not belong to the firm and cannot be requisitioned by it. Nothing was stolen. Nothing was rushed. The exchange remained intact.

Alex stands.

He does not wait for ceremony.

He does not announce a transformation.

He picks up his beanie, slides his tablet under his arm, and walks toward the elevators at an unremarkable pace. This is not an escape. It is a handoff—from one operating mode to another.

As the elevator doors close, his reflection catches briefly in the polished metal. He does not see a Junior Designer. He does not see a rebel or a runaway.

He sees a Pilot—someone who understands instruments, terrain, and limits, and knows when a system has taken him as far as it can.

Outside, the rain has returned to Brooklyn, light and steady. Alex steps into it without urgency. The city feels the same. The future does not.

The Tuesday Morning Crisis has resolved—not into certainty, but into context.

Alex is no longer reacting to what comes next.

He is positioned for it.

He's directing it.

NEW RULES FOR THE HUMAN MOAT

Alex steps back from the whiteboard and looks at what remains. Not a system. Not a framework. A posture.

The Human Moat is not something you build once and defend aggressively. It is something you maintain—quietly, continuously—through the way you allocate attention in a world where execution has become inexpensive and judgment has not.

What follows are not tactics. They are corrections. Updated rules that replace assumptions inherited from an era when labor was scarce, output was slow, and effort could still stand in for value.

. . .

Release the Clock

You are not paid for your time.

You are paid for your judgment.

Time-based measurement is a coordination tool from an earlier economic regime. It worked when human effort was the limiting factor—when nothing moved faster than a person could type, calculate, or draw.

That constraint no longer applies.

When a system completes the mechanical portion of work in seconds, the remaining hours are not surplus and not a loophole. They are capacity—capacity that exists for observation, synthesis, and decision-making that cannot be automated.

Used well, that capacity improves outcomes.

Used poorly, it collapses back into activity for its own sake.

The Human Moat begins when reclaimed time is invested in discernment rather than additional motion.

Work at the 100:1 Ratio

Do not ask the machine for *the* answer.

That framing assumes the answer exists independently of judgment.

Instead, ask for range. Ask for breadth. Let the system do what it does best: generate options without fatigue or attachment. Then do what only a human can do—recognize which option carries intent, consequence, and context.

You are not searching for polish.

You are not searching for correctness.

You are searching for the option that would be costly to defend if it were wrong.

Volume belongs to systems.

Selection remains human.

This ratio preserves authorship in an environment where output is abundant.

. . .

Honor the Audit

Most people misallocate effort.

They overinvest in generation and underinvest in evaluation. They treat the act of producing as the work and the act of deciding as overhead.

The opposite is now true.

A small portion of effort belongs to articulating intent—clear constraints, real goals, bounded scope. The majority belongs to audit: filtering, rejecting, and naming what matters.

This is where value concentrates.

The Human Moat is not the ability to create endlessly.

It is the ability to decide, calmly and precisely, what should persist.

Cultivate the Human Moat

Systems excel at consistency.

They excel at synthesis.

They excel at speed.

They do not inhabit context. They do not experience consequence. They do not carry a point of view that risks exclusion.

So the moat is not built by resisting systems, but by complementing them.

Taste.

Friction.

Clear points of view.

These are not inefficiencies. They are stabilizers—ways of ensuring that decisions remain accountable to the world they affect.

Work that carries responsibility does not scale cleanly. That is not a defect. It is protection.

Operate Within Institutions with Clarity

Many people will continue to work inside organizations. That is neither a failure nor a compromise. Institutions exist to coordinate effort, distribute risk, and sustain complex outcomes over time.

Within those structures, clarity matters.

Complete assigned work carefully and reliably.

Use systems to reduce clerical load.

Invest remaining attention in understanding people, incentives, and second-order effects.

Organizations provide infrastructure.

Individuals provide judgment.

When those roles are respected, both function better.

Alex understands now that none of this is about leaving systems behind.

It is about alignment—about occupying the role that remains valuable when execution accelerates and averages rise.

The Human Moat is not opposition to automation. It is the space where human responsibility still operates: where decisions exclude, where consequences are felt, and where meaning survives abundance.

The baseline will continue to rise.

The Average will continue to flatten.

That is not a threat.

It is clarification.

And for those who learn to stand comfortably in judgment—without panic, without urgency, without illusion—what remains is not less work, but better work.

Work that can be owned.

Work that can be defended.

Work that lasts.

12

THE INFINITE GAME

The Lie: The goal is to win the AI era by finding a stable advantage and locking it in.

The Truth: There is no permanent advantage—only continuous repositioning. Ownership in the infinite game is not control over assets, but responsibility for direction, values, and consequence as conditions change.

THE EVOLUTION OF THE OWNER

The Brooklyn skyline shimmers in the early morning light—a rigid grid of glass and steel that looks, from Alex's window, like a vast motherboard glowing under the pressure of eight million lives moving at once. The illusion is tempting: a city as a machine, humming along according to design.

It is 8:00 AM on a Tuesday.

One year ago, this hour was defined by a single, crushing sensation in Alex's chest. The sound of a notification—sharp, clean, inescapable—had felt like a verdict. A machine that never slept, never stalled, never asked permission had just demonstrated that it could do what he did faster, cheaper, and without fatigue. His question then was narrow and urgent: *How do I survive the machine?*

That question no longer organizes his thinking.

Today, the problem has widened. It is no longer about relevance in the next cycle, or income in the next quarter. The question has become more dangerous precisely because it is less desperate: *How wide can I build the world that depends on my decisions?*

This is not an emotional shift. It is a structural one.

Alex has moved beyond the life of operating inside other people's frames—beyond the rhythm of freelance work that treats autonomy as mobility and resilience as adaptability. That life rewarded responsiveness. It did not reward responsibility. When conditions changed, you adjusted. When incentives shifted, you followed.

Ownership begins where that logic fails.

As the founder and principal of The Lab Strategic, Alex no longer sells effort or execution. He no longer competes on speed or novelty. His role now is to decide which questions should not be accelerated, which tradeoffs must be surfaced rather than smoothed over, and which directions are worth committing to even when the data is incomplete.

This is a different posture entirely.

Agencies optimize within briefs. Platforms scale what already works. Tools increase throughput. Ownership, by contrast, absorbs uncertainty. It accepts that some decisions cannot be A/B tested, and that some consequences will only become visible long after the original choice has faded from memory.

The Lab Strategic is not a design agency or a marketing shop because those categories belong to a finite game—one where success is measured by winning a contract, shipping a deliverable, or beating a competitor to a milestone. Alex's work now unfolds on a longer horizon. His responsibility is not to maximize output, but to preserve coherence as conditions shift.

He has moved from selling syntax—the mechanics of *how* something is done—to selling semantics: the authority to decide *why* something should exist at all, and what it must remain aligned to over time.

In a world flooded with infinite, low-cost content, this inversion becomes unavoidable. Execution is abundant. Variation is cheap. The scarce resource is not ideas, but *direction*. Not activity, but *continuity*. Not intelligence, but the willingness to stand behind a trajectory when the incentives to drift are constant and subtle.

Ownership in the infinite game is not about locking in advantage. It is about carrying consequence forward—about being answerable not just to outcomes, but to what those outcomes make possible next.

Alex understands now that there will be no final configuration that solves this problem. No structure that cannot be eroded. No moat that does not require upkeep. The work is not to win once, but to keep choosing—deliberately, visibly, and with an awareness that every decision sets the boundary conditions for the ones that follow.

That is what the infinite game demands.

And that is the cost of being the owner.

THE FOSSILIZATION OF THE STATIC OWNER

To understand what is at stake in the Infinite Game, Alex has learned to look not at failure, but at **stability**—the kind that hardens quietly over time.

On his way into the studio one morning, he takes a longer route than usual. He passes the bodega where nothing has changed in years. He walks by the subway entrance, watching the same flows of people moving on the same schedules. A few blocks down, he stops in front of a local print shop he used to rely on regularly, back when his own work moved at the speed of his hands.

The shop has been there since the late nineties.

The owner, Mr. Henderson, still unlocks the door every morning at the same hour. He still runs the same presses. Still stocks the same papers. Still trusts the same sequence of steps that once guaranteed quality and predictability. Henderson is not careless. He is not incompetent. He is diligent, experienced, and deeply invested in his craft.

That is precisely the problem.

Henderson is what Alex has come to think of as a *Static Owner*—not because he lacks skill, but because he believes that skill, once earned, should entitle him to permanence. In his mental model, mastery is a destination. Once reached, it should hold.

In Henderson's world, value is cumulative. You put in the hours, learn the hard parts, endure the frustration, and eventually the work stabilizes around you. The tools change slowly. The customers learn what to expect. The system rewards consistency.

For decades, this was true.

When Henderson talks about automation, there is no panic in his voice. There is something quieter and more personal: offense. Not fear of competition, but resentment that something external would devalue the effort he already paid for in full.

"It's all junk now," he says, tugging at a stubborn sheet caught in the rollers. The shop smells of solvent and old paper. "People don't want computer-made trash. They want craftsmanship. They want to know someone suffered for it."

Alex listens without interrupting.

He recognizes the impulse. He has felt it himself.

There was a time when Alex believed the same thing—that endurance conferred legitimacy, that visible effort was proof of seriousness, that pain was the entrance fee for respect. The system trained him that way early. School. Work. Reputation. All of it reinforced the same rule: *do the hard thing long enough, and you earn the right to stop adapting.*

But markets do not honor sunk costs.

Henderson's shop still functions, but only by converting personal strain directly into price. Because the work cannot be delegated or compressed, every order consumes his time and body. What once looked like dedication now reads as friction. Delivery stretches from hours to days. Costs rise. Customers drift—not because they don't respect the craft, but because they no longer experience the struggle as value.

Henderson is not losing because he is wrong about quality.

He is losing because he is playing a **Finite Game** in an environment that no longer has a finish line.

In a finite game, endurance makes sense. You push through the hard years in exchange for eventual stability. You defend what you've built. You wait for validation to arrive in the form of retirement, reputation, or relief.

The Infinite Game does not offer that bargain.

The rules change without notice. Tools improve asymmetrically. New entrants do not respect old boundaries. Stability is temporary, and adaptation is not a phase—it is the work itself.

Alex understands now that Henderson is not an outlier. He is a preview.

Static ownership is not a personality flaw. It is what happens when responsibility calcifies around past success. When yesterday's alignment is mistaken for tomorrow's protection. When skill is treated as a shield instead of a resource that must be repositioned continuously.

Nothing catastrophic has happened to Henderson. The shop still opens. The machines still run. But the space between effort and outcome has widened so slowly that it feels natural.

That is how fossilization happens.

Not through collapse, but through continuity.

And Alex knows, uncomfortably, that without deliberate repositioning, the same gravity applies to him.

THE VOID OF THE COMMODITY OWNER

Alex continues his walk toward his cornerstone client, The Bitter Bean. The route is familiar enough that he usually takes it without thinking, but today he slows. A few blocks on, he stops near a newly opened automated café kiosk positioned on a high-traffic corner.

It occupies the kind of location entrepreneurs fight over. Constant foot traffic. Clear sightlines. Office buildings on three sides. The kind of place where success is supposed to be inevitable if the model is right.

This is the other extreme.

If Henderson represents the refusal to change, this represents something just as common: the belief that the safest response to uncertainty is **complete surrender to optimization.**

The owner of the kiosk did not resist the machine. They embraced it fully. Every decision that could be delegated was. Branding generated in seconds. Menu items selected by algorithms trained on national averages. Marketing copy scheduled precisely, written by systems that never pause to ask whether anyone is actually listening.

Nothing here feels careless.

Nothing here feels improvised.

The kiosk is clean. Efficient. Predictable. Its surfaces reflect light evenly. The menu boards update without flicker. The ordering interface responds instantly. By the metrics that once defined good business sense, it is exemplary.

Alex watches for a few minutes.

People pass. Some glance. A few slow, curious. One person approaches, taps through the menu, collects a cup, and leaves without looking back. There is no line behind them. No one sits. No one waits.

What Alex notices first is the sound—or the lack of it. No overlapping conversations. No small negotiations at the counter. No low background noise of people deciding to stay a little longer than they planned. The silence is not calm. It is vacant.

The space feels less like a café and more like an interface—something designed to be moved through rather than occupied. A place optimized for transactions, not for presence.

The Commodity Owner made a rational bet. They assumed that by removing human variance—by eliminating inconsistency, judgment, and friction—they would arrive at reliability. And in a narrow sense, they were right. Everything here behaves exactly as designed.

But as Alex stands there longer, another absence becomes harder to ignore.

Nothing feels *chosen*.

Every element looks as though it could belong anywhere else. The colors are correct. The proportions are correct. The pricing is correct. But none of it feels anchored to this block, this corner, this morning. It is correct in the abstract and unrooted in practice.

Alex recognizes the temptation immediately.

This path is appealing precisely because it feels safe. If everything is automated, then no one has to stand behind a decision. Defaults replace judgment. Outcomes can always be attributed to the model, the market, the data. Ownership becomes administrative rather than directional.

He understands why someone would choose this. He understands how easily he could have.

But something essential thins out in the handoff.

The kiosk performs the *syntax* of a café flawlessly while remaining indifferent to the reasons people seek one out in the first place. It does not know why someone might want to linger. Or why a place becomes familiar. Or why small, unoptimized irregularities can signal care rather than incompetence.

As Alex watches, he realizes that this is not failure in the obvious sense. The kiosk may survive. It may even scale. But it will never accumulate memory. It will never become *someone's place.*

Henderson is too rigid to adapt.

This is too hollow to hold meaning.

Both are playing finite games. One defends the past. The other dissolves into the average. Neither accepts responsibility for steering forward when the rules refuse to stay still.

The Infinite Game does not punish either choice immediately. It allows both to persist for a long time, slowly drifting away from relevance without collapsing.

That is what makes the danger easy to miss.

The threat is not extinction.

It is emptiness.

And standing there on the sidewalk, Alex feels the uncomfortable recognition that without deliberate ownership, either path is easy to slip into—quietly, rationally, and without ever noticing the moment when something essential was handed away.

THE SCALING OF THE SOUL

Alex arrives at The Bitter Bean just as the neighborhood is waking into itself. He unlocks the door with his phone and steps inside before the street has fully decided what kind of morning it will be. The smell reaches him first—yeast, roasted beans, faint sweetness from something baked earlier than planned. It's the kind of sensory signal no dashboard captures and no model predicts. Human Data arrives before metrics do.

Marcus is already inside. He stands near the roaster, listening more than looking, making small adjustments that are difficult to explain but easy to recognize once you've learned the language of the room. He tilts a valve slightly. He pauses. He waits. Nothing about the movement is rushed. Nothing about it is accidental.

Marcus isn't just a client anymore. He is a living demonstration of what happens when ownership adapts without dissolving—when a person stays responsible for direction even as tools change beneath their feet.

They sit together in the back office. This is not a space for execution. No screens are demanding attention. No timers are running. Alex has come to think of it as a *second cockpit*—not a place where work happens, but where work is *aimed*.

Alex understands now that Business Owner Alex is not a departure from being a Pilot. It is the next stage of it.

To stay ahead of rising capability, he cannot simply acquire more skills. Skills are static coordinates, and the machine maps them instantly. Certifications decay. Techniques diffuse. Best practices flatten into averages. Competing on skill alone only delays replacement.

What remains is posture.

He has to play the Infinite Game.

In a finite game, the rules are stable and the objective is to win. You try to become the best designer. You try to sell the cheapest coffee. You defend a narrow advantage and hope conditions remain friendly long enough for it to pay off.

The Infinite Game offers no such rest.

The rules shift without warning. Tools accelerate asymmetrically. New players enter without permission. The only objective is continuity—remaining capable of meaningful action as the environment refuses to hold still.

Alex opens a visualization from The Lab Strategic—not to impress Marcus, but to orient him.

"The machine handles the Known," Alex says, carefully. "The things that already have language. Patterns that repeat. Work that can be averaged. Our job isn't to beat that. Our job is to stay responsible for what *doesn't* resolve cleanly."

Marcus leans forward. He doesn't interrupt.

"We don't compete on price," Alex continues. "We don't compete on volume. We don't try to outrun scale. We compete on Context—on understanding why this place exists, who it's for, and how it should feel when someone walks in at seven in the morning before they've decided who they are that day."

Alex sees now that for a small business owner, AI is not a replacement. It is an **exoskeleton.** It multiplies reach without diluting intent—*if* someone remains accountable for direction.

In the old world, a corporation like Global Coffee Corp. could overwhelm a place like this through sheer headcount. Thousands of Horses pulling in parallel, producing enough Average output to drown anything local. Scale itself was the weapon.

Today, Marcus does not need to match that force.

He has Alex.

And Alex has the Dream Stack.

Together, they operate with leverage that would have been unthinkable a decade ago. The machine absorbs the repeatable work. The structure compresses execution. What remains for Alex is the only activity that does not scale cleanly, does not automate, and does not decay with repetition: connecting people to place, place to memory, and memory to intent.

This is what scaling looks like in the Infinite Game.

Not the expansion of output.

The expansion of responsibility.

Alex understands now that ownership is not about control. It is about *staying present* where decisions still carry consequence—long after optimization has done everything it can.

FROM TIME ARBITRAGE TO NON-STATIONARY VALUE

Alex studies the expansion proposal on his screen, not as a plan to be executed, but as a field of decisions waiting to be shaped. Across the city, other coffee shops are reacting to automation as if it were an approaching storm—something to brace against, something to survive.

Alex does the opposite.

He incorporates the machine deliberately and without ceremony. AI manages roaster curves with greater consistency than any human could sustain at scale. Inventory forecasting updates continuously, adjusting for weather, foot traffic, and local events. Payroll reconciliation runs quietly in the background, removing a category of error that once consumed entire afternoons. The repetitive logistics—the work that demanded attention without offering insight—simply stop asking for it.

At first glance, this looks like efficiency.

But Alex has learned not to confuse surface effects with structural change.

What this shift produces is not merely saved time. It produces what he privately calls the **Boredom Dividend**—the return of unclaimed attention. Not empty hours, but *unassigned cognition*. The portion of the week that used to vanish into low-yield execution quietly reappears.

Tuesday morning comes back.

Not as leisure.

Not as slack.

But as space.

This is the moment where most people stop. They treat time arbitrage as the win. Do the same work faster. Produce more with less. Fill the recovered hours with additional output and call it progress.

Alex understands why that instinct is strong.

He also understands why it fails.

Time savings are stationary. Everyone eventually gets them. What begins as leverage collapses into baseline. Speed diffuses. Efficiency normalizes. The advantage evaporates the moment it becomes visible.

So Alex does not reinvest the recovered hours into more Doing.

Instead of kerning logos for four hours, he spends those same four hours inside The Lab Strategic doing something that does not settle into equilibrium. He researches the **Spiky Point of View** that will define Marcus's next fifty locations. He traces how neighborhoods change before the data reflects it. He listens for contradictions customers cannot articulate yet. He shapes the narrative horizon of the business rather than responding to its current demands.

This is the shift from **time arbitrage** to **non-stationary value.**

Time arbitrage says: *do the same thing faster.*

Non-stationary value says: *move to where the value will be next.*

Alex is no longer reacting to tasks or chasing revisions. He is deciding which questions are worth asking before they become obvious. He is positioning Marcus's business ahead of imitation rather than racing against it.

He isn't a Task-Taker anymore.

But he isn't a "Dream-Maker" in the romantic sense either.

He is responsible for direction.

And responsibility, Alex now understands, is the only form of value that does not collapse under automation—because it must be re-assumed continuously, under conditions that refuse to stay still.

THE VECTOR MAP VS. THE HUMAN HORIZON

The sun has fully crested the Brooklyn skyline, turning glass towers into slow-burning pillars of light. From Alex's studio—the physical headquarters of The Lab Strategic—the city looks less like a threat than a system in motion. The light hitting his monitors feels different than it did a year ago.

Back then, it felt like a countdown.

A spotlight trained on approaching irrelevance.

Today, it feels like illumination.

Alex leans back in his chair and lets the room settle. The machines are running, but nothing is demanding him. On the center monitor, a complex visualization rotates in a patient orbit—a dense constellation of glowing points suspended in a dark, three-dimensional field.

This is the Vector Map.

Each point represents a capability. A pattern. A direction in which machine output can accelerate. Some clusters are familiar. Others are still forming. Together, they sketch the expanding perimeter of what automated systems can now generate—quickly, cheaply, and at scale.

For many people, this map induces vertigo.

They look at its density and mistake it for depth. They see range and assume wisdom. From the outside, it is easy to conclude that the machine is developing judgment—that it is becoming something like a thinking entity, capable of replacing the messy, uncertain work humans once did by default.

Alex understands why that conclusion is tempting.

From a distance, comprehensiveness can resemble intelligence. Scale can feel like understanding. Speed can masquerade as insight.

But months inside the Lab have clarified the distinction for him—not as an argument, but as experience.

The machine is not becoming more *judgmental.*

It is becoming more *complete.*

It maps more territory. It fills in more vectors. It answers more questions, more quickly, across more domains. What it does not do is decide which direction matters when conditions refuse to hold still.

That work still lives elsewhere.

Alex zooms out until the Vector Map occupies only part of the screen. Beyond it lies something harder to render and impossible to automate fully: the **Human Horizon**. This is not a space of outputs, but of orientation. It is where judgment is exercised under uncertainty, where values are chosen without guarantees, where responsibility persists even when optimization has finished its job.

The Horizon is not shrinking as the Vector Map expands.

It is moving.

And that movement is the opportunity.

The mistake most people make is treating AI as a finish line—something to outrun, or something to submit to. Alex has learned to treat it as terrain. The faster the terrain fills in, the more important it becomes to know where you are standing and why.

This is where hope enters—not as reassurance, but as clarity.

When machines absorb execution, humans are not left with nothing. They are left with the work that cannot be averaged: deciding what should exist next, what should endure, and what should be allowed to disappear. They become stewards of direction rather than participants in a race.

Alex understands now that the Infinite Game is not about winning against the machine.

It is about staying oriented as capability accelerates.

The Vector Map will continue to grow. That is inevitable. But the Human Horizon will always remain open—because no system, no matter how comprehensive, can assume responsibility for where the world ought to go.

That responsibility does not vanish in the age of AI.

It returns.

WHERE AVERAGE GOES TO ZERO

To understand why Alex is no longer afraid, you have to shift perspective. Not toward what the machine *is*, but toward **where it operates.**

The machine does not reason in the human sense. It does not interpret meaning. It navigates space.

Inside it, language, images, and ideas are arranged as points in a vast, multidimensional terrain. "Coffee" occupies one region. "Morning" sits nearby. "Caffeine" is closer still. The machine does not know the taste of coffee or the way steam curls on a cold Tuesday. It does not register the small alertness that arrives after a third cup.

What it knows is proximity.

As systems improve, they do not invent new territory. They **densify existing ground.** They fill in gaps. They refine distances. The map grows more complete, not more adventurous. Over time, the known world becomes increasingly well charted.

This is not a flaw. It is the point.

As the Vector Map fills, the statistical middle collapses toward zero cost. What was once expensive—average logos, competent copy, serviceable strategies—becomes abundant. Not because quality disappears, but because **familiar quality becomes trivial to reproduce.**

Alex rotates the visualization slowly, watching clusters brighten where the terrain has been thoroughly explored.

"The machine is a mapmaker," he says, almost to himself. "And the map it's building is a record of where we've already been."

This is the Syntactic Trap—not because the machine is wrong, but because it is faithful. It aggregates what exists. It reflects what has already worked. Its apparent intelligence is retrospective, not directional. It does not pull the world forward. It renders the past frictionless.

The more comprehensive the map becomes, the stronger its gravity toward the center. The Beige is not a mistake. It is the natural consequence of aggregation. The machine converges not on genius, but on the **mathematically perfect middle**—the place where variance disappears and nothing offends.

Alex understands now that this convergence is inevitable.

And that is why he is calm.

When Average becomes free, it stops being a competitive arena. It becomes infrastructure. The value migrates outward—not into novelty for novelty's sake, but into regions the map cannot pre-define because they do not exist yet.

The machine owns the center of the map.

The opportunity lives at the horizon.

Not in opposition to the machine, but beyond its geography—

where judgment, responsibility, and direction are still being decided in real time.

THE EMPTY ROOM PARADOX

Alex leans forward and zooms into a dim region at the outer edge of the glowing nebula. Compared to the dense clusters nearer the center of the Vector Map, this area looks almost unfinished—thin, irregular, sparsely populated.

He has learned to pause here.

Regions like this make people uncomfortable. They look like mistakes. Like blind spots. Like places the map has failed to complete. Early on, Alex felt the same instinctual pull to correct them—to fill them in, to smooth them out, to ask the machine to try harder.

Now he resists that reflex.

He refers to regions like this as Empty Rooms.

Not empty because nothing could exist there.

Empty because nothing has stabilized there yet.

For a long time, Alex avoided these zones. There was too much risk. Too little precedent. Nothing to point to when a client asked, *Why this?* The center of the map was safer. The center always had examples. Benchmarks. Case studies. Proof.

The center also stopped producing anything that mattered.

Standing here now, Alex doesn't feel excitement. He feels less exposed The kind that comes when you realize there is no optimization pass left to run. No data you can add that will resolve the uncertainty. Whatever happens next will happen because *someone chooses it.*

This is where the money is, he realizes—not as a boast, and not as ambition, but as a structural consequence.

An Empty Room is not an error in the system. It is not a gap waiting to be filled. It is a coordinate the machine cannot reach yet because the conditions required to define it do not exist in the data.

There is no dominant pattern. No averaged style. No grammar that has hardened into expectation.

It is the Unknown—not as mystery, but as responsibility.

Alex pulls up a project for a new client: a high-end tailoring shop attempting to describe itself as "post-luxury." The phrase sounds confident, but it doesn't locate anything yet. It gestures without committing.

The machine responds exactly as it should.

It scans the Vector Map and returns a logo that blends the visual grammar of Rolex and Apple—precise geometry, restrained symmetry, polished minimalism. The confidence score is high. The associations are clean. Nothing about the output is wrong.

It is elegant.

It is correct.

It is also completely interchangeable.

Alex studies it longer than he needs to. He knows what the client will say if he presents this. *It looks expensive. It looks professional. It looks like it should work.*

And it probably would.

That is the danger.

The logo sits perfectly centered inside the Luxury Cluster—surrounded by other signals that once meant distinction and now mean compliance. It does not offend. It does not linger. It does not demand a second look. It disappears into the background noise of correctness.

Alex does not delete it.

He does not argue with it.

He lets it remain where it belongs—at the center.

Then he moves outward.

He begins anchoring the brand's identity in something the map cannot smooth away: the rust patterns on old Brooklyn subway cars. Textures shaped by pressure, time, neglect, and endurance rather than refinement. Surfaces that record contact. That show wear without apology.

This is not nostalgia.

It is not rebellion.

It is inheritance.

The choice is slower. Harder to justify. There is no slide that proves it will work. No dataset that guarantees reception. He introduces friction where the machine removed it. He introduces weight where polish had become default. He reframes luxury not as flawlessness, but as permanence—the ability to remain intact after use, after years of contact with real bodies and real weather.

The machine flags the coordinates immediately.

The confidence score drops.

The system categorizes the move as an anomaly.

From the map's perspective, this is an error.

Alex sits with that discomfort.

When he presents the direction to the client, he does not lead with explanation. He lets them feel it first. The silence stretches. No one rushes to approve. For a moment, Alex wonders if he has misjudged the room.

Then something shifts.

The client doesn't say, *That's clever.*

They don't say, *That's different.*

They say, *That feels right.*

Not because the choice confirms what they already believed, but because it gives form to something they sensed without language. The brand does not explain itself. It locates itself—in place, in time, in consequence.

Alex understands now why Empty Rooms always feel risky.

They cannot be validated in advance. There is no benchmark that makes them safe. Someone has to step into them first and accept responsibility for what happens next.

That is the paradox.

As the Vector Map becomes more complete, the value of the unexplored does not disappear—it concentrates. But it only becomes accessible to those willing to stand behind a decision that cannot yet be justified by precedent.

The machine can tell you where everything has already been.

Only a human can decide where to go next—and remain accountable for the choice.

THE INFINITE GAME OF EVOLUTION

Alex understands now that the Infinite Game is not about defending a position.

It is about **continuously relocating your coordinates**—often before it is obvious that you need to move.

In a Finite Game, the map *is* the world. You choose a position, invest in it, and work to hold it as long as possible. You learn a skill—logo design, coding, copywriting—and you try to become exceptional enough that others cannot dislodge you. The rules reward endurance. Stability is the prize.

For a long time, this made sense.

But the machine is a perfect Finite Game player.

It does not tire. It does not protect identity. It does not hesitate to occupy territory once the path is clear. When a coordinate becomes well defined—when the work can be described, taught, and evaluated consistently—the machine moves in and fills it completely. Logo design. Coding. Copywriting. One by one, these positions lose friction.

Not because they were unimportant.

Because they became **legible.**

Alex no longer experiences this as threat. He experiences it as topography.

"The sea level is rising," he notes—not with alarm, and not with drama, but with precision. As the machine fills more of the map, the value of fixed coordinates compresses. If something can be done on demand, at scale, with predictable results, it becomes a commodity by definition.

The mistake is trying to stand still while this happens.

To remain valuable above the rising waterline, the Context Architect cannot anchor to a single skill or role. Skills are stationary. Titles are stationary. The map does not stop expanding to protect them.

Evolution is not optional.

But it is also not linear.

Looking back, Alex can trace the shifts that brought him here—not as a ladder climbed, but as a series of relinquishments.

The Maker

He began by doing the work directly—drawing pixels, shaping layouts, executing tasks. Craft mattered. Precision mattered. But over time, execution became a bottleneck rather than an advantage.

The Manager

He moved from producing artifacts to directing tools. The work multiplied, but so did coordination. The problem shifted from *how to do the work* to *how to prevent the work from consuming everything.*

The Director

He stepped back again—this time from systems themselves. Orchestration wasn't enough. Someone had to evaluate outputs, reject the smooth but hollow, and protect clients from convincing nonsense. Judgment became central.

The Architect

Eventually, Alex found himself operating beyond the center of the map altogether—entering Empty Rooms where the machine had no precedent to follow. Here, he was no longer optimizing or supervising. He was deciding what should exist in the first place.

None of these roles replaced the previous ones.

They subsumed them.

And none of them are permanent.

Alex understands that the Infinite Game does not end with becoming an Architect. The map will continue to fill. Today's Empty Rooms will become tomorrow's averages. What requires judgment now will eventually become infrastructure.

Evolution, in this game, is not about reaching a final identity.

It is about staying willing to move—again and again—without waiting for permission, without nostalgia for past mastery, and without mistaking familiarity for safety.

The goal is not to outrun the machine.

It is to remain responsible for direction as the ground keeps shifting beneath your feet.

VALUE CANNOT SIT STILL

Alex glances at the clock. It reads 10:30 AM.

In his old life—the life of the 9:15 AM Criminal—this hour carried weight. It meant proof. Four hours logged. Six remaining. A checkpoint in a long, visible march toward permission to rest. Value was measured by strain you could point to and presence that could be verified. If nothing hurt yet, the day hadn't earned its legitimacy.

The clock enforced that logic relentlessly.

Now, the clock still moves, but its authority has thinned. Not because time disappeared, and not because the day became easier—but because time stopped being the scarcest input. By allowing the Exosuit to absorb the Syntactic labor of the business, Alex removed time pressure as the governing constraint.

What surfaced in its place was something heavier.

Responsibility.

Alex is no longer a Graphic Designer. That identity dissolved quietly, without ceremony. But what replaced it is not a title he can defend. He has become a Meaning-Maker, and that role carries a rule he cannot negotiate with:

Any position the machine can learn is already decaying.

The moment a technique stabilizes—when it can be described clearly, taught reliably, and repeated at scale—its value begins collapsing toward zero. There is no malice in this. No injustice. It is simply what happens when something becomes legible.

This means Alex's responsibility is not to protect his current advantage.

It is to abandon it.

Early.

That abandonment is never comfortable. Each move feels like stepping away from ground that still appears solid. There is always a temptation to stay longer, to extract a little more value, to wait for clearer confirmation that the ground is giving way. The Infinite Game does not offer that certainty.

This is the owner's burden.

Alex must continuously relocate his point of value ahead of the map—toward Empty Rooms where context still precedes data, and judgment still arrives before optimization. He does not optimize for throughput. He does not optimize for retention. He optimizes for **displacement**: the ability to move before the machine finishes mapping the terrain beneath his feet.

On his screen, tokens stream by—millions of new coordinates added to the global Vector Map. Clusters brighten. Gaps close. Regions that once required human attention flatten into infrastructure.

Alex watches without anxiety.

He does not feel urgency.

He does not feel relief.

He feels orientation.

Each completed cluster tells him where *not* to stand. Each area of consolidation clarifies where the next boundary of responsibility will emerge. The more thoroughly the machine renders the Average frictionless, the more sharply the Unique concentrates its value—briefly, precariously, and only for those willing to move.

The machine is clearing the forest.

Not maliciously.

Not strategically.

Simply by doing what it does best.

The Architect's responsibility is not to mourn what disappears.

It is to decide—again and again—what should be built next, knowing that whatever he builds will someday require leaving behind.

Value cannot sit still.

And neither can the person responsible for it.

THE PARADOX OF THE FINAL TOKEN

Inside the shop, the lights have shifted to their evening setting, casting a warm amber glow across the counters and reclaimed wood. Marcus is closing down for the night, wiping surfaces, stacking chairs, moving with the unhurried satisfaction that comes from knowing the day produced something tangible. Orders were filled. Conversations happened. People stayed longer than they needed to.

Alex stands just outside, the door closed behind him, the street quieting into its late rhythm. He pulls his phone from his pocket—not out of urgency, but habit—and checks the dashboard for his firm.

The machine is still working.

The Exosuit does not sleep. It is processing at speeds no human system can match, quietly folding new information into the Vector Map with a density that would have been inconceivable not long ago. Ethiopia harvest reports update automatically. Brooklyn demographic shifts reweight projections. The roaster's heat curves adjust in response to subtle changes in humidity and load.

None of this requires attention anymore.

From the outside, this looks like intelligence accelerating. Like the system is approaching something like awareness. Like it is climbing toward a finish line humans can no longer see.

Alex recognizes the distinction without needing to articulate it.

The system is not discovering purpose.

It is completing coverage.

It is filling in a map that has no destination and no sense of arrival. Each token does its work and disappears, replaced immediately by the next. Progress is measured only by density. There is no moment where the system pauses to ask whether the map means anything—or where it should go next.

Alex watches the stream slow just enough to register on his screen.

"The machine is a library that can read itself," he says quietly, more observation than argument. "But it still doesn't know why it's reading."

It has flawless syntax.

It can locate every word relative to every other word.

It can trace patterns across unimaginable scale.

But it cannot feel the weight of a secret.

It cannot sense when a choice matters more than it can be justified.

It cannot decide which direction is worth committing to when the data refuses to settle.

Standing there, Alex understands why the Infinite Game is the only posture that holds in a world where the map never stops expanding.

Finite Games promise rest. They offer endpoints: retirement, market dominance, stability earned through endurance. You play well, you win, and the motion stops.

That promise no longer applies.

As the machine completes the Average—rendering it frictionless, abundant, and forgettable—the horizon of the Unique does not collapse. It does not retreat. It shifts.

It moves outward, into spaces that cannot be pre-validated. Into moments where someone must choose without assurance and remain accountable after the choice is made.

The final token will never arrive.

There will always be another coordinate.

Another cluster.

Another completion.

What remains constant is the need for someone to decide, again and again, what the map is *for*.

Alex pockets his phone and turns back toward the shop. Marcus locks the door, nods once, and they start walking down the block together.

The machine continues its work.

So does the responsibility.

WHEN TIME STOPS EXPLAINING VALUE

Alex still remembers Corporate Alex—the version of himself working inside a large, structured organization. He remembers the dashboards, the status indicators, the shared calendars that attempted to synchronize hundreds of people across time zones and priorities. He remembers the fluorescent light not as cruelty, but as context: a system designed for coordination at scale.

Those systems were not irrational.

They were built for a different era.

The forty-hour week was never about punishment. It was a proxy. A way to align effort when outcomes were difficult to measure directly. Time became the visible stand-in for contribution, not because it was precise, but because it was legible. Presence could be counted. Duration could be verified. In environments where work unfolded sequentially and tools moved slowly, this approximation worked well enough.

The problem was never work.

The problem was mistaking the proxy for the thing itself.

Over time, the proxy hardened into belief. If value could not be seen unfolding across hours, it was assumed not to exist. Activity became proof. Endurance became credibility. People learned to equate contribution with strain, and systems learned to reward what could be observed rather than what endured.

That belief lingers—even now.

Alex understands that this is why the machine unsettles so many organizations. It doesn't challenge effort. It challenges the usefulness of time as the primary unit of measurement. When execution compresses, duration stops correlating cleanly with value. The old signals flicker. The dashboards still glow, but they no longer tell the full story.

Through The Lab Strategic, Alex hasn't rejected structured work or institutional coordination. He has simply adjusted what he optimizes *within* it. He has learned that time is no longer the currency of modern work.

It is the outcome.

What matters is not how long something takes, but whether it survives selection—whether it remains useful, meaningful, and relevant after the environment changes.

By allowing the Exosuit to absorb the repeatable Doing, Alex hasn't escaped responsibility. He has intensified it. He is no longer trading hours for permission to proceed. He is accountable for direction—inside projects, inside organizations, and inside decisions that persist beyond any single reporting cycle.

His days still have structure.

They still contain effort.

They still require discipline.

What has disappeared is the belief that value must announce itself through exhaustion.

Curiosity has replaced anxiety as his navigational instrument—not as indulgence, but as early detection. Curiosity is how he senses where the map is thinning, where assumptions are breaking, where the next Empty Room might be forming.

This posture is not an exit from work.

It is an evolution of how work is understood.

The ghost of the forty-hour week fades not because people stop showing up, but because time alone is no longer sufficient to explain where value comes from—or where responsibility truly lives.

THE FINAL LAUNCH

Alex pauses at the threshold of the shop and looks back once more before turning toward the door. The space has settled into itself. Nothing is calling for attention. Nothing is trying to impress.

Earlier in the process, the machine had proposed a different solution—one derived cleanly from the Vector Average of high-performing Brooklyn cafés. Brushed steel. White LED lighting. Crisp edges. A design that scored perfectly across every measurable dimension.

Alex didn't argue with it.

He simply chose something else.

He chose reclaimed wood that carries the faint trace of prior use. Lighting that behaves less like an instrument and more like a presence—warm, uneven, forgiving. Materials that will age, weather, and change rather than remain permanently new. A point of view that does not peak on opening day, but deepens over time.

None of these choices are optimal in isolation.

Together, they are coherent.

The machine can identify where patterns have already converged. It can show where the crowd is moving now. What it cannot do is decide which direction is worth committing to when the answer cannot be justified in advance.

That responsibility remains human.

Standing there, Alex recognizes something about the work he's been doing—both here, and in the pages of the book you're reading now. It isn't a warning. It isn't an instruction manual. It's an orientation aid. A way of seeing how value moves when averages collapse and certainty evaporates.

Not a call to abandon systems, but an invitation to **inhabit them differently.**

The Tuesday Morning Crisis no longer defines his weeks. Not because the machine disappeared, and not because effort vanished, but because Alex stopped treating time as the terrain and started designing for direction. He learned to work *with* the current instead of bracing against it—shaping vessels rather than resisting water.

He pulls on his beanie and steps out into the evening. He doesn't check his phone. He doesn't audit the day. There will be time for that later.

For now, he walks.

The air is cool. The street is active but unhurried. Somewhere behind him, the machine continues its work—quiet, relentless, invaluable.

And ahead of him, the path remains open.

Not because the future is predictable.

But because it is navigable.

THE FINAL RULES FOR THE INFINITE GAME

As Alex walks home, he notices how tempting it would be to turn what he's learned into a list. A set of rules. Something clean enough to follow and stable enough to rely on.

That impulse is understandable. It's how finite games work.

But the Infinite Game resists that kind of closure. Any rule precise enough to enforce is already too rigid to survive what comes next.

What Alex carries instead are orientations—ways of noticing when value is drifting, when certainty is becoming cheap, when a once-rare skill is hardening into infrastructure. He's learned to watch where judgment still matters, where outcomes cannot be averaged, where responsibility remains human because no one else can assume it.

He's learned that speed eventually equalizes, but taste does not. That physical trust becomes more valuable as digital fluency becomes abundant. That proximity to real consequences—customers, materials, decisions that endure—creates signals no system can simulate fully.

He's also learned that structured environments are not enemies. They are contexts. Sometimes they constrain. Sometimes they enable. What matters is not whether one works inside them or outside them, but whether one understands what is being measured—and what is no longer being explained by those measurements.

Most of all, Alex has learned to pay attention to that quiet feeling he once dismissed as idleness. The spaciousness that appears when unnecessary friction is removed. The moments where no one is demanding output yet something important is taking shape.

That feeling is not an endpoint.

It is a signal.

It doesn't tell you what to do next.

It tells you that you're finally in a position to decide.

The Infinite Game doesn't begin with a rulebook.

It begins with responsibility—and the willingness to carry it forward without knowing where it will lead.

CONCLUSION

The Sky Is Open

WHY IT ALWAYS RAINS IN BROOKLYN

The Brooklyn rain is falling again.

It is a Tuesday morning—exactly one year since the Tuesday Morning Crisis first entered Alex's life. He stands at the wide industrial window of his studio, not in front of a dashboard or a deadline, but simply watching the city move under pressure.

Below him, the streets dissolve into motion. Gray umbrellas collide and separate. Yellow taxis throw water sideways as they cut through oil-slicked puddles. The city does what it always does: it absorbs weather and keeps going.

His attention settles briefly on a young man in a soaked suit sprinting toward the subway entrance, leather briefcase pressed tight against his chest. The grip is instinctive—as if holding something solid might keep the rest of the morning from slipping.

Alex recognizes the posture without judgment.

It's the stance of someone who believes speed offers shelter. Someone who thinks momentum can substitute for orientation. Someone trying, reasonably, to stay upright in conditions that feel increasingly unpredictable.

Alex has worn that posture before. Not because he misunderstood the world, but because it was the only posture the world seemed to reward. Move faster. Stay later. Absorb more rain than the next person and call it resilience.

For a long time, that belief felt practical. Even responsible.

The storm was never the problem.

The problem was believing it could be outrun.

THE WEATHER OF THE MACHINE

In the old world—the world this book began in—we were taught to expect predictable weather. We were told that if we followed the Sequential Method, attended the right schools, and mastered the Syntax of our craft, the climate would remain stable. Effort would be rewarded. Progress would move forward in a straight line. Hard work, applied consistently, would eventually be met with calm skies.

That assumption held for a long time.

But AI did not arrive as a single new tool or a passing storm. It altered the climate itself.

The rain falling over Brooklyn is not an accident of the day. It is the Beige Tsunami rendered atmospheric—the steady, indifferent downpour of Average content, Average code, and Average solutions. The clouds are saturated now. The Vector Map is so dense with prior human output that overflow has become inevitable. Every time a machine produces a perfectly acceptable paragraph, a statistically sound design, or a competent strategic recommendation, another drop joins the rain.

This isn't malice.

It isn't intention.

It's physics.

For many people, this new weather feels personal. Long-standing skills lose traction. Familiar signals stop working. The instincts that once kept careers upright begin to fail quietly. The natural response is to look for shelter—to reinforce what worked before, to protect existing structures, to wait for the storm to pass.

That response is understandable. It's human.

The difficulty is not that people are reacting incorrectly. It's that the weather they're reacting to is no longer temporary. What feels like disruption is, in fact, the new environment. The rain isn't something happening *to* work. It's what work now moves through.

Alex learned this slowly, without drama. Not through rebellion or escape, but through observation. When conditions change at scale, protection is rarely the right strategy. You don't survive a flood by holding an umbrella tighter. You survive it by changing how you move.

When the ground becomes unreliable, stability comes from buoyancy.

You don't argue with the rain.

You design something that floats.

THE INFINITE SATURDAY MORNING

Alex turns away from the window and takes in the studio around him.

It doesn't resemble the places he used to work. There are no dashboards flickering for attention. No ambient pressure to perform visibility. No signal demanding proof of effort. The room is not optimized for throughput. It is optimized for judgment—for thinking clearly, slowly, and in full contact with consequence.

What changed was never the space itself.

It was the posture inside it.

The Tuesday Morning Crisis was not caused by a machine. It wasn't even caused by work. It emerged from a misalignment that had been tolerated for years—the quiet acceptance of a life measured primarily by compliance with someone else's clock. AI did not remove Alex from that arrangement. It revealed it. It made visible a transaction that had been normalized for so long it no longer registered as a choice.

He didn't escape the system.

He redefined where he stood within it.

The machine absorbed the Doing.

Alex absorbed the responsibility.

That exchange changed everything.

What Remains Human

If you are reading this, you are likely standing somewhere between familiarity and unease.

Nothing has collapsed. Your work still exists. Your skills still function. But something feels different now—lighter in some places, thinner in others. You may have noticed that what once felt valuable now feels easier to replace. That effort no longer guarantees insulation. That speed, once protective, now attracts scrutiny.

This is not failure.

It is orientation.

The question in front of you is not whether the machine will improve. It will.

The question is whether *you* will remain stationary as it does.

A Human Moat is not a title, a role, or a lifestyle change. It is a posture.

It begins when you stop asking *how to compete* and start asking *where substitution breaks*. When you notice which decisions you are uniquely willing to stand behind—and which ones you've been outsourcing to habit, policy, or precedent.

Some people will build that moat inside organizations.

Some will build it across clients.

Some will build it in teams, classrooms, studios, or kitchens.

The location doesn't matter.

The responsibility does.

The Quiet Test

A simple test begins to clarify everything:

- Are you paid primarily for **execution**, or for **judgment**?
- When conditions change, do people ask you for **speed**, or for **direction**?
- If your tools disappeared tomorrow, would your value remain legible?

The machine is indifferent to these questions.

You are not.

As the terrain fills in—as Average becomes abundant and cheap—the remaining advantage concentrates not in effort, but in selection. In deciding what *not* to do. In choosing where friction is appropriate. In standing visibly behind choices that cannot be justified by optimization alone.

This is not about working less.

It is about being harder to replace.

The Open Sky

Alex checks the time. It's just after noon.

In another life, this would have been a checkpoint—a marker in a day already accounted for. Now, it's simply a moment.

He closes the studio door and steps outside. The rain is still falling, steady and unremarkable. He doesn't hurry. He doesn't shield himself. He lets it register.

The world no longer feels like something to outrun.

It feels navigable.

The machine is humming.

Average is everywhere.

And the sky is still open.

What the machine will do next is not the question.

Whether you will choose to become a Human Moat—and accept what that choice demands—is.

The Infinite Game does not announce its beginning.

You enter it the moment you decide to stand somewhere the machine cannot stand for you.

APPENDIX

SOURCES, FRAMEWORKS, FICTIONALIZATION, AND CLARIFICATIONS

This book is a work of narrative nonfiction. It combines illustrative scenarios, composite characters, condensed timelines, and conceptual frameworks to explore structural shifts in automation, professional leverage, and human judgment in the age of artificial intelligence.

The purpose of this appendix is to:

1. Distinguish fictionalized elements from real-world references.
2. Clarify the status of legal and institutional examples.
3. Acknowledge intellectual influences where applicable.
4. Define the scope and limitations of the analytical frameworks introduced.

This appendix is not intended as a comprehensive academic citation index, nor as legal or technical advice.

FICTIONAL AND COMPOSITE ELEMENTS

Several individuals, organizations, and scenarios depicted in this book are fictional or composite constructions.

Alex is a composite character representing patterns observed among knowledge workers in professional, creative, and technical roles adapting to automation-driven shifts in leverage and responsibility.

Chad is a narrative device used to personify large language model behavior. Chad does not represent any specific artificial intelligence product, vendor, model architecture, or version. The character is used for explanatory clarity only and should not be interpreted as implying agency, consciousness, intent, or personality in actual AI systems.

The Neon Roast, The Lab Strategic, Julian, Susan, and other named individuals or entities are fictional composites. Any resemblance to real persons, organizations, cases, or events is coincidental and unintended.

LEGAL ILLUSTRATIONS AND CASE REFERENCES

Certain legal cases, quotations, and judicial figures referenced in the narrative are intentionally fictionalized.

In particular, the case involving color trademark enforcement and the quoted judicial opinion attributed to a judge are fictional constructs designed to illustrate a known phenomenon in generative AI systems: the production of plausible but fabricated content when prompts are not grounded in verified sources.

These illustrative legal references are not real case law and must not be interpreted as legal precedent. The book does not offer legal advice, and readers should not rely on narrative examples for legal decision-making.

INTELLECTUAL AND HISTORICAL FOUNDATIONS

The arguments presented in this book draw on established work in economics, philosophy, systems theory, and labor history.

The transformation of labor from outcome-based craft to time-compensated task work reflects industrial developments associated with factory systems and the assembly line, including practices popularized by Henry Ford and principles associated with scientific management as articulated by Frederick Winslow Taylor.

The distinction between finite and infinite games draws from the work of James P. Carse in *Finite and Infinite Games*.

Observations regarding labor market polarization and the erosion of routine middle-skill work are consistent with research on task automation and routine-biased technological change, including work by David Autor and collaborators.

Discussion of tacit knowledge, bounded rationality, and limits of formalization reflects themes explored by Michael Polanyi and Herbert A. Simon.

References to the "Chinese Room" thought experiment acknowledge its origin in the work of John Searle. The discussion of machine intelligence and fluency builds on foundational questions raised by Alan Turing. These references are included for intellectual context; the book does not attempt to relitigate philosophical debates surrounding artificial intelligence.

The metaphorical use of the term "semantic gravity" acknowledges terminology developed by Karl Maton within Legitimation Code Theory. In Maton's framework, semantic gravity refers to the degree to which meaning is context-dependent or abstracted. The usage in this book adapts the term metaphorically to describe convergence effects in statistical language systems and should not be interpreted as a formal application of Legitimation Code Theory.

AI SYSTEM BEHAVIOR AND HALLUCINATION

Descriptions of generative AI behavior reflect widely documented properties of large language models in academic and industry research. These systems generate statistically plausible language based on learned probability distributions and do not independently verify factual accuracy.

The phenomenon commonly described as "hallucination" refers to the generation of false but coherent content in the absence of grounding mechanisms. This is a documented limitation of current model architectures and is not presented as malicious intent or system-level agency.

Interrogation techniques described in the narrative—such as enforced citation, adversarial questioning, or role separation—are conceptual adaptations of validation practices used in safety-critical engineering and risk-sensitive system design. They are not technical guarantees of correctness.

ORIGINAL ANALYTICAL FRAMEWORKS

The following terms are introduced in this book as original conceptual lenses:

- The Human Moat
- The Exosuit
- The Fast Food Trap
- The Product Timeline Tax
- The Saturday Morning Feeling
- The Dream Stack
- The Citation Cage
- The Zero-Sum Gate

These constructs are descriptive frameworks developed for explanatory clarity. They are not empirical models, predictive systems, proprietary methodologies, or legally protected processes.

The term "Context Architect" originated in a prior volume of this trilogy and is referenced here for conceptual continuity.

SCOPE AND RELIANCE

This book provides analytical interpretation and strategic commentary. It does not constitute legal, financial, regulatory, or technical advice.

Readers are responsible for independent verification of claims, legal references, and business decisions derived from the themes discussed.

CLOSING CLARIFICATION

The central argument of this book is that as execution becomes abundant, responsibility becomes decisive. The frameworks presented are tools for reflection and positioning, not guarantees of outcome.

The reader's judgment remains primary.

ACKNOWLEDGMENTS

This work was shaped by years of operating inside systems where failure carries real consequence. I'm grateful to the engineers, operators, compliance professionals, executives, and business owners who allowed these ideas to be tested under pressure—inside regulated environments, safety-critical systems, and organizations where correctness mattered more than speed. Their questions, resistance, and lived constraints informed this work far more than theory ever could.

I'm also indebted to the intellectual traditions that clarified the limits of automation and the boundaries of machine agency. Long before artificial intelligence became a cultural fixation, disciplines such as systems engineering, philosophy of mind, and safety-critical design established a necessary distinction between execution and judgment. These ideas form the quiet foundation beneath the arguments in this trilogy, even as they are adapted to a world where execution has become effectively instantaneous.

Finally, my thanks to my wife for her patience during the long stretches of focus this work required. Their steadiness made it possible to pursue clarity without urgency and rigor without compromise.

ABOUT THE AUTHOR

Sean Pan,

Sean Pan approaches artificial intelligence from environments where failure is not abstract and correctness is not optional. His perspective was shaped not by consumer software or growth-stage product culture, but by industrial automation and digital signal processing—domains where errors produce physical consequences and late discovery is unacceptable.

His formal training began at the University of California, Davis, where, while studying Electrical Engineering, he also pursued a rigorous inquiry into the philosophy of artificial intelligence within mathematically grounded curricula emphasizing formal logic, symbolic representation, and the known boundaries of computation. He later completed a Bachelor of Science in Electrical Engineering at San José State University and earned an MBA in Technology Management, integrating technical rigor with organizational accountability.

Sean's career unfolded inside zero-tolerance systems spanning industrial control environments, military systems, and critical energy infrastructure. In these contexts, defects do not result in feature updates; they trigger shutdowns, financial loss, or safety risk. That discipline—where constraints must be respected before execution—continues to shape how he evaluates modern AI systems and the behaviors forming around them.

Today, Sean serves in a leadership role within a Fortune 35 insurance and financial services organization, overseeing a nine-figure revenue portfolio and advising teams operating under regulatory, economic, and reputational constraint.

Across the Semantic Trilogy—*The Empty Room*, *The Context Architect*, and *The Human Moat*—Sean examines a single throughline:

where machine execution ends and human judgment begins. His work helps leaders, builders, and professionals reposition their value in a world where execution has become abundant, but responsibility, authorship, and consequence remain irreducibly human.

www.ingramcontent.com/pod-product-compliance
Lightning Source LLC
LaVergne TN
LVHW090855250926
848801LV00039B/180/J
* 9 7 9 8 9 9 4 6 2 9 6 4 2 *